IMAGES
of America

LARGO

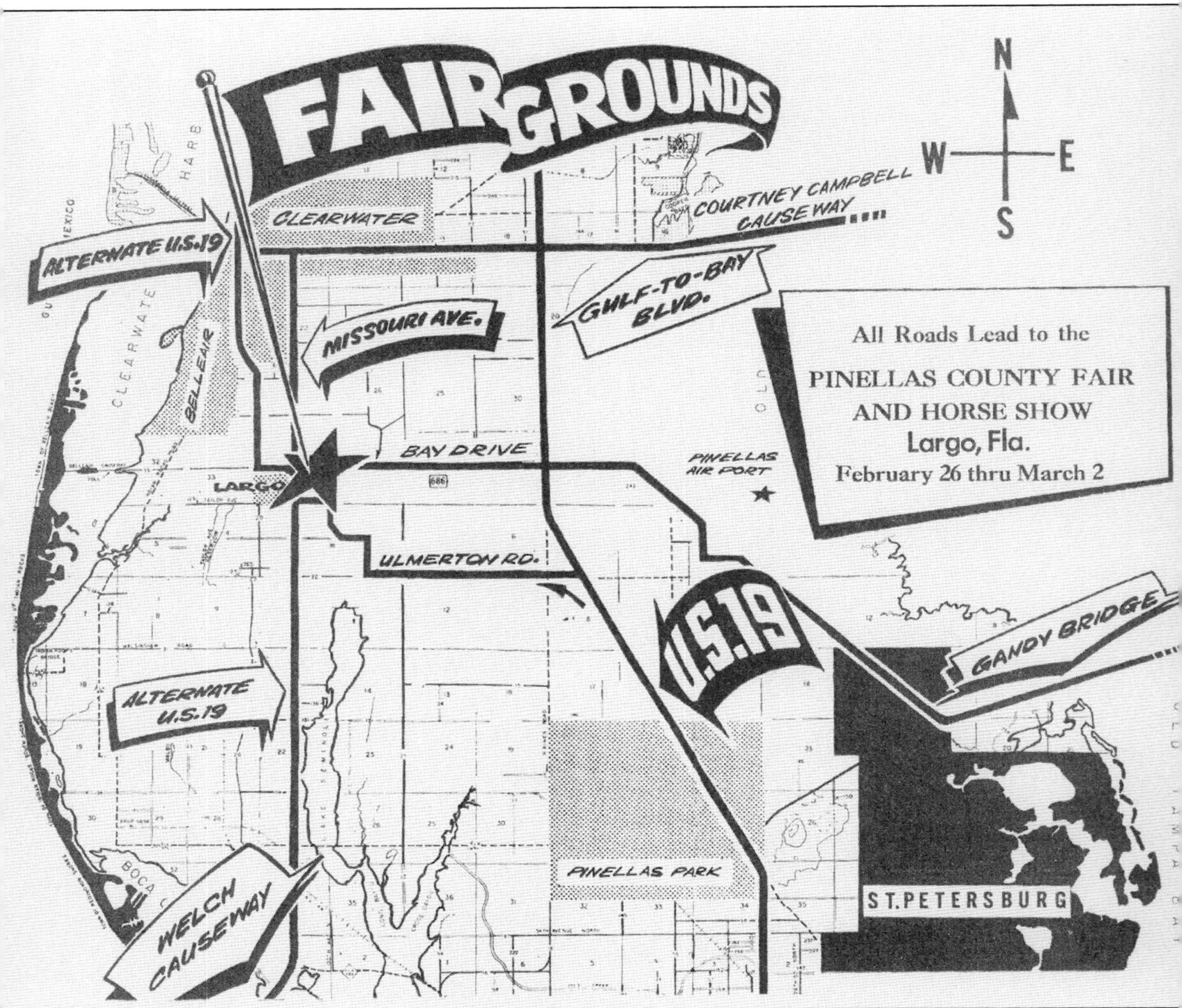

A 1957 map touted the close proximity of the fairgrounds to the rest of Pinellas. Two convenient routes across Tampa Bay—the Courtney Campbell Causeway and the Gandy Bridge—allowed fairgoers to arrive from Tampa and points further east. At that time, eastbound Ulmerton Road ended as a dirt path beyond Roosevelt Boulevard. (Courtesy of the Archives and Library at Heritage Village.)

On the Cover: Field workers gather oranges in the Largo area during the 1890s. The arrival of railroad service a few years earlier led to the development of many new groves around the small settlement of Largo. (Courtesy of the Tampa Library, University of South Florida.)

IMAGES
of America

LARGO

James Anthony Schnur

ARCADIA
PUBLISHING

ISBN 978-0-7385-8221-4

Published by Arcadia Publishing
Charleston, South Carolina

Printed in the United States of America

Library of Congress Control Number: 2010939279

For all general information, please contact Arcadia Publishing:
Telephone 843-853-2070
Fax 843-853-0044
E-mail sales@arcadiapublishing.com
For customer service and orders:
Toll-Free 1-888-313-2665

Visit us on the Internet at www.arcadiapublishing.com

To members of the Largo Area Historical Society and Pinellas County Historical Society for their efforts to preserve our community's history

CONTENTS

ACKNOWLEDGMENTS

The author wishes to express his appreciation to the executive board and officers of the Pinellas County Historical Society (PCHS). Under president Fran Johnson's tenure, PCHS has reaffirmed its commitment to preserving Heritage Village, a cultural treasure in the Largo area. The staff, volunteers, and docents at Heritage Village, as well as Ellen Babb, the village's operations manager, have also provided immeasurable support during the research and writing of this book.

Colleagues at the University of South Florida (USF) St. Petersburg—especially the staff and librarians at Nelson Poynter Memorial Library—offered insight, guidance, and technical support. I extend a deep debt of appreciation to Raymond Arsenault, Carol Hixson, Marta Jones, Gary Mormino, Tina Neville, Jerry Notaro, J. M. "Sudsy" Tschiderer, and Berrie Watson. Friends and family, including Carolyn Schnur Hoffman and Annie Miller, offered editorial suggestions. Lindsay Harris Carter and Maggie Tiller Bullwinkel at Arcadia Publishing worked with me throughout the process. The sage guidance and support of historical society members, colleagues, friends, family, and the excellent staff at Arcadia made this an enjoyable task.

My greatest debt of gratitude must be shared with my wife, Phuongdung Schnur. She endures my long hours away from home while at work, researching local history, and watching the Tampa Bay Rays from my perch at Tropicana Field. Without her endless love and amazing patience, this project would have never happened.

Except for the cover image and those supplied by the author, all images in this volume appear courtesy of the Archives and Library at Heritage Village (HV), the Burgert Brothers Photographic Collection of the Tampa-Hillsborough County Public Library System (THPL), and the Earl R. Jacobs III Collection of Francis G. Wagner's Photographs at Nelson Poynter Memorial Library at the University of South Florida St. Petersburg (USFSP).

Introduction

Before Spanish explorers set foot upon Florida's west coast, indigenous cultures enjoyed the bountiful seafood and wildlife along the Pinellas Peninsula and in the Tampa Bay region. Expeditions by Panfilo de Narvaez in 1528 and Hernando de Soto in 1539 ultimately led to the demise of these pre-Columbian cultures. Much of Pinellas remained uninhabited until the early 1800s, except for occasional fishing parties or itinerant Cuban fishing rancheros along the Gulf Coast. The United States took possession of Florida from the Spanish crown under the Adams-Onis Treaty of 1819. Although territorial politics brought newcomers to many sections of northern Florida, the Pinellas Peninsula remained a remote and inaccessible location due to a lack of infrastructure and the occasional wars with Seminole Indians during the antebellum period.

The few settlers living in the Largo area before the Civil War were able to benefit from elevated land with excellent drainage, making the area a great region for crop cultivation. In 1844, as federal officials prepared Florida for statehood the following year, a surveyor named A. M. Randolph came to the area to set up township and range boundaries so land could later be sold or homesteaded. At one point, he was unable to place a post into the ground because of the location of a large lake. He called this 500-acre body of water Lake Tolulu, though the reason for this name remains a mystery. By the 1870s, members of the Lowe, Meares, and McMullen families had developed groves and farmsteads at Anona and near Lake Tolulu.

John Gideon Blitch migrated to the Largo area in 1875, before the site adjacent to the lake had a formal name. He married Cimodocia Carolyn Hammock of Anona a couple of years later. According to differing stories, Gideon's daughter Lulu may have been a source for the small settlement's name, as the Orange Belt Railroad planned to arrive in the area in 1888, and the location of the whistle-stop for the train required a name. By some accounts, Gideon wanted to call the location Lulaville, and some of the railroad workers also thought that the site should be named in honor of Gideon's 10-year-old daughter. Others have claimed that the name Luluville (with a u rather than an a) recognized the settlement's location near Lake Tolulu. Whichever story one wishes to believe, the large lake (or *lago largo* in Spanish) was later known as Lake Largo, and the early residents referred to the community as Largo by the time that Gideon had established the first post office at his house later that year.

Since those early days, Largo has grown into the third largest city in Florida's most densely populated county. The city occupies a prominent geographical position at the center of Pinellas County. Although present-day boundaries between Largo and neighboring communities seem difficult to distinguish, settlers and residents of Largo have played an important role in shaping the history of Pinellas since the late 1800s. From a handful of pioneers who homesteaded before the Civil War to the developers who leveled citrus groves to construct mobile home communities for retirees, the human footprint on this area illustrates the evolving chapters of the "Florida dream."

Rather than focusing solely upon the land within Largo's municipal limits, this book examines the city and neighboring areas in a broader context. Before 1900, the Largo area extended as far south as Bay Pines and Long Bayou, including all of the present-day areas of Seminole and Oakhurst. Communities to the north and west, including Anona, Belleair, and Belleair Bluffs, have a history of development closely aligned with that of Largo. Areas to the south and southeast, including Pinellas Park and the unincorporated sections of High Point and Lealman, also looked to Largo as a source of agricultural and commercial support when other areas, most notably St. Petersburg, rechanneled their energies into real estate speculation. As these outside areas developed their own sense of community, the images and narratives in this book return to Largo and its expanding boundaries.

The book's five chapters paint a picture of the region from its early settlement through its recent redevelopment. The first chapter describes the folkways and activities of pioneer settlers before and after the arrival of the railroad in 1888. Historians in Florida often recognize the iron horse on rails for its ability to bring snowbirds and seasonal visitors to the opulent hotels opened by Henry Flagler and Henry Plant. Early settlers of Largo appreciated the rail because it allowed them to expand their agricultural output, not the number of hotel rooms.

Subsequent chapters examine the development of Largo and surrounding areas by placing the time period within the context of the city's four notable nicknames. The second chapter traces the expansion of "Citrus City" from its incorporation in 1905 until the end of the 1920s. As the agricultural heartland of Pinellas, Largo became the home of Pinellas County's fairgrounds and the "Fair City" gained regional prominence for its groves, farms, and pastureland through the early 1950s. Although developers began to replace trees with subdivisions for families and retirees on a large scale by the mid-1950s, Largo's open spaces and lack of skyscrapers made it an appropriate site to serve as the county's "Clean Air Capital." By the 1980s, suburban sprawl covered much of the area. Businesses moved from downtown stores to new shopping centers carved from former groves. The final chapter looks at Largo's efforts to refine its sense of community and redevelop its core while remaining a "City of Progress."

Largo's history reflects the incredible transformations that have shaped Pinellas County during the last century. Although Largo lacked the tourist resorts and amenities of St. Petersburg (the "Sunshine City") during the boom years along southern Pinellas, the bright and warm sun did, indeed, shine upon Largo as well. The crops and livestock from Largo's fields fed the land boom elsewhere, just as the warm sense of community in the Largo area makes it a preferred place for many in the Tampa Bay region today.

One

PIONEERS AMONGST THE PINES 1800s–1904

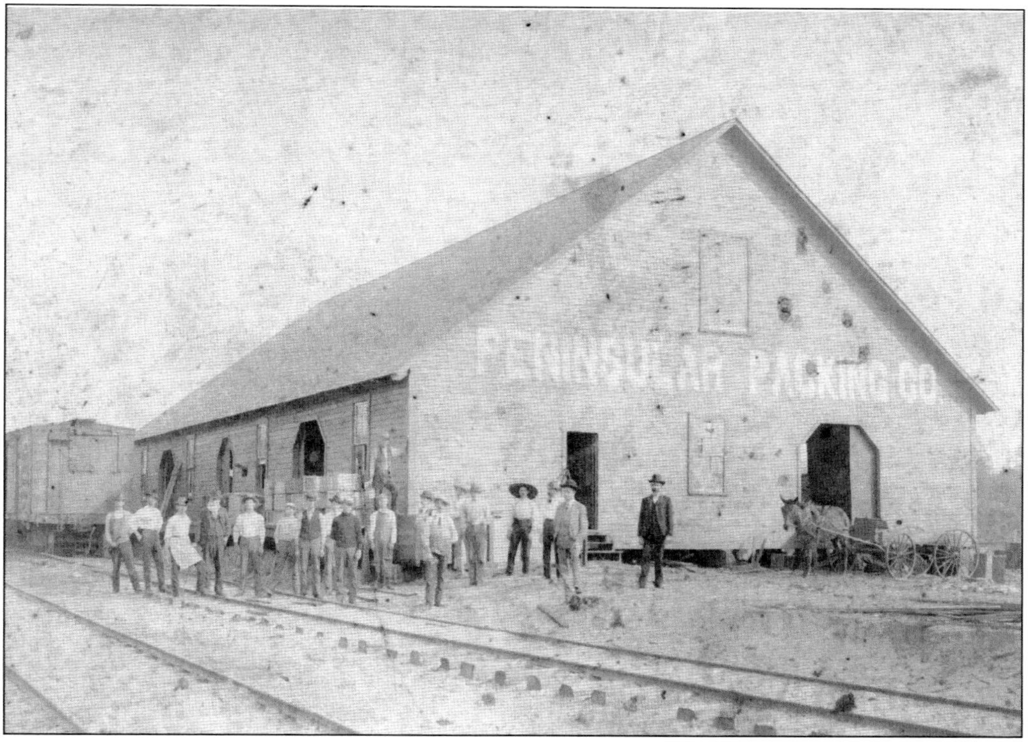

John S. Taylor Sr. oversaw activities at the old yellow building of the Peninsular Packing Company, which once sat along the railroad tracks north of Bay Drive. During the early days, packinghouses lacked machinery. Workers stood around large tubs, washing, drying, and polishing fruit by hand. Taylor appears on the far right in a suit and hat. (John S. Taylor Collection, HV.)

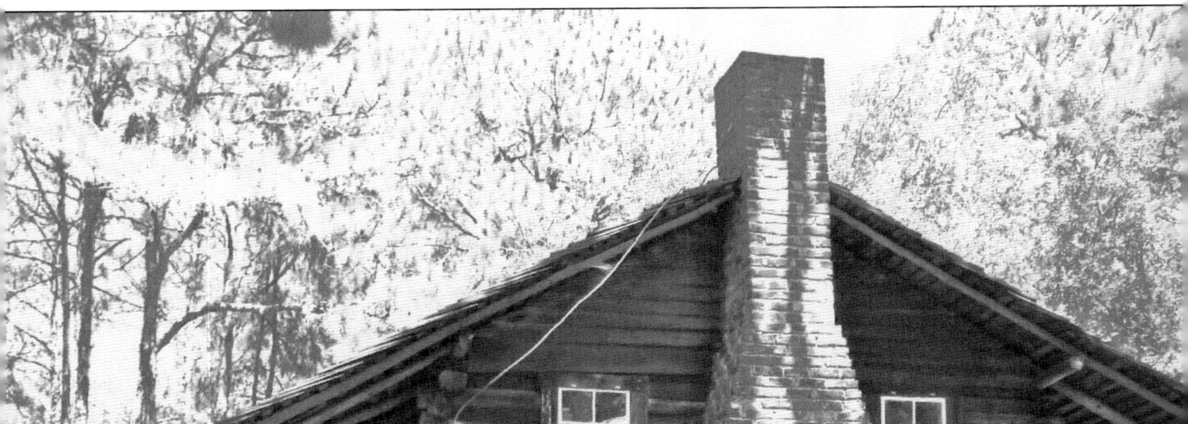

Between 1841 and 1871, each of the seven McMullen brothers raised in Quitman, Georgia, migrated to the Pinellas Peninsula. The first to arrive, James Parramore McMullen, entered territorial Florida during the waning months of the Second Seminole War (1835–1842) and before statehood (1845). Suffering a bout of consumption (tuberculosis), he lived in solitude along the upper Pinellas Peninsula and enjoyed a bountiful supply of seafood, wildlife, and sunshine while recovering. James returned to Georgia after his tuberculosis went into remission and told his family that the largely unpopulated area was "the closest thing to heaven" he could imagine. James soon returned to Florida, married Elizabeth Campbell of Melendez (a settlement renamed Brooksville in 1856), and homesteaded in the area near the corner of Old Coachman Road and Northeast Coachman Road. At this site, that McMullens built the log house that was relocated to Heritage Village near Largo in July 1977 to ensure its preservation. (Author.)

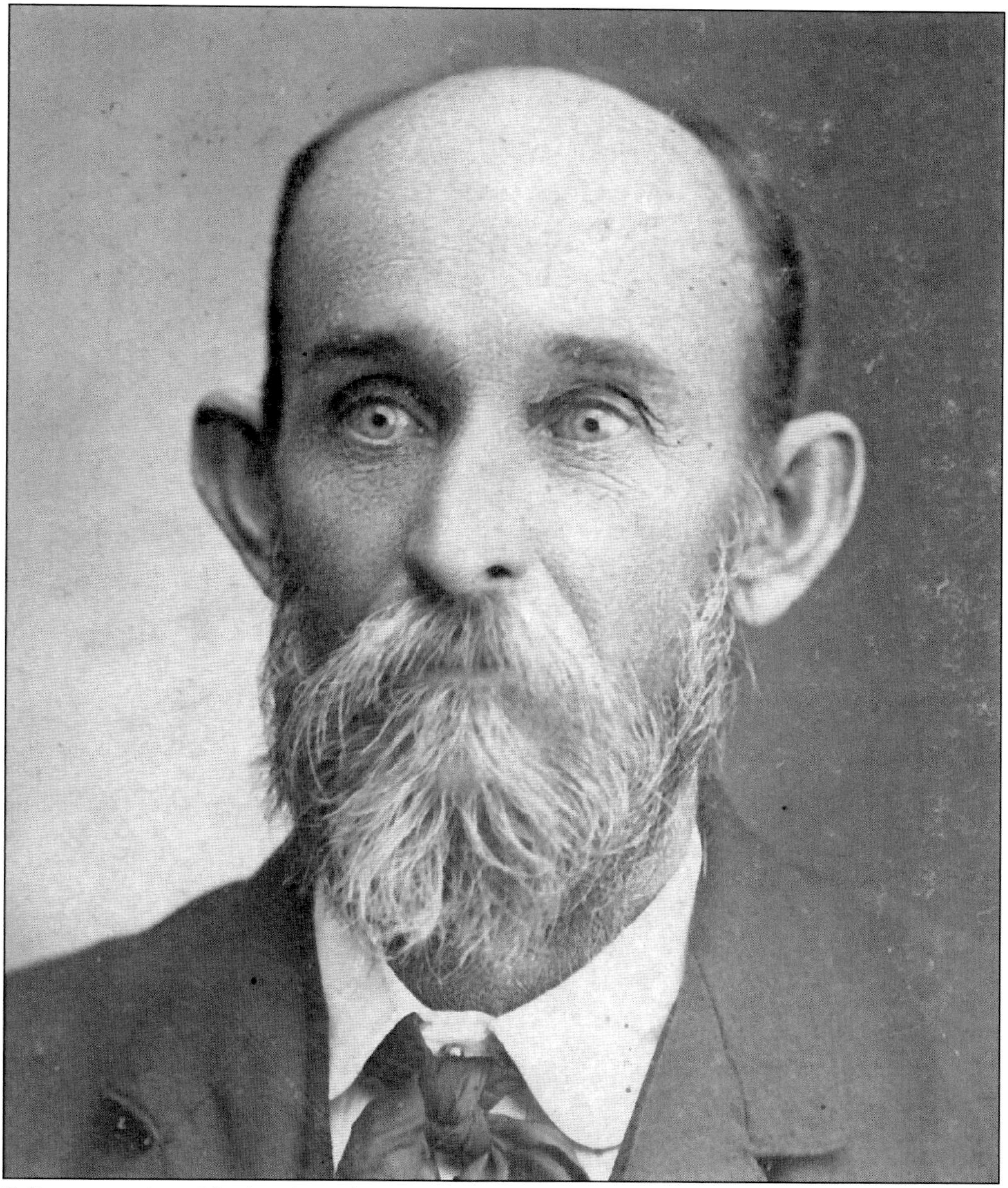

Following in his older brother's footsteps, Daniel McMullen, the fourth brother, became the second family member to formalize a land claim on the Pinellas Peninsula. This image shows "Uncle Dan" during his later years. Like his brother James, he spent some time near Brooksville and fell in love with a member of the Campbell family; Dan married Margaret Ann Campbell, Elizabeth's younger sister, in November 1851. The newlyweds then obtained a homestead near the present-day area of Rosery Road and Missouri Avenue that also included a portion of the Markley Grove property. Although Dan and James lived a few miles apart, the uninhabited land between Largo and Clearwater allowed them to raise substantial herds of livestock and cultivate a variety of crops. The other McMullen brothers—David, John, Malcolm, Thomas, and William—arrived during the 20 years following the establishment of Dan's homestead. They owned land that covered a wide area between Safety Harbor and Lealman, with many of them owning some acreage in the Largo area. (HV.)

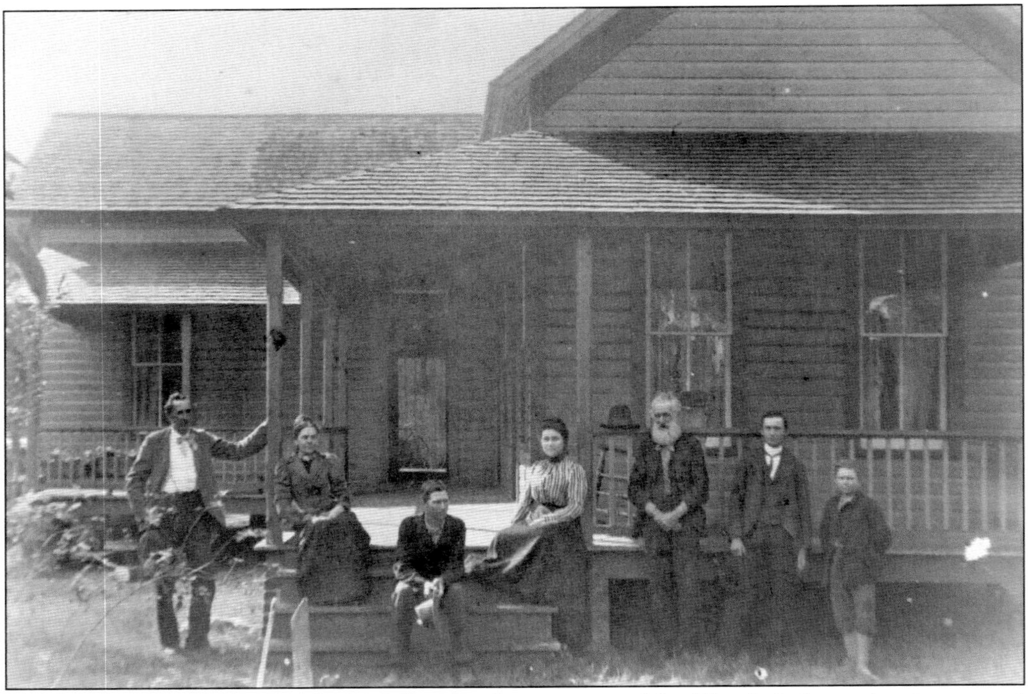

During the Civil War, Daniel McMullen fought in a unit of the Florida Infantry headquartered in Brooksville and served as a member of the Florida Cow Cavalry, which provided the hides, tallow, and meat needed to sustain the Confederate war effort. He returned to the Largo area in the fall of 1865 and became one of the biggest cattle ranchers in the Tampa Bay region. In August 1868, Dan and his family moved into a home they built on their land near Rosery Road. The image above shows this structure as it appeared in about 1900, with a white-bearded Uncle Dan pictured third from the right. The McMullen home, shown below in 1985 before its move to Heritage Village and following restoration, was continuously occupied by family members for more than 120 years. (Both, HV.)

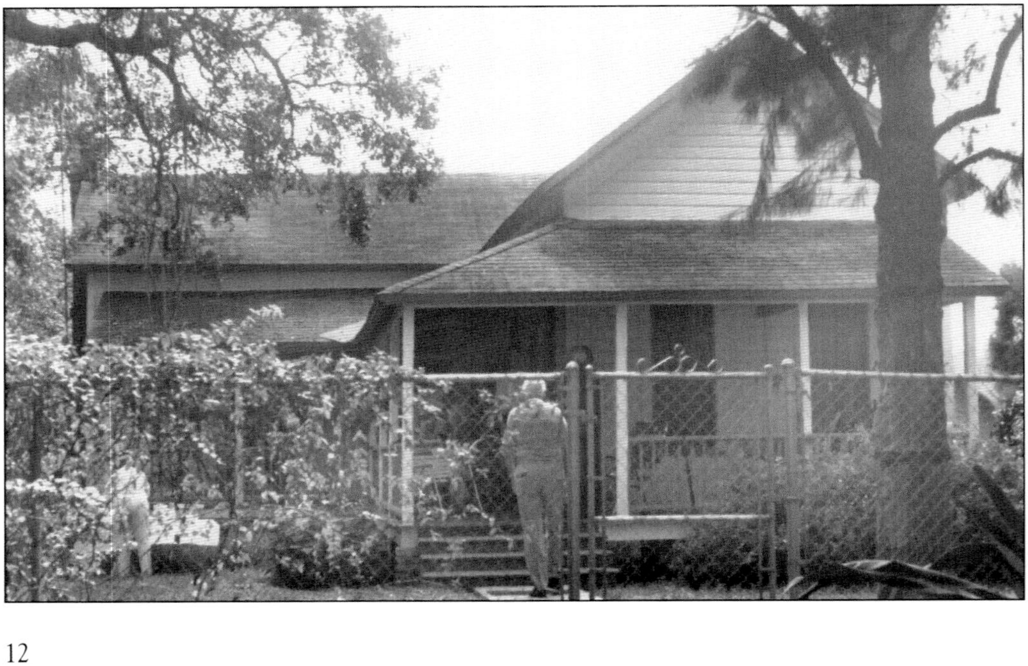

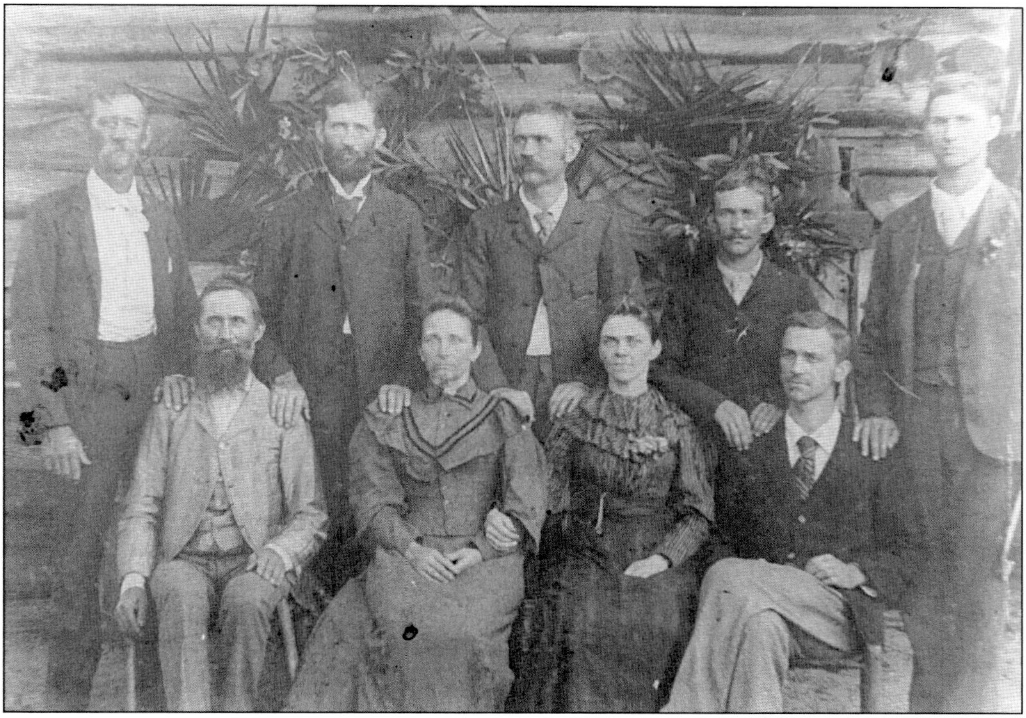

McMullen family members pose for a picture in the mid-1890s with kith and kin from the Belcher and Hardage families at the smokehouse near the 1868 home. Smokehouses played an important role in preserving meats at a time when refrigeration was nonexistent in remote regions. Local residents used a variety of woods—but never pine, due to the turpentine odor it left on the meat. (HV.)

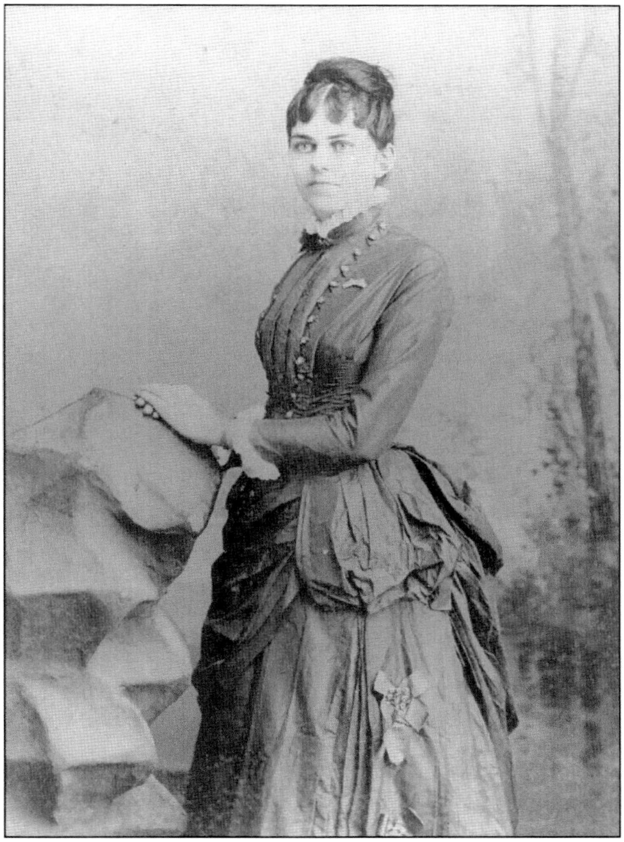

One of Dan and Margaret Ann McMullen's daughters, Margaret Nancy Ann, lived on the family property for over 80 years. Born Margaret Nancy Ann McMullen in 1865, "Aunt Nannie" raised her younger siblings after her mother became ill in the mid-1870s. She married James N. Hardage in January 1902. She lived in the McMullen home until her death in 1957. (HV.)

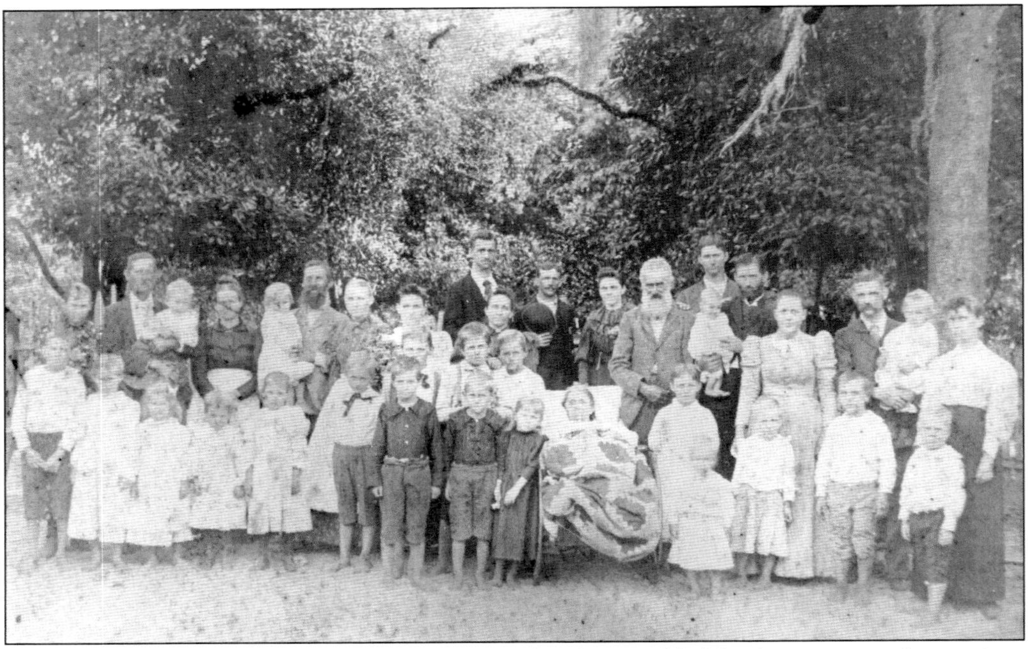

Daniel and Margaret Ann Campbell McMullen's family assembled for this portrait taken at their Largo homestead on June 9, 1895. At time of Daniel McMullen's death in August 1908, he had 65 children, grandchildren, and great-grandchildren. Most of them remained in the Largo area. Margaret Ann passed away in April 1909. (HV.)

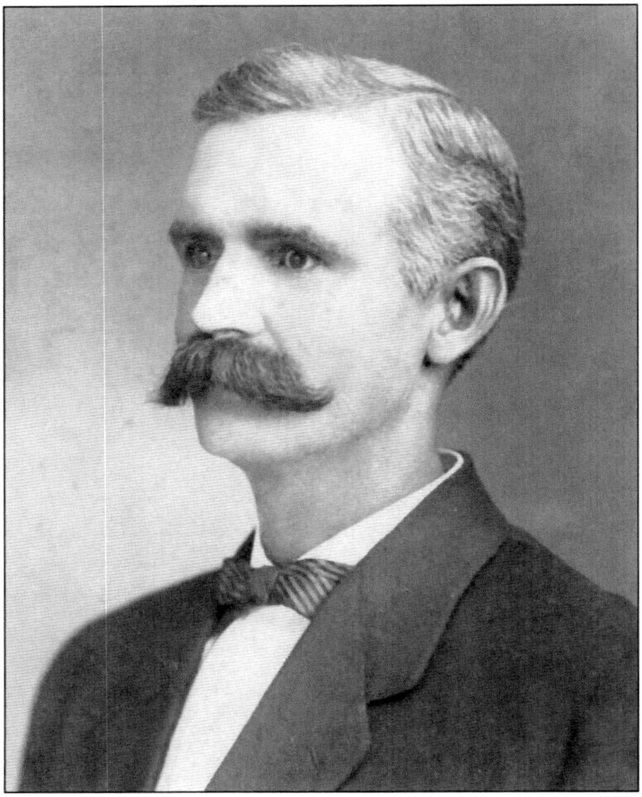

John S. Taylor Sr. moved from Brooksville to the Clear Water Harbor area at the insistence of James Stevens, the "father of Clearwater." Taylor bought land from Stevens in March 1850. He later sold it to members of the Turner and Whitehurst families. Taylor relocated to the Largo area and began a trend of commercial and political leadership that continued in the family for generations. (John S. Taylor Collection, HV.)

While the McMullens and Taylors hailed from Georgia, others arrived in the late 1850s from the Bahamas by way of Key West. Capt. John Thomas Lowe sailed his boat, the *Seadrift*, along the Gulf Coast, arriving at the Narrows in 1859. Members of the Lowe and Meares family settled at Lowe's Landing after acquiring land for $1.25 an acre. At right, Lowe appears in his uniform after he had enlisted in Company K, 7th Florida Infantry, of the Confederate army in April 1862. Below is an image caputred of Lowe shortly before his death in 1921. Lowe and his children, especially sons Jefferson T. and Wesley, played an important role in the development of Anona. (Both, HV.)

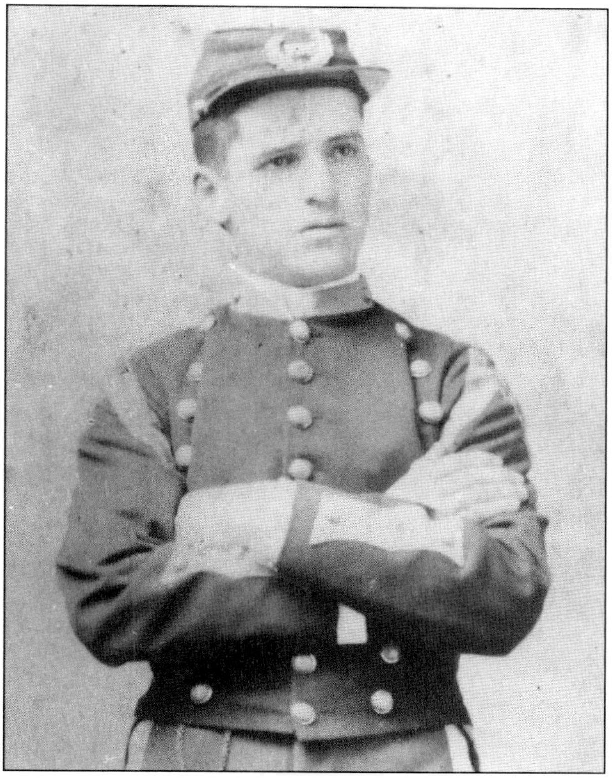

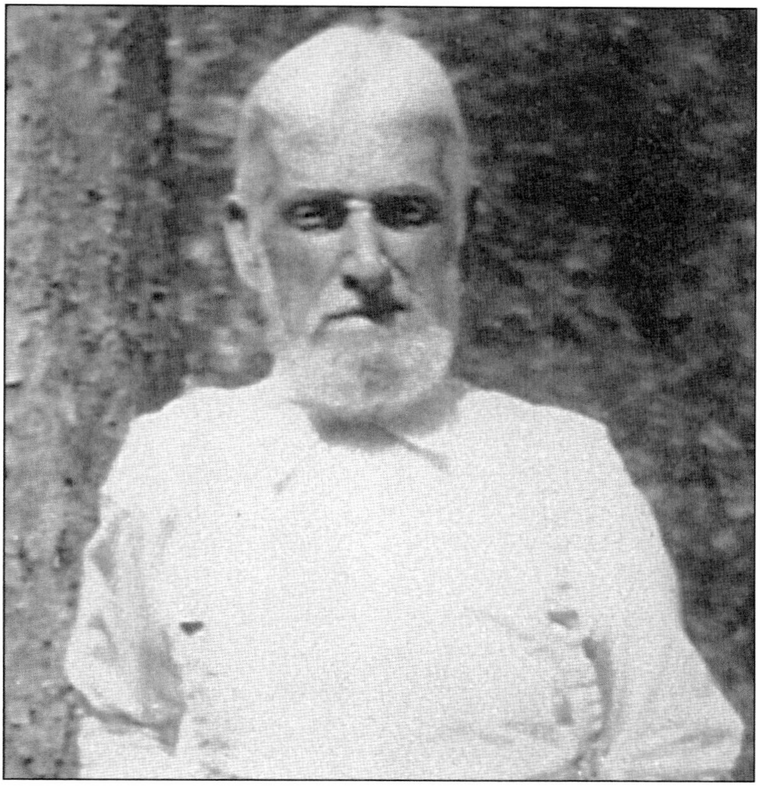

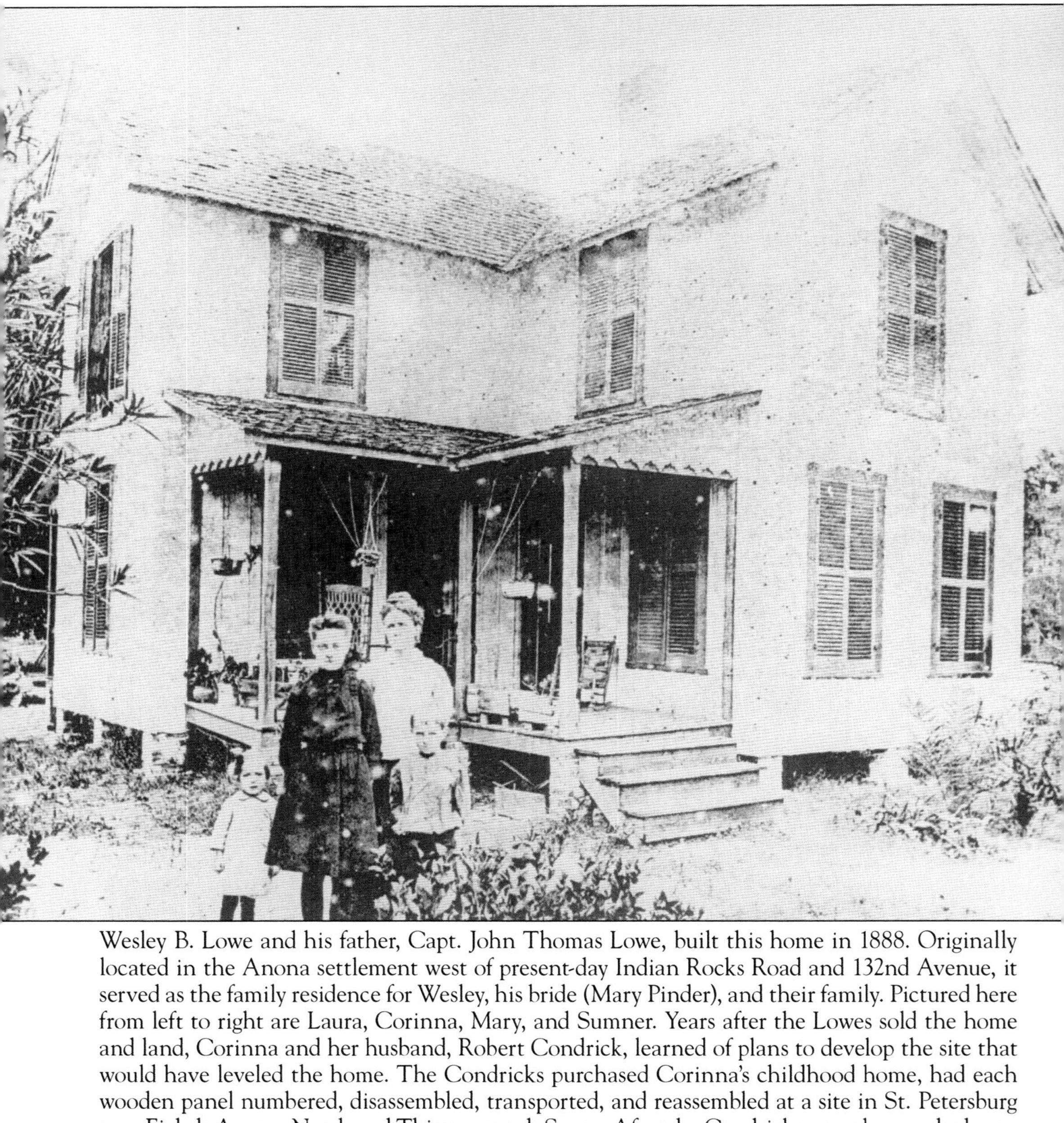

Wesley B. Lowe and his father, Capt. John Thomas Lowe, built this home in 1888. Originally located in the Anona settlement west of present-day Indian Rocks Road and 132nd Avenue, it served as the family residence for Wesley, his bride (Mary Pinder), and their family. Pictured here from left to right are Laura, Corinna, Mary, and Sumner. Years after the Lowes sold the home and land, Corinna and her husband, Robert Condrick, learned of plans to develop the site that would have leveled the home. The Condricks purchased Corinna's childhood home, had each wooden panel numbered, disassembled, transported, and reassembled at a site in St. Petersburg near Eighth Avenue North and Thirty-seventh Street. After the Condricks passed away, the home moved a second time (this time in one piece) to 3511 Second Avenue South, the Haas Museum complex. In 1991, the home moved one last time back to the Largo area as a signature structure at Heritage Village. (HV.)

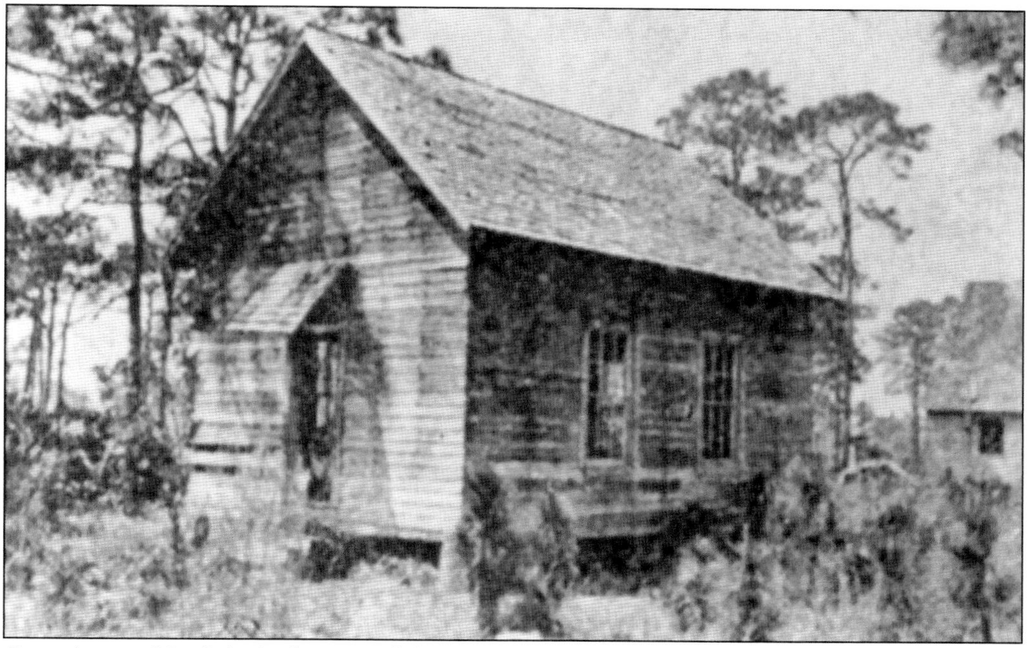

Capt. August "Gus" A. Archer joined the Lowe and Meares families as they sailed from Key West to Anona in 1859. Archer later moved his family to an area near Bay Pines, where he established a general store and helped the Thevenet family build a school on their land near Seminole Boulevard and Fifty-fourth Avenue North. This early school served students by the 1880s. (HV.)

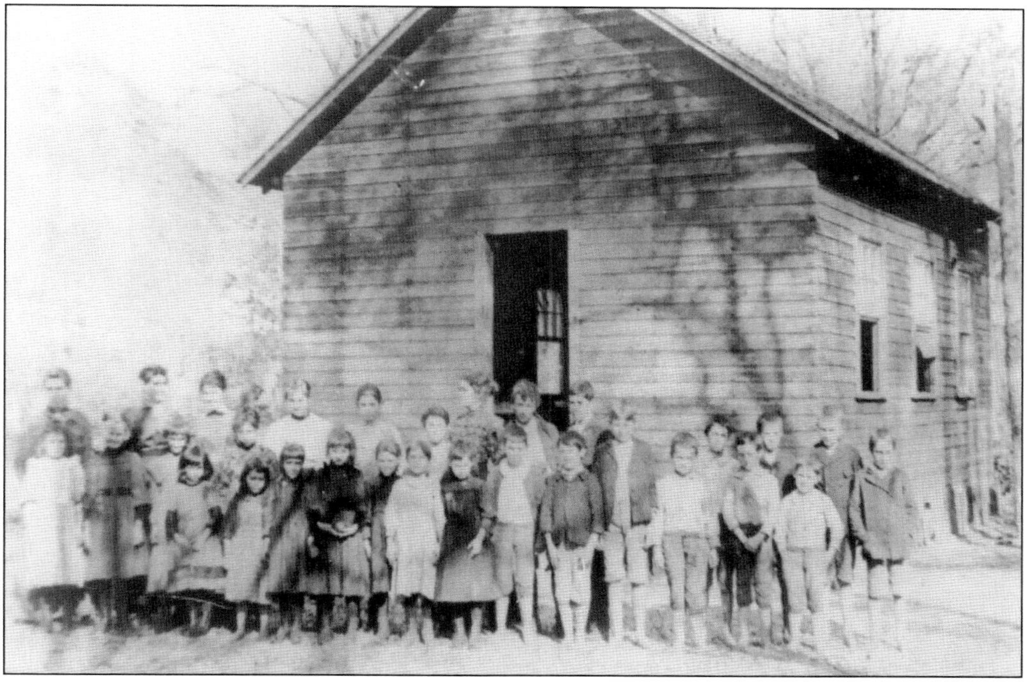

The first formal school at Anona opened in 1874. Built with lumber that pioneers sailed down from Cedar Key, this wooden structure served as both a schoolhouse and a Methodist church for pioneers of the area. This image from about 1900 shows the school after it was moved and rebuilt in the 1890s. (HV.)

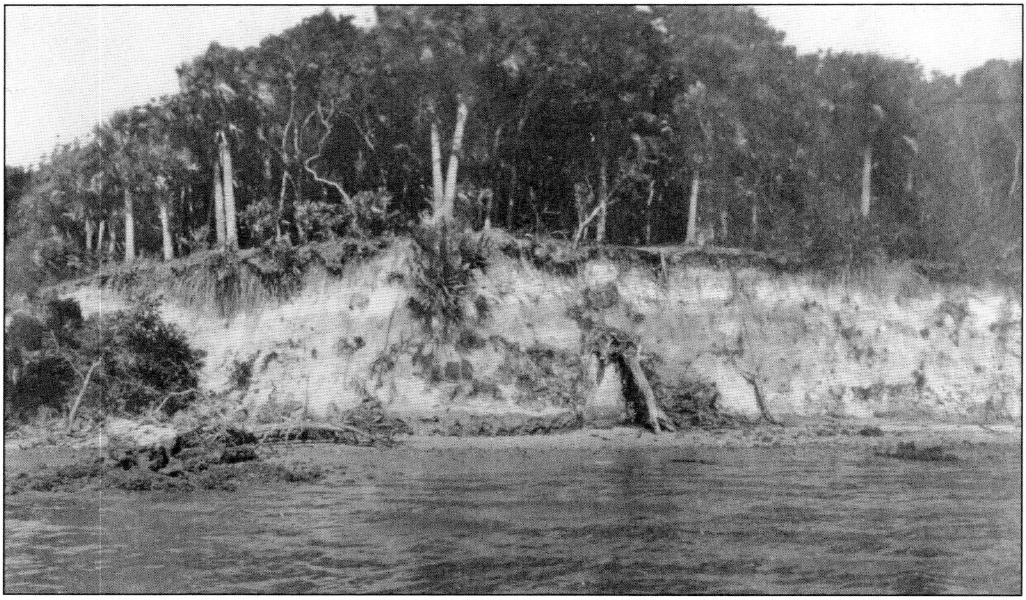

Philip James (P. J.) Bayly came from an English family. As a young man, he farmed in Australia and New Zealand. While traveling along Florida's coast, he met some early settlers of the Anona area and purchased a nearby site in 1883. His holdings included acreage where West Bay Drive becomes the Belleair Causeway, a place known as Bayly's Bluff. Taver Bayly, Philip's son, remembered endless harvests of stone crabs and an abundance of fish along the family's coastal property, shown in this photograph from around 1900. (HV.)

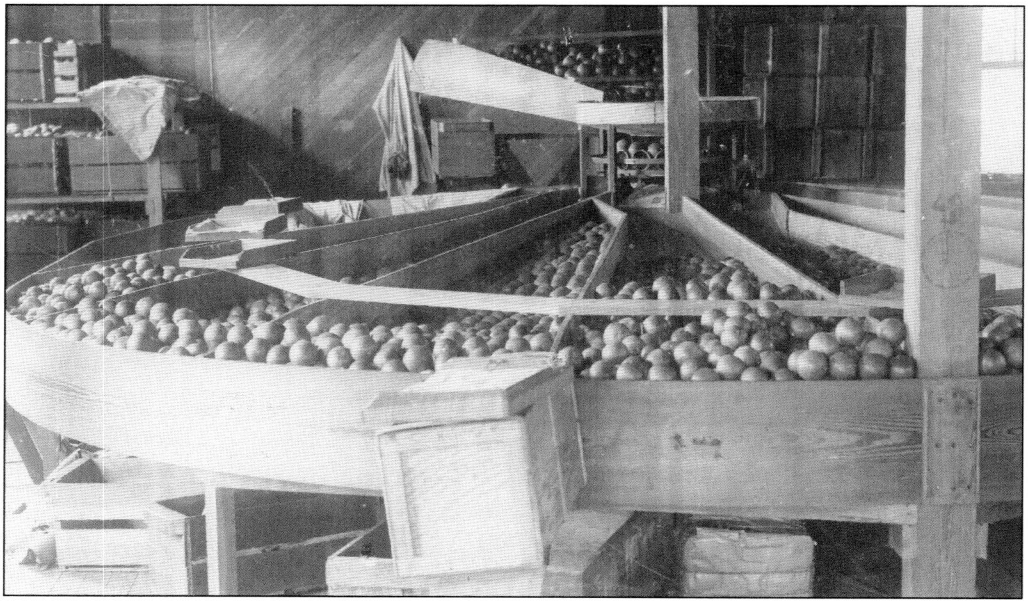

P. J. Bayly and his family operated a grove along the Intracoastal Waterway. The site's topography and the warmer waters that washed upon its sandy shores protected Bayly's citrus from the devastating freezes of late 1894 and early 1895. Fruit from Bayly's grove became a staple on Southern Railway trains and the dining room of the Belleview Biltmore Hotel. His harvests even won acclaim in the White House. This interior view of his packinghouse at Sandsfoot grove shows fruit during the harvesting season. (HV.)

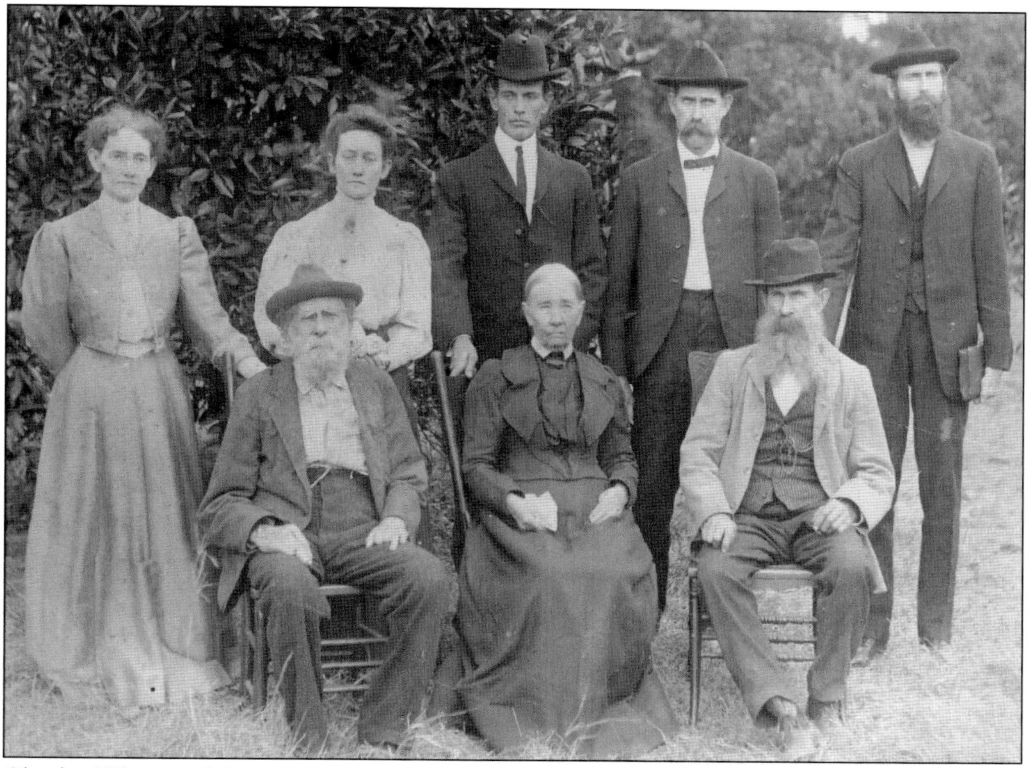

Charles Wharton Johnson was a sea captain based out of Cedar Key with a mail route along Florida's sparsely settled west coast. He ran his boat aground on the bluffs south of the Clear Water Harbor settlement in the early 1870s and homesteaded on the site. Soon he moved a few miles southeast to the center of what later became Largo. Charles, wife Catherine Kurtz, and eldest son Levin William appear in the first row above. Charlotte "Lottie" Kurtz, Lela Catharine, Louis Steele, George Ward and Charles Powell—the other surviving children—stand in the rear. The dock in the picture below existed a short distance south of Johnson's original tract, near Bayly's land. Dr. Payne, a retired physician from the Midwest, established a grove and built this dock, which became a popular gathering place by 1900. (Both, HV.)

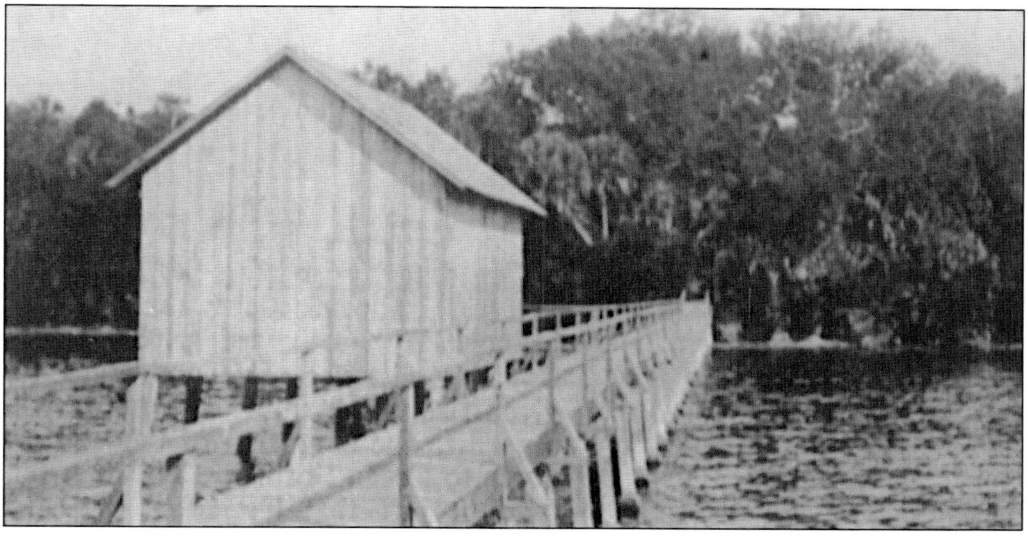

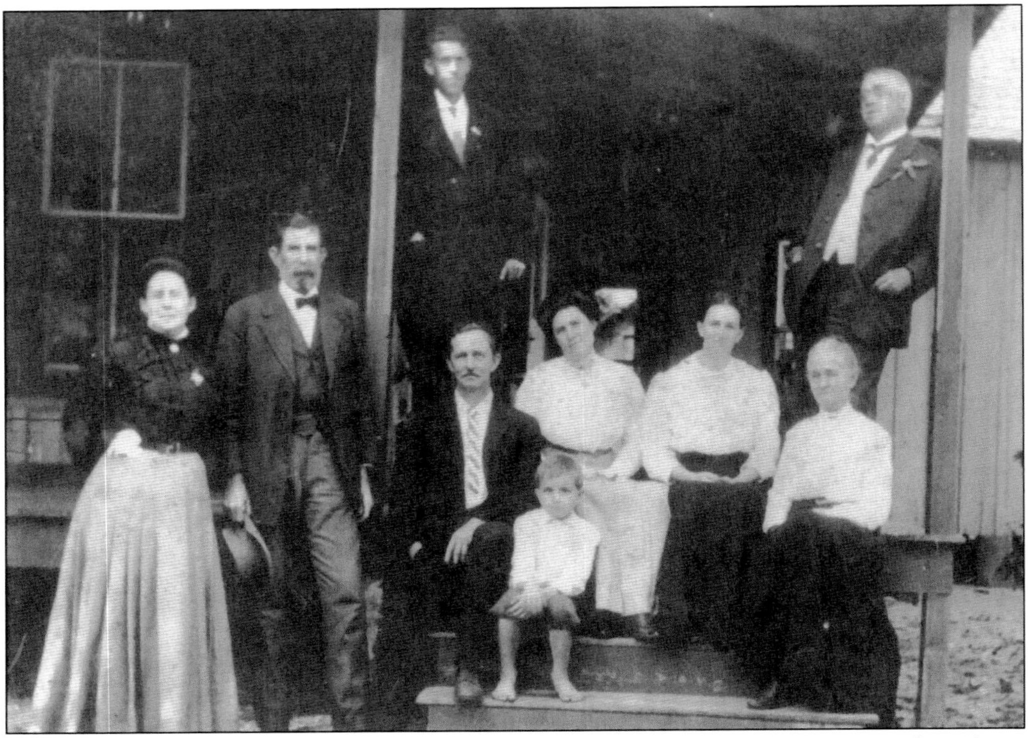

William Alexander Belcher, holding his hat above, hailed from Virginia. Fearing tuberculosis, Belcher came to the area in 1870, and he married into the McMullen family. The Belchers farmed and grew citrus along Belcher Road, south of Allen's Creek. During the late 1800s, Largo residents without boats wanting to reach Tampa often traveled along the creek until they reached Belcher's property. A school board member and commissioner representing Hillsborough County, he also served in the Florida legislature and in 1885 led the first unsuccessful attempt to separate Western Hillsborough into a new county. The Belchers replaced their log cabin with the home seen below in 1898. Some of the others gathered at the Kilgore estate above include Dr. Payne (standing on the right side of the porch), Barnard and Augusta B. "Gussie" Kilgore, and Sara M. Belcher (William's wife). (Both, HV.)

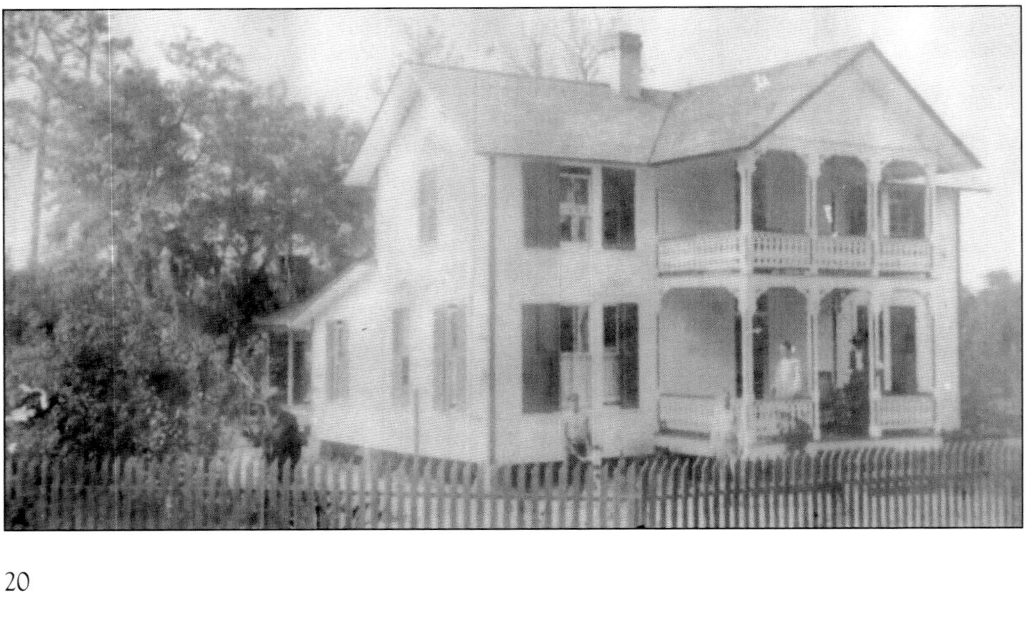

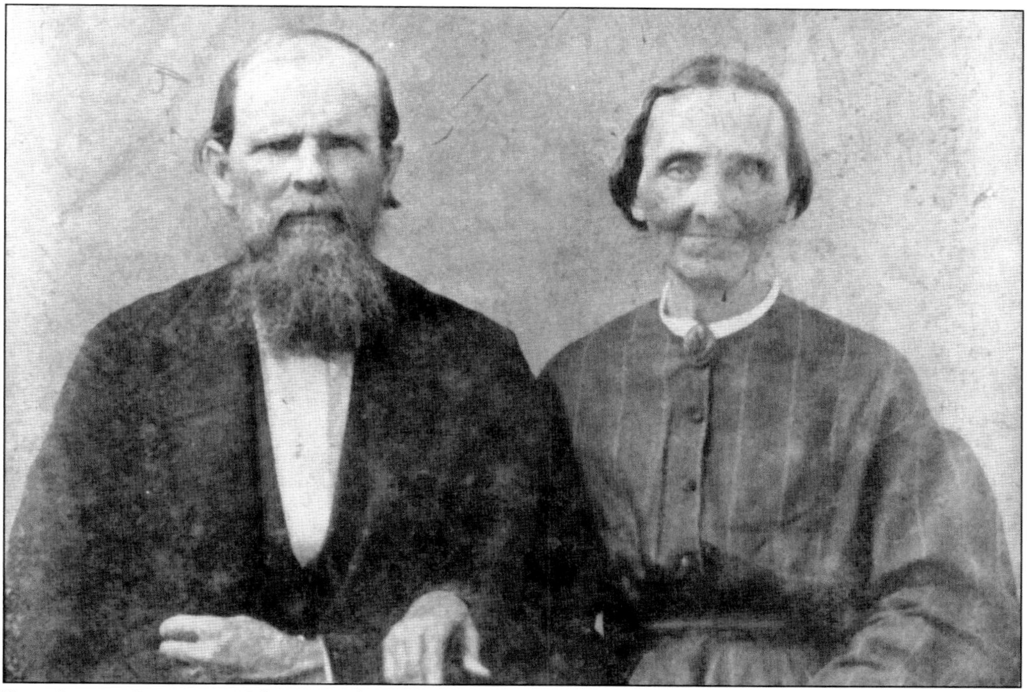

Rev. James Summers Kilgore and wife Rhoda Chapman brought their children to the Anona area in the mid-1850s from South Carolina. An early pastor at Anona Methodist Church, Kilgore conducted weddings of the pioneer Hart, McMullen, Meares, and Whitehurst families. Reverend Kilgore passed away in October 1886 and became one of the first people buried at the Anona Cemetery. (HV.)

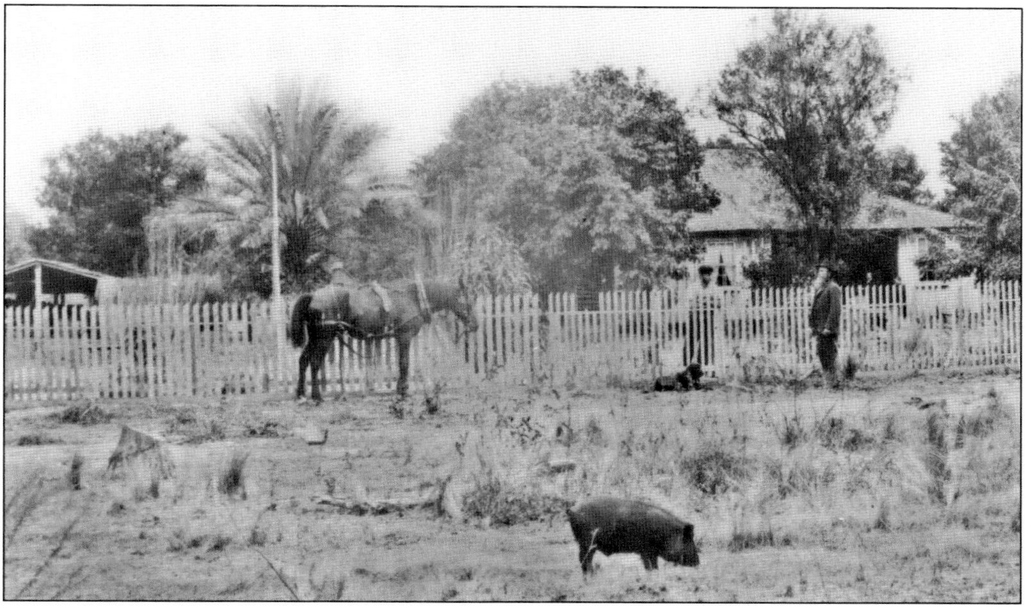

Reverend Kilgore's son Samuel Henry Kilgore also homesteaded in the area. A bearded Sam and his son James appear in this image from about 1900 taken along West Bay Drive, east of Indian Rocks Road. Although they originally lived on opposite sides of the Largo region, nuptial ties brought together members of the Kilgore and Belcher families. (HV.)

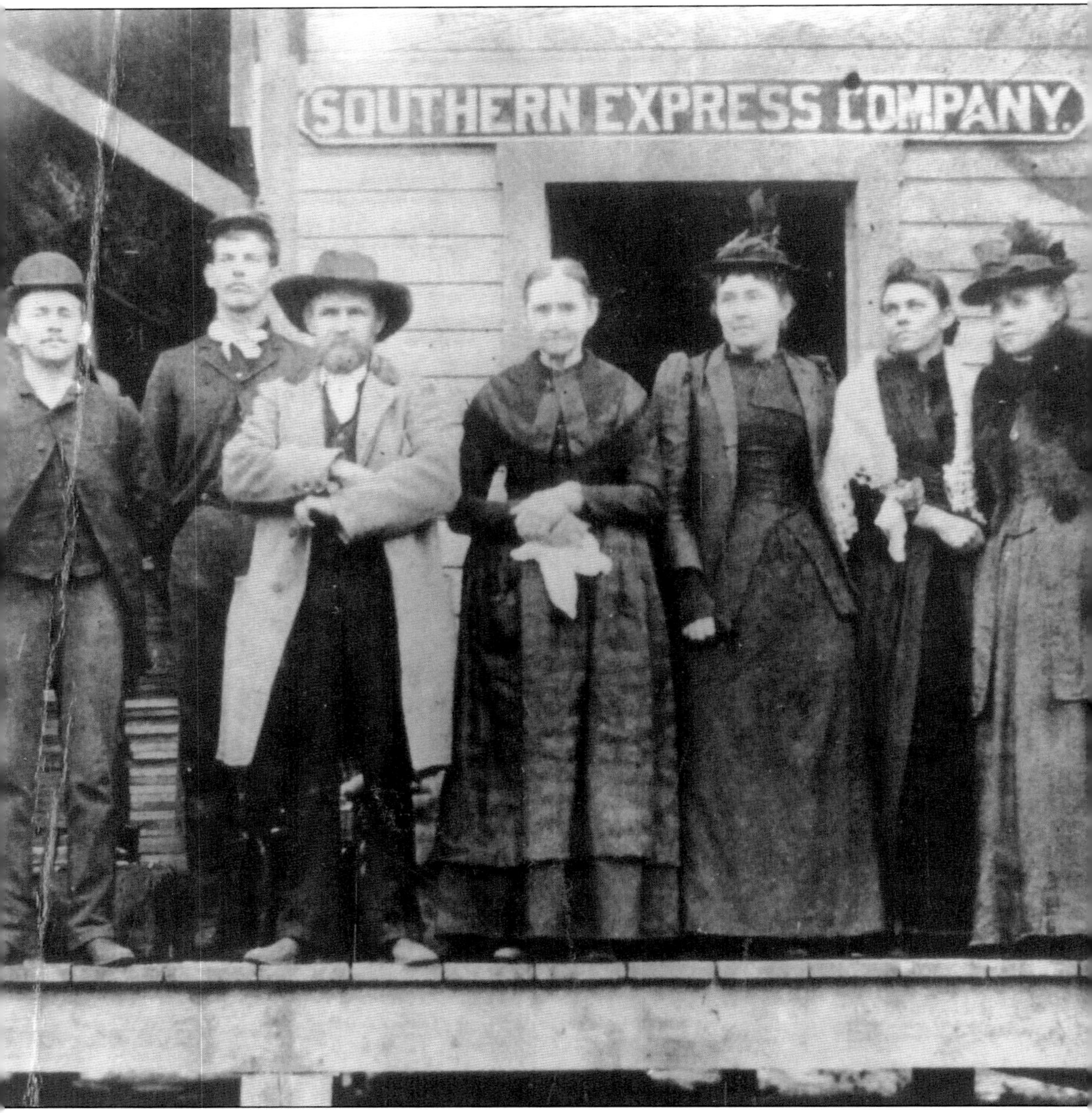

The arrival of the Orange Belt Railway in the spring of 1888 opened the frontier around Largo to widespread agricultural development. With few settlers in the region, the original Largo depot was a flag station. If a customer wanted the train to stop, they had to flag it down. If no passengers waited for a train on its run to or from St. Petersburg, a railroad worker on the train would use a hook to grab the mailbags at the Largo stop while the train kept moving. The settlement's small railroad terminal did provide an essential connection with the outside world. Pioneer residents from left to right in this 1890s picture are Robert L. McMullen, Louis Johnson, Joel Morris, Aunt Polly Lewis (Polly McMullen), Blanche McMullen, Margaret Nancy McMullen, and Florida Morris. (HV.)

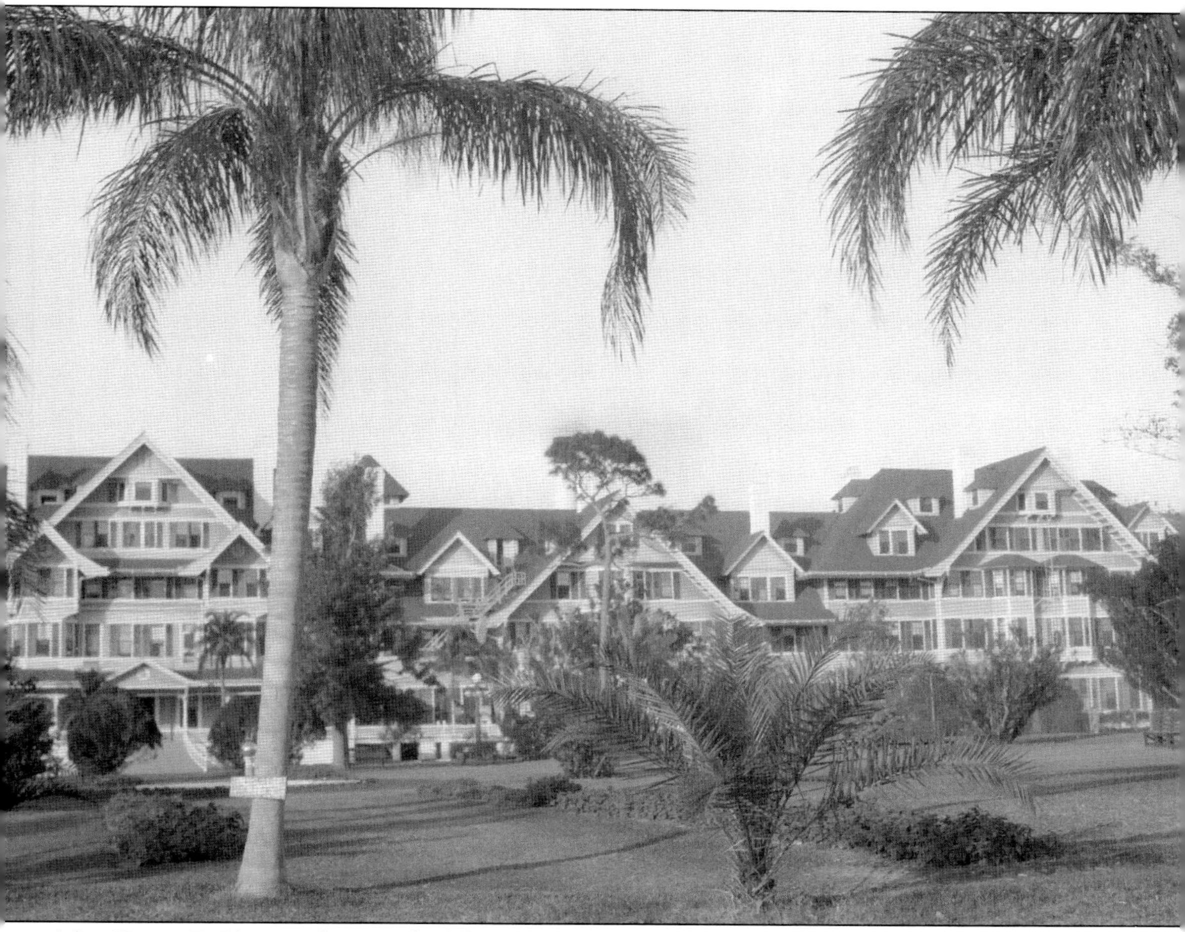

After Henry B. Plant took control of the Orange Belt Railway, the tract of land Capt. Charles W. Johnson sold became the site of one of the earliest Tampa-St. Petersburg regional rivalries. With his elegant Tampa Bay Hotel redefining the skyline of the small town of Tampa, Plant had hoped to build another hotel along the waterfront of the small village of St. Petersburg near the southern terminus of the Orange Belt. When St. Petersburg's few residents scoffed at Plant's plans, the railroad magnate acquired the Johnson site north of Largo and built the opulent Hotel Belleview. This majestic wooden structure opened for its first season on January 17, 1897, leaving St. Petersburg's landowners waiting another 15 years for the real estate boom to reach their area. Plant died in June 1899, but his hotel—later renamed the Belleview Biltmore Resort— thrived for more than a century. The municipalities of Belleair and Belleair Bluffs, communities neighboring Largo, evolved around the hotel. (USFSP.)

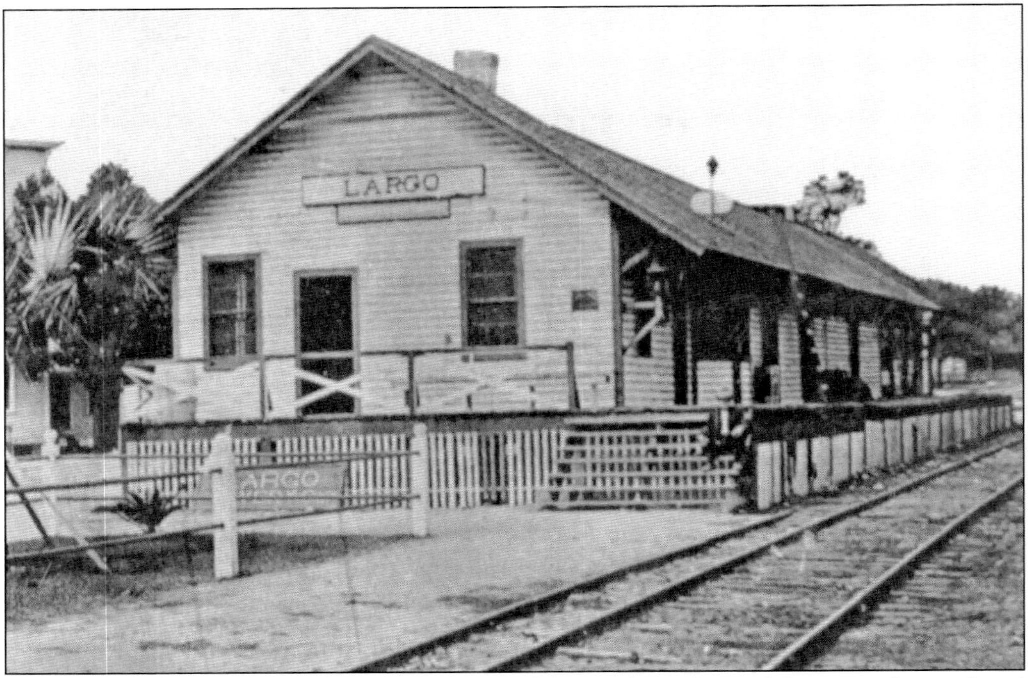

Farmers and landowners in the Largo area heralded the iron horse for its ability to send agricultural commodities to distant markets. Largo's station became a focal point of business activities for much of the west-central Pinellas frontier. Note the advertisement for the Largo Livery Company near the platform. (HV.)

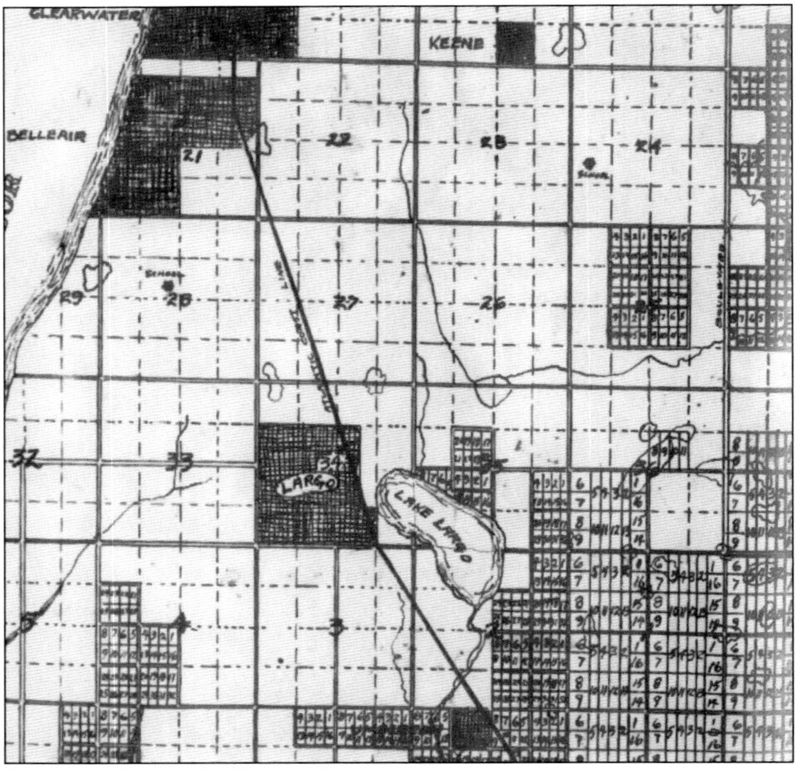

The original Largo settlement, shown here in a 1910 survey map, remained landlocked even after its formal incorporation on June 6, 1905. The nearest body of water, Lake Largo, occupied a site between present-day Seminole Boulevard and Starkey Road, with a northern boundary near Bay Drive. Today the greater Largo area stretches across Pinellas from Boca Ciega Bay to Tampa Bay. (HV.)

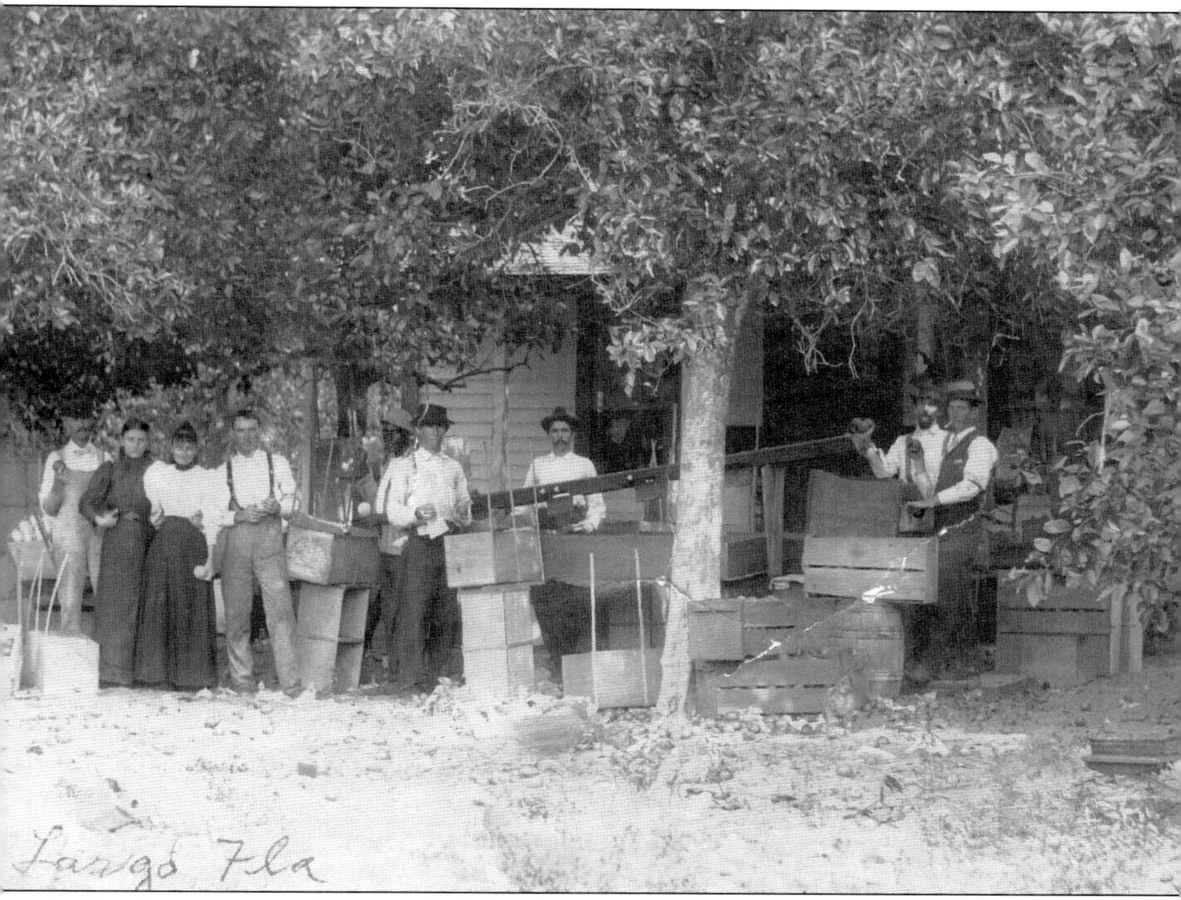

Lacking factories, many farmers packed their harvests outdoors. In this image from about 1900, workers in the Largo area posed for a camera in fancier-than-usual attire while boxing citrus. Notice the way they sorted and arranged fruit, as well as the abundance of citrus on the ground adjacent to the boxes. An African American laborer wearing simpler attire appears in the background at the center of the photograph. (HV.)

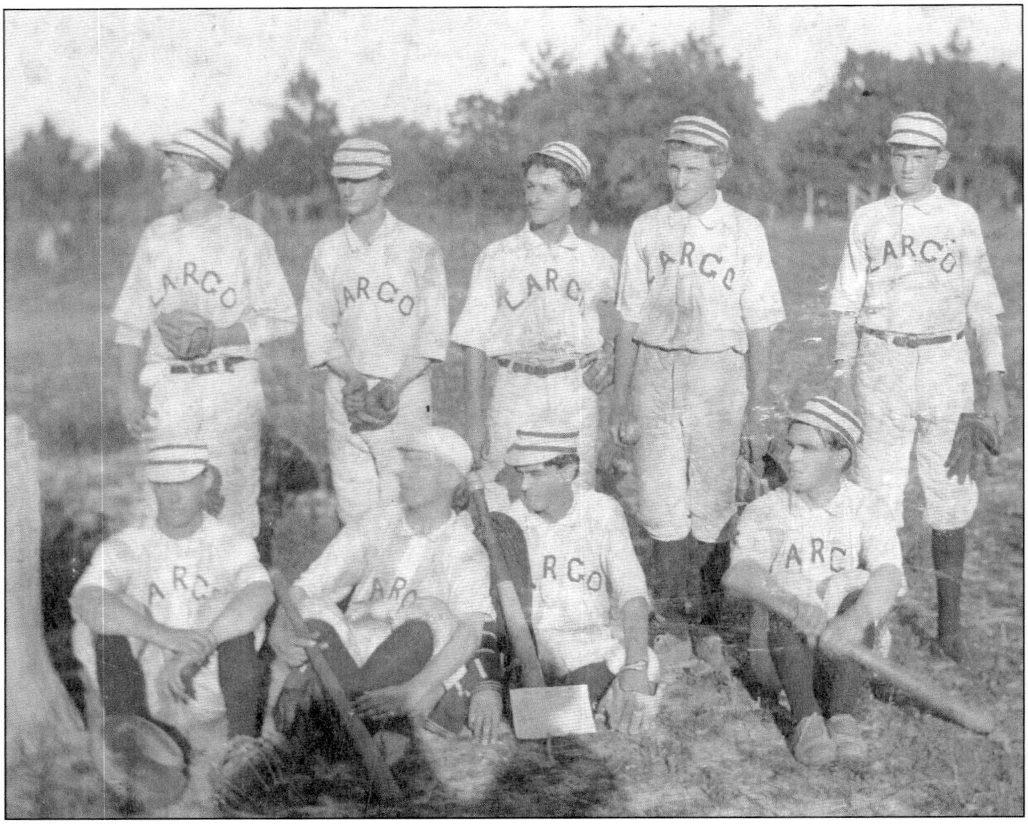

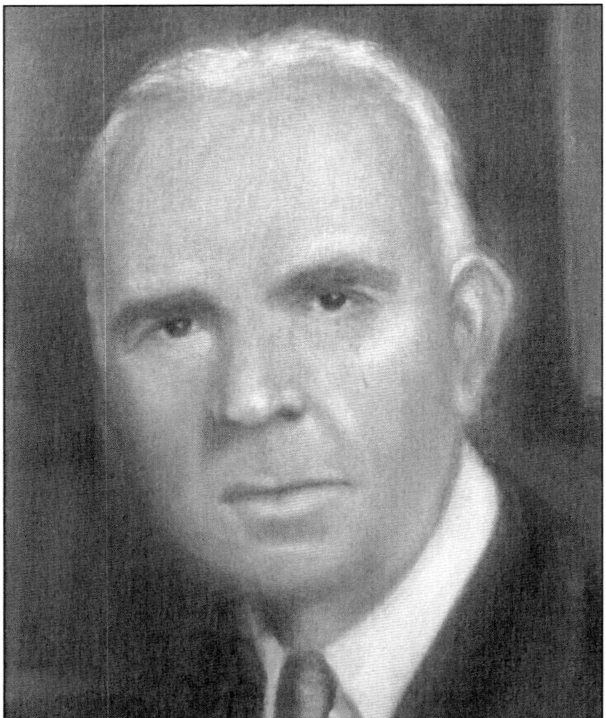

Shortly after 1900, more than a decade before spring training became an annual ritual in the Tampa Bay region, members of this Largo baseball team pose for a picture. One of the players sitting at right in the first row, Melvin Arthur McMullen, had an impressive legal career after his playing days ended. A grandson of Uncle Dan and son of "Uncle Eli," young Melvin was born in the Largo area in December 1885. He earned his law degree in 1912, the same year his father began a 17-year tenure as the first tax collector of Pinellas County. Melvin joined his father as a constitutional officer when he served as the state attorney for Pinellas from 1915 through 1921. Melvin passed away in May 1955 at the age of 69. A courthouse portrait of McMullen appears at left. (Both, HV.)

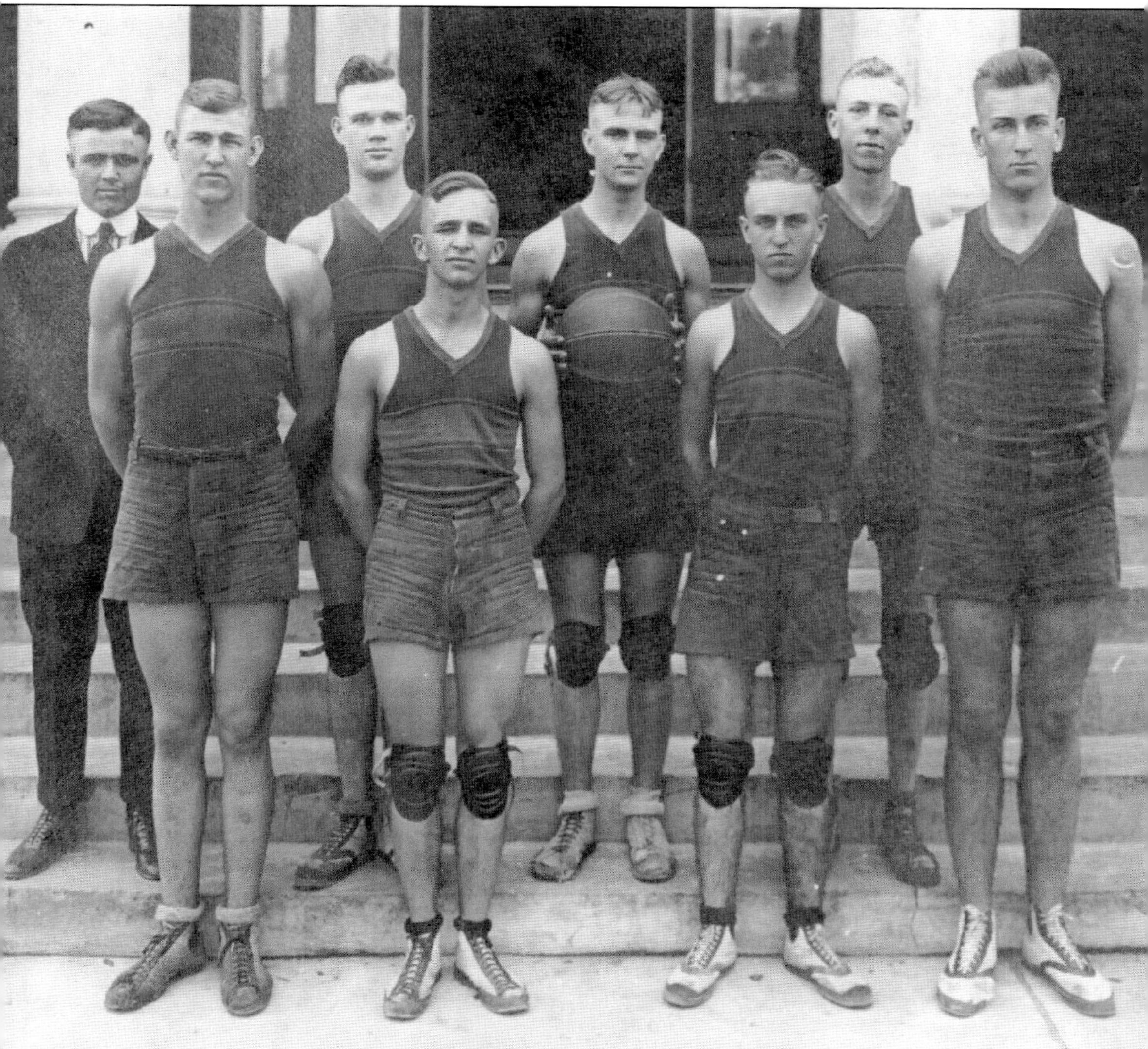

Melvin's younger brother, Chester Bartow McMullen, also won acclaim in sports before following his brother and father in public service. He holds the basketball in this photograph from the 1920 Largo High School yearbook. Other players on the varsity squad included Lloyd Knight, Stansel Taylor, Morris Campbell, Ray Tyler, Leslie Jackson, and Roland Ochs. Born in Largo in December 1902, Chester graduated from Largo High in 1920 as a star athlete and highly regarded student. After earning a law degree from the University of Florida, Chester retuned to Pinellas. He worked as a county prosecutor in 1927 and 1928 before following in Melvin's footsteps by serving as state attorney for Pinellas from 1931 through 1950. He served one term as a member of the Democratic Party in the U.S. House of Representatives from 1951 through 1953. After his Congressional term ended in January 1953, he returned to Clearwater. He passed away in November 1953. (HV.)

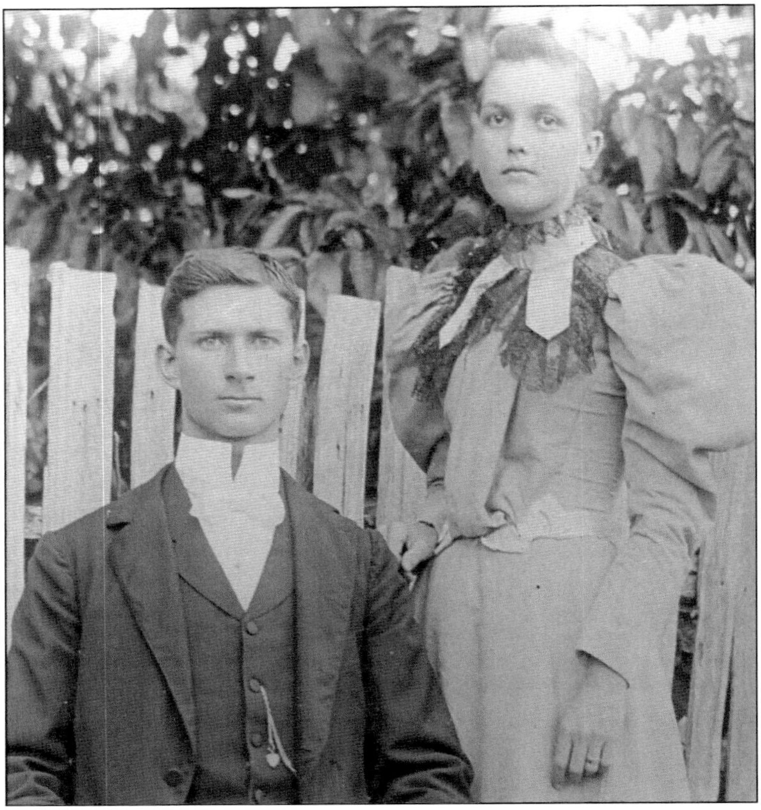

Family ties remained strong on the frontier. Daniel McMullen's youngest son, Charles Breckenridge McMullen, married Mattie Abigail Caruthers in June 1895. Charles and Mattie, pictured here, lived adjacent to Uncle Dan for many years and took care of him and Margaret Campbell McMullen. When Mattie unexpectedly passed away in 1908, Charles's older sister Margaret Nancy "Aunt Nannie" Hardage helped raise their children. (HV.)

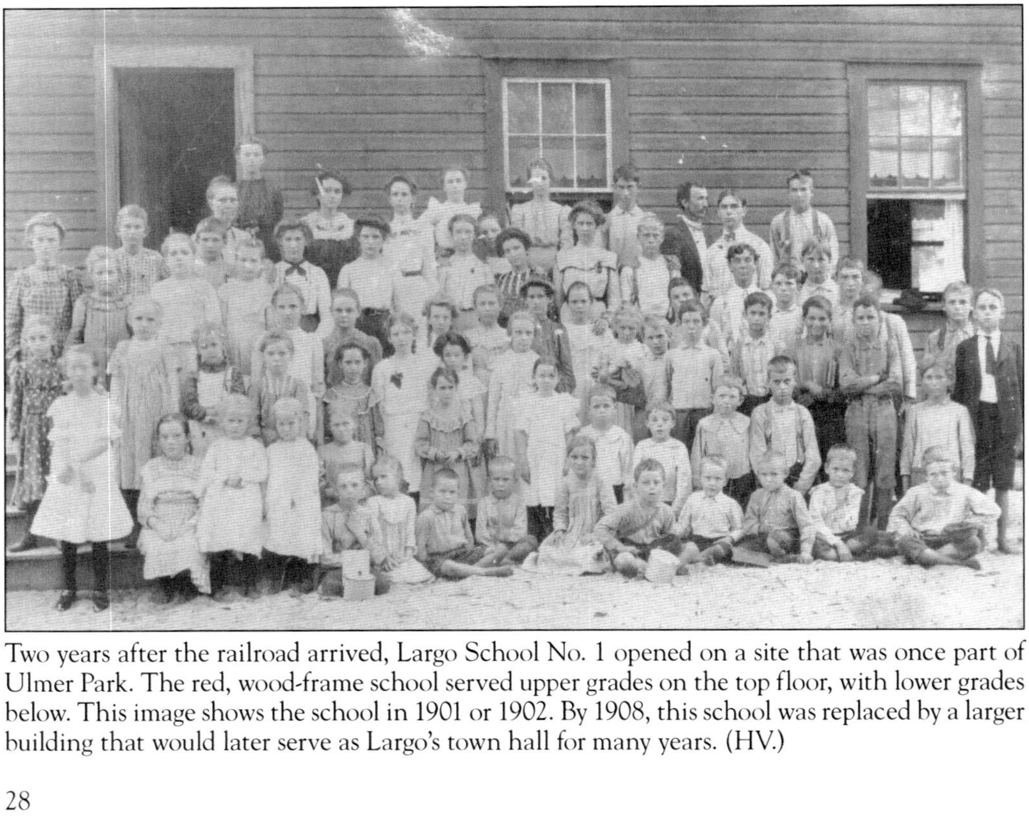

Two years after the railroad arrived, Largo School No. 1 opened on a site that was once part of Ulmer Park. The red, wood-frame school served upper grades on the top floor, with lower grades below. This image shows the school in 1901 or 1902. By 1908, this school was replaced by a larger building that would later serve as Largo's town hall for many years. (HV.)

Two

A Small Town Grows Into Citrus City 1905–1929

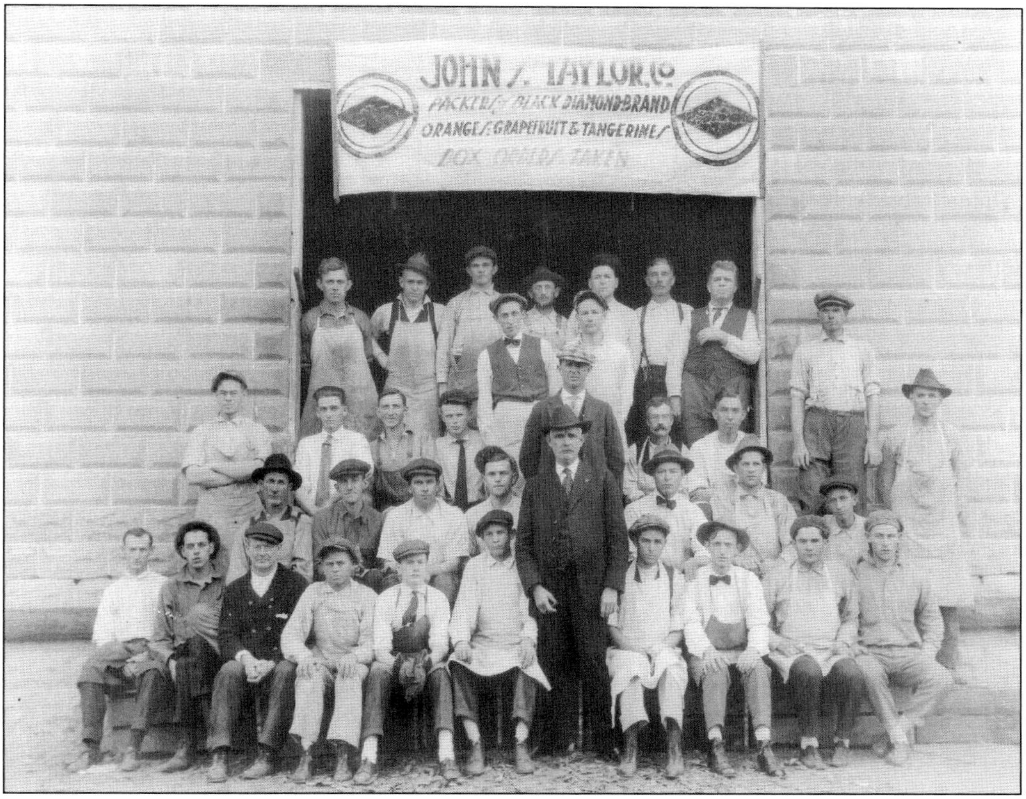

This image from the early 1910s shows John Stansel Taylor, William Fletcher "W. Fletch" Belcher, and employees at the John S. Taylor Packing House. By 1910, five years after Largo became an incorporated town, Taylor, Belcher, and John Archibald Campbell controlled four substantial packing plants and perhaps 8 to 10 smaller ones on groves in the Anona and Largo areas. (HV.)

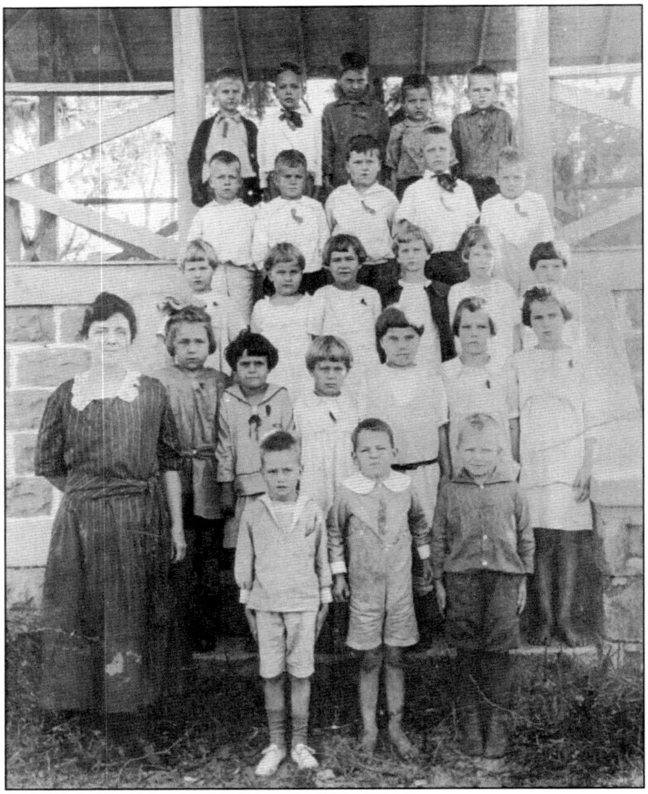

James Dieffenwierth came to the area in 1880 and homesteaded. He and his father, Phillip, donated 1 acre of land for a two-story school (Largo School No. 1) on a site in 1890 that later became Town Park. During much of the 20th century, this location (later renamed Ulmer Park) became a popular gathering place. At left, a group of students from the elementary school enjoy a visit to the park's bandstand in 1921. Controversy ensued in the 1990s when city officials decided to sell part of the park to a firm that planned to redevelop the area, including the former town hall site south of West Bay Drive. Townhouses and newer stores surround the smaller version of the park that remains; this site continues to offer a relaxing place to stop in downtown Largo. (Left, HV; below, author.)

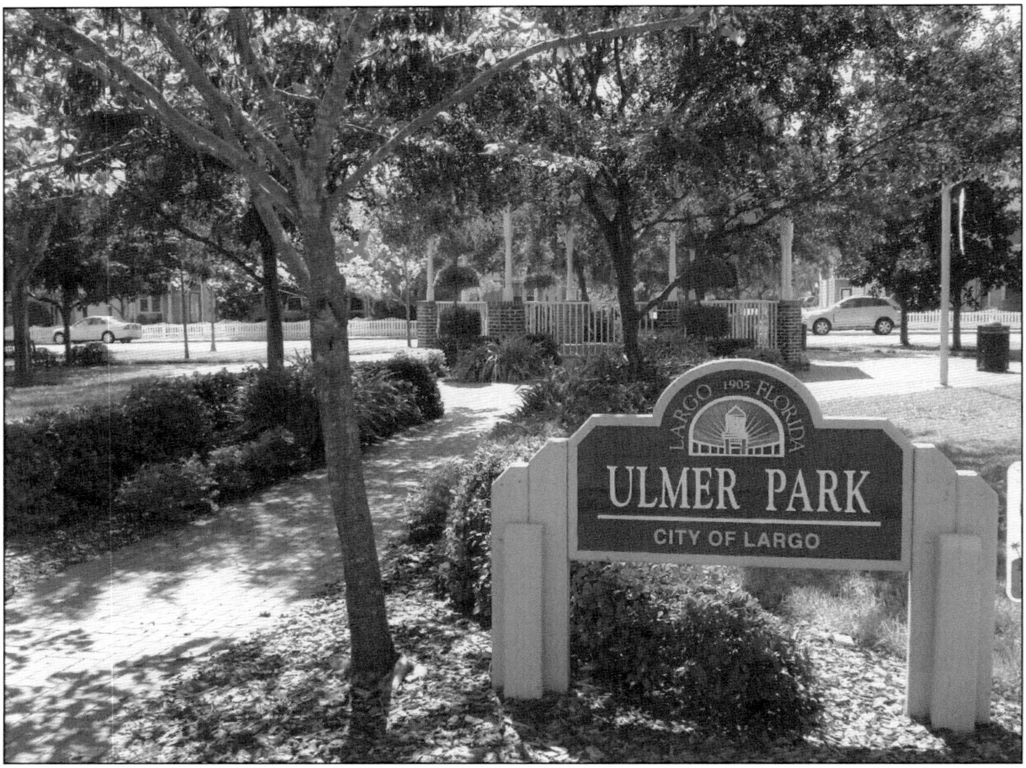

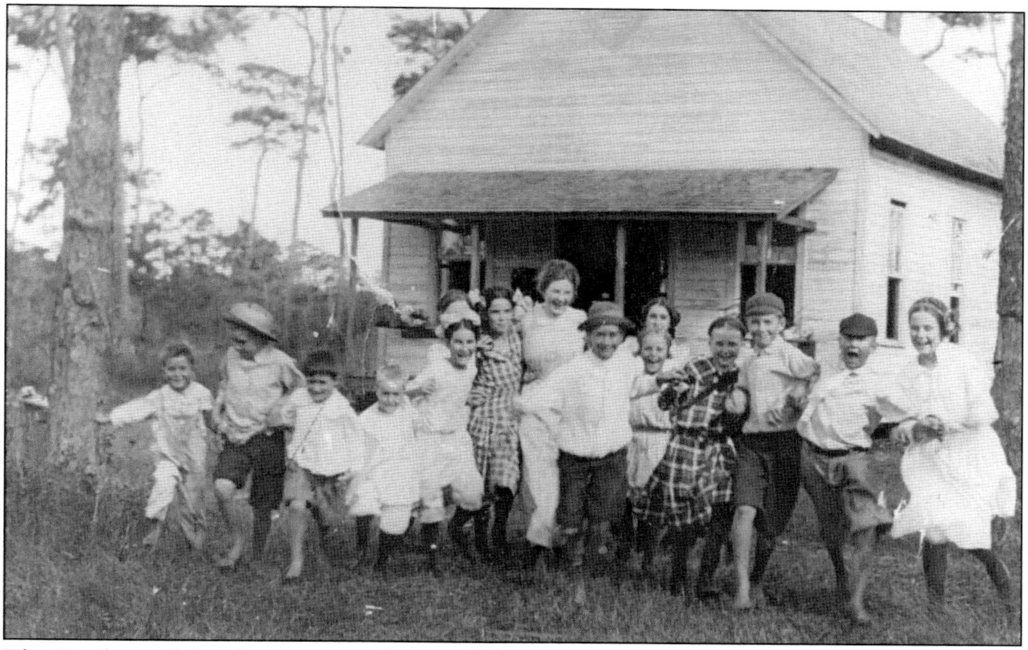

The Pinehurst School intermittently served the western Largo area. Located near the present intersection of Pinehurst Avenue and Lentz Road, this one-room schoolhouse occupied a site east of Indian Rocks Road and midway between West Bay Drive and Mehlenbacher Road. Above, a teacher and students (many of them shoeless) enjoy recess in or about 1905. The image below, from a 1919 superintendent's report, illustrates changes to the campus after the removal of nearby pine trees and the addition of outbuildings. The school's low enrollment led to its occasional closure. In 1913, approximately 30 students attended grades one through eight; only 10 students attended Pinehurst in 1940. The school board closed the school in 1948, and sold the site for $4,000 the following year. The area is now part of Belleair Bluffs. (Both, HV.)

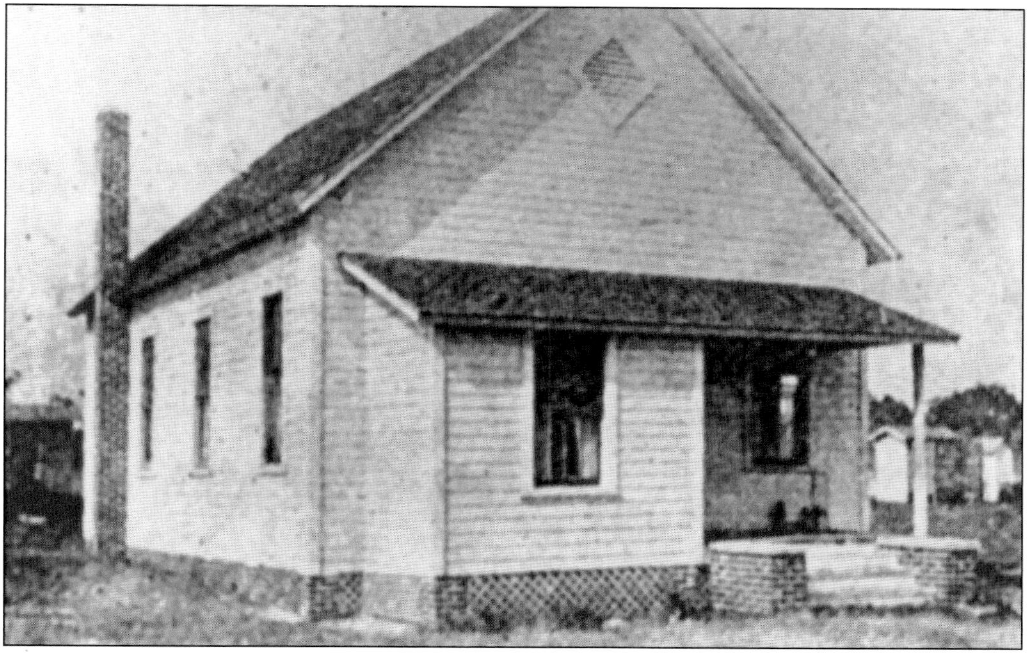

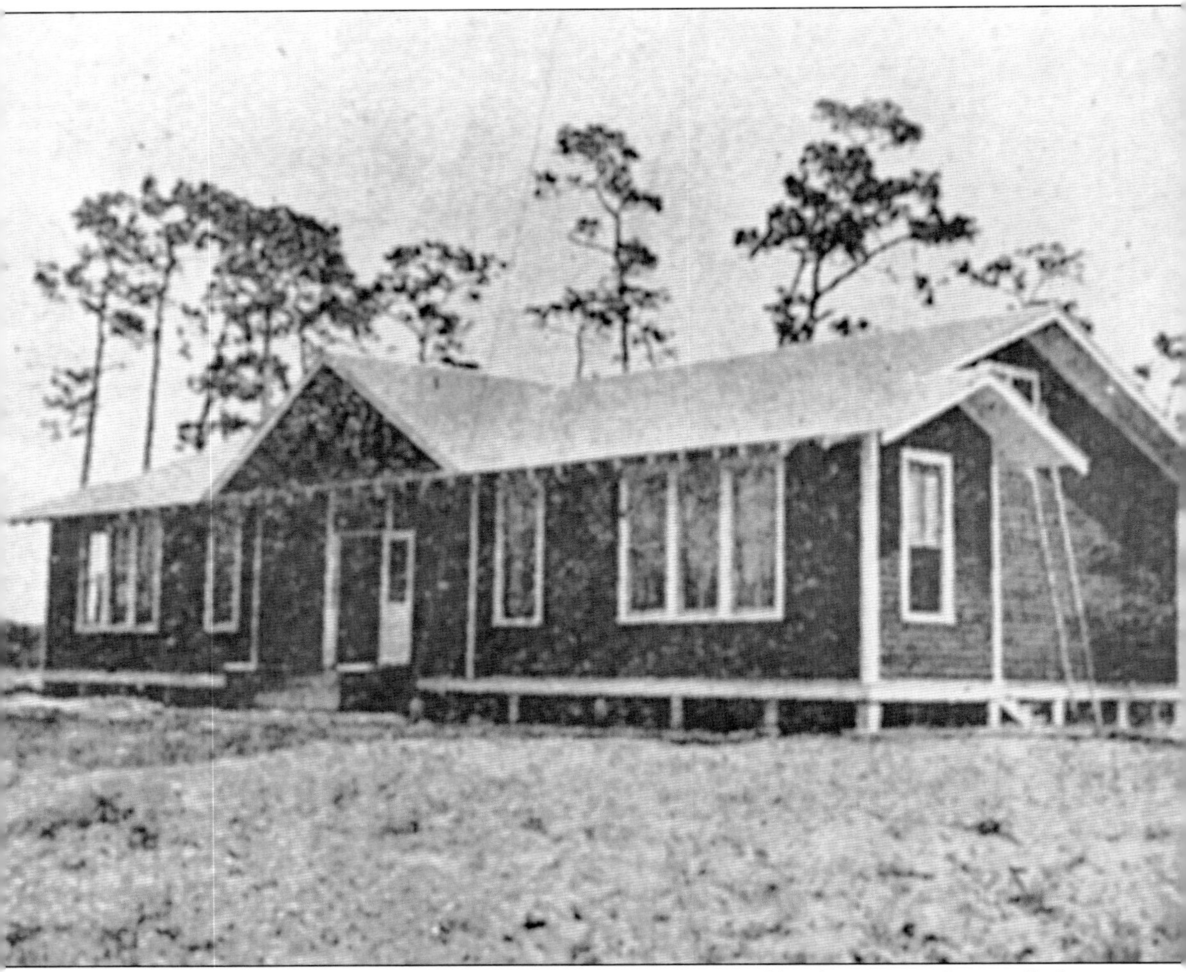

The Keene School serves as one of the area's earliest portable classrooms. Originally known as Midway School when classes began in 1882, it occupied a site east of Largo near Robert C. McMullen's home. By 1909, the facility moved to a remote path known as Keene Road. Students referred to their school in the woods as "Skunk Hill." The school closed from 1912 until 1915, and later reopened with some improvements by the time this image appeared in a 1919 superintendent's report. After closing again in the mid-1920s, the City of Clearwater bought the building for $200 and moved it to an athletic field. Keene Road received its name from Arthur Horace Duncan, a native of Keene, New Hampshire, after he homesteaded on 160 acres near the intersection of Keene and Druid Roads in the late 1870s. Long before the Keene School opened, Duncan and others in the area operated profitable groves and a nursery. (HV.)

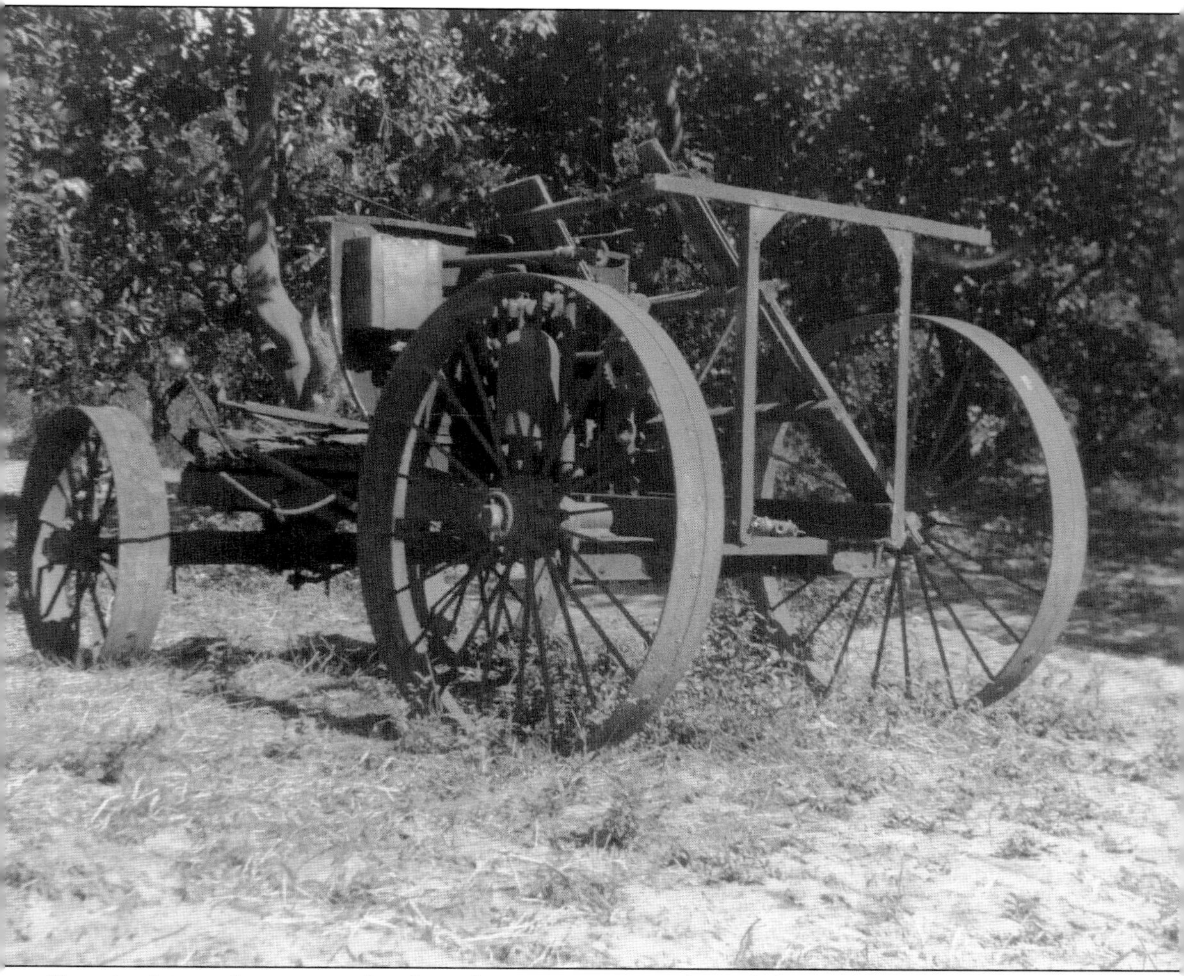

Even in this rural setting, technological innovations transformed the landscape and redefined agricultural practices. This photograph shows a citrus sprayer from the late 1920s. Machinery such as this allowed farmers and citrus grove operators to expand the amount of acreage under cultivation. By the mid-1910s, a number of engineering projects rechanneled freshwater lakes, created canals to control flooding, and allowed groves to flourish throughout the central Pinellas peninsula. In addition to citrus and other crops commonly grown by truck farmers, some pioneers even began to harvest upland rice and other exotic crops along a narrow dirt trail once referred to as Ulmerton Boulevard, now the site of busy Ulmerton Road. (HV.)

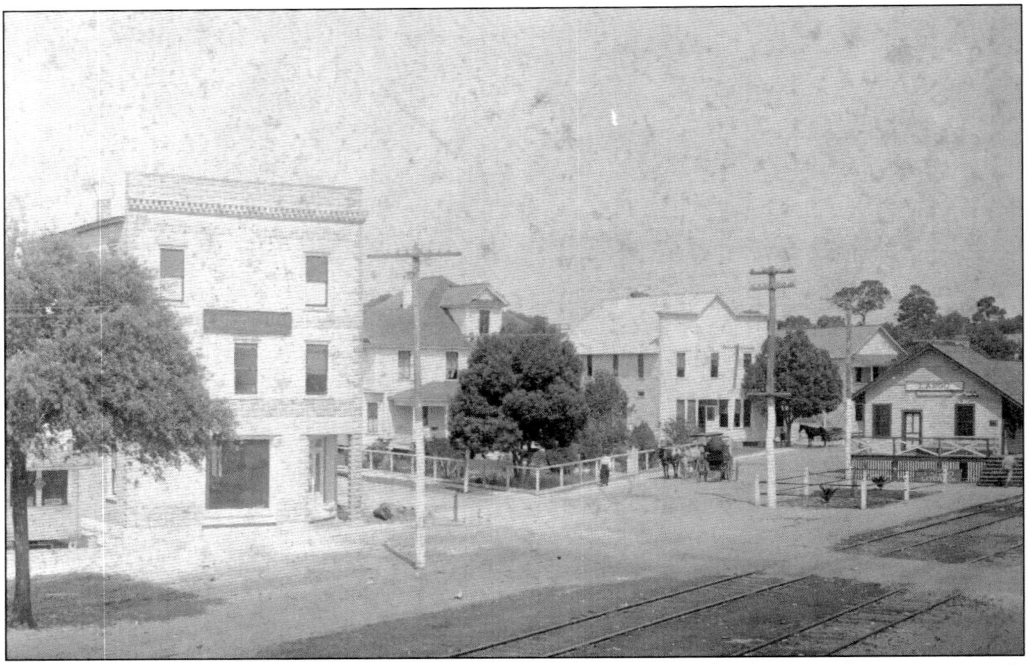

By 1910, the small town incorporated five years earlier began to take shape at the junction with the Atlantic Coast Line Railroad. The above image facing northwest shows John S. Taylor's three-story office building on the left, the Largo Hotel (first in the area) behind the tree, the annex building with its post office facilities, and behind the depot, Largo's first drugstore. Within a few years, brick roads replaced many of the sand trails, and automobiles outnumbered horse carriages on the town's streets. Below, delivery drivers prepare the fleet at the Taylor packinghouse for deliveries, around 1915. (Both, HV.)

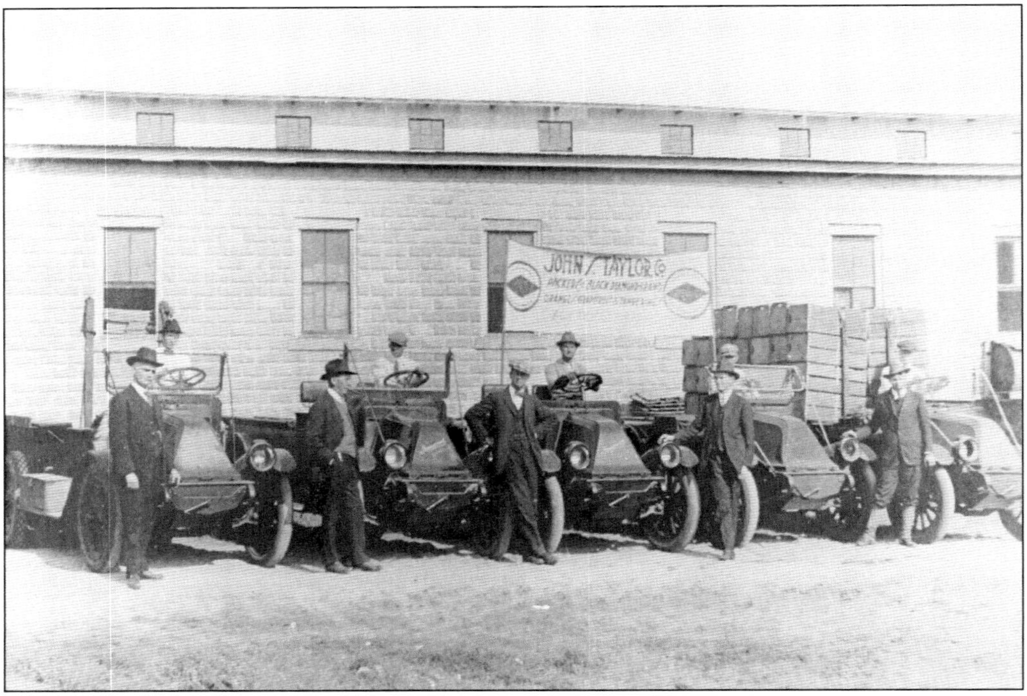

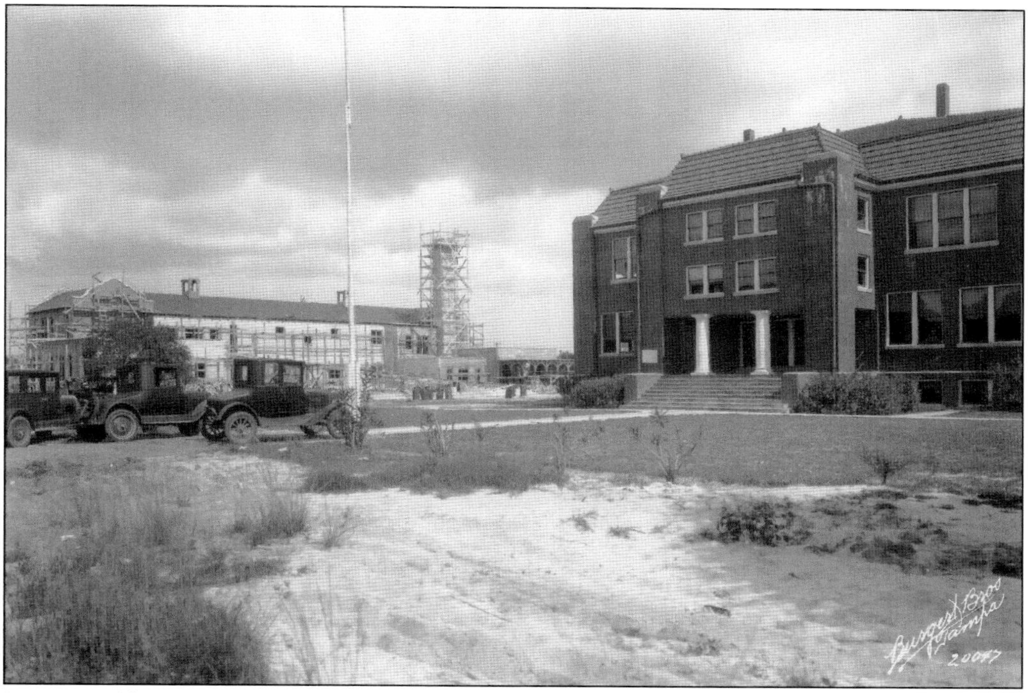

Largo quickly outgrew its smaller schools. A new facility between St. Petersburg and Clearwater, the first offering a full curriculum through high school, opened on a larger campus along Bullock Street (Fourth Street Southwest) in 1914. The prominent structure replaced a four-room schoolhouse at Town Park that became city hall. By 1924, the site expanded with an addition (seen above to the left) south of the original building as enrollment increased. (THPL.)

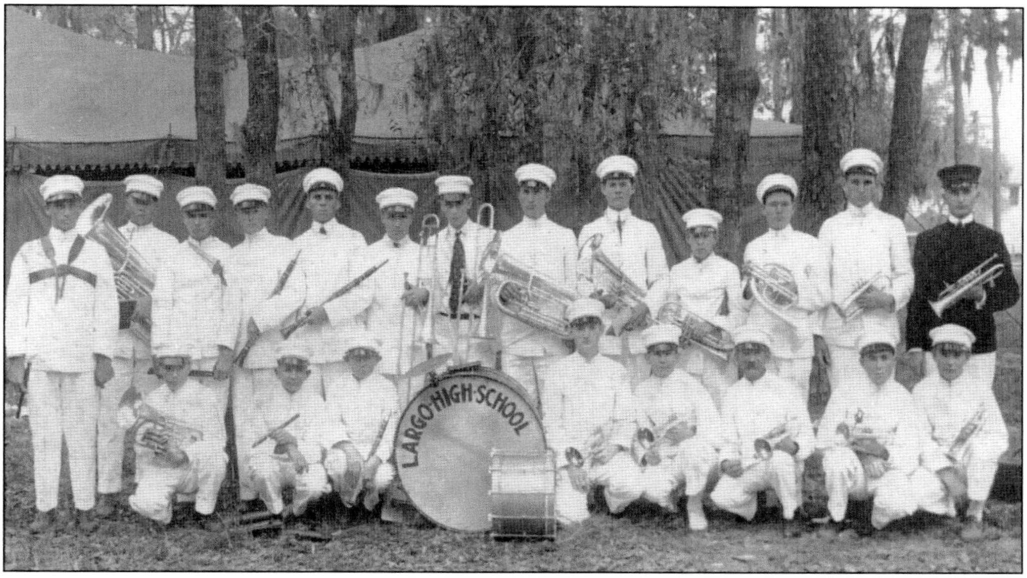

Since the earliest days of Largo High School, talented bands have entertained the community. Long before the internationally renowned Largo Band of Gold won awards nationally and overseas, Largo's early bands played before enthusiastic crowds. The first organized school band struck a note in 1915. This picture shows them at the first county fair in 1917, an event held that year at Town Park. (HV.)

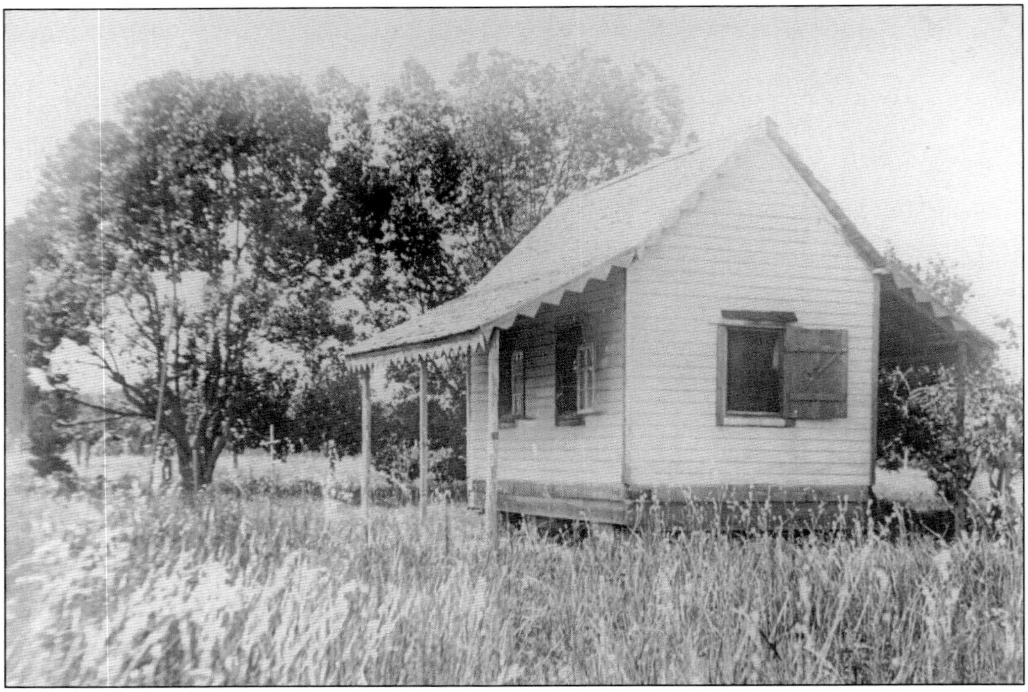

Members of the Brumby, Leach, and Meares families settled south of Largo in an area known as Oakhurst. This region encompassed the acreage west of present-day Lake Seminole and south of Walsingham Road. Many of the early settlers of Oakhurst had migrated from Anona in the late 1800s. Robert Leach came over from England. These pioneers encountered deer, bears, and even an occasional panther along the narrow paths they forged into the wilderness. At the time these images of the Meares and Leach homesteads were taken around 1910, few others lived along the then narrow dirt path of Ridge Road near its current intersection with Park Boulevard. Most of the Oakhurst area later became part of Seminole. (Both, HV.)

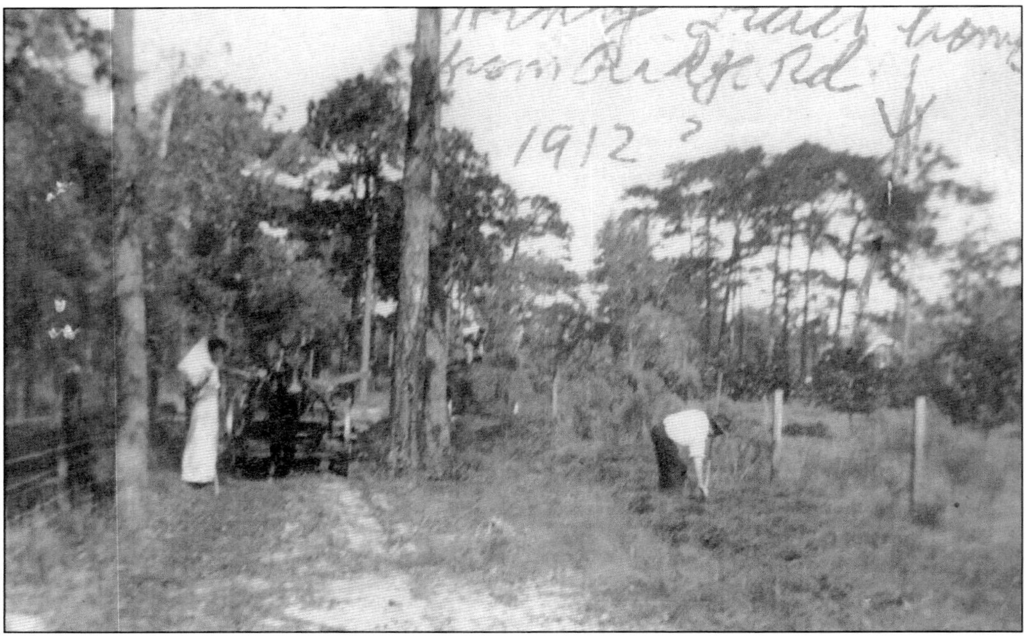

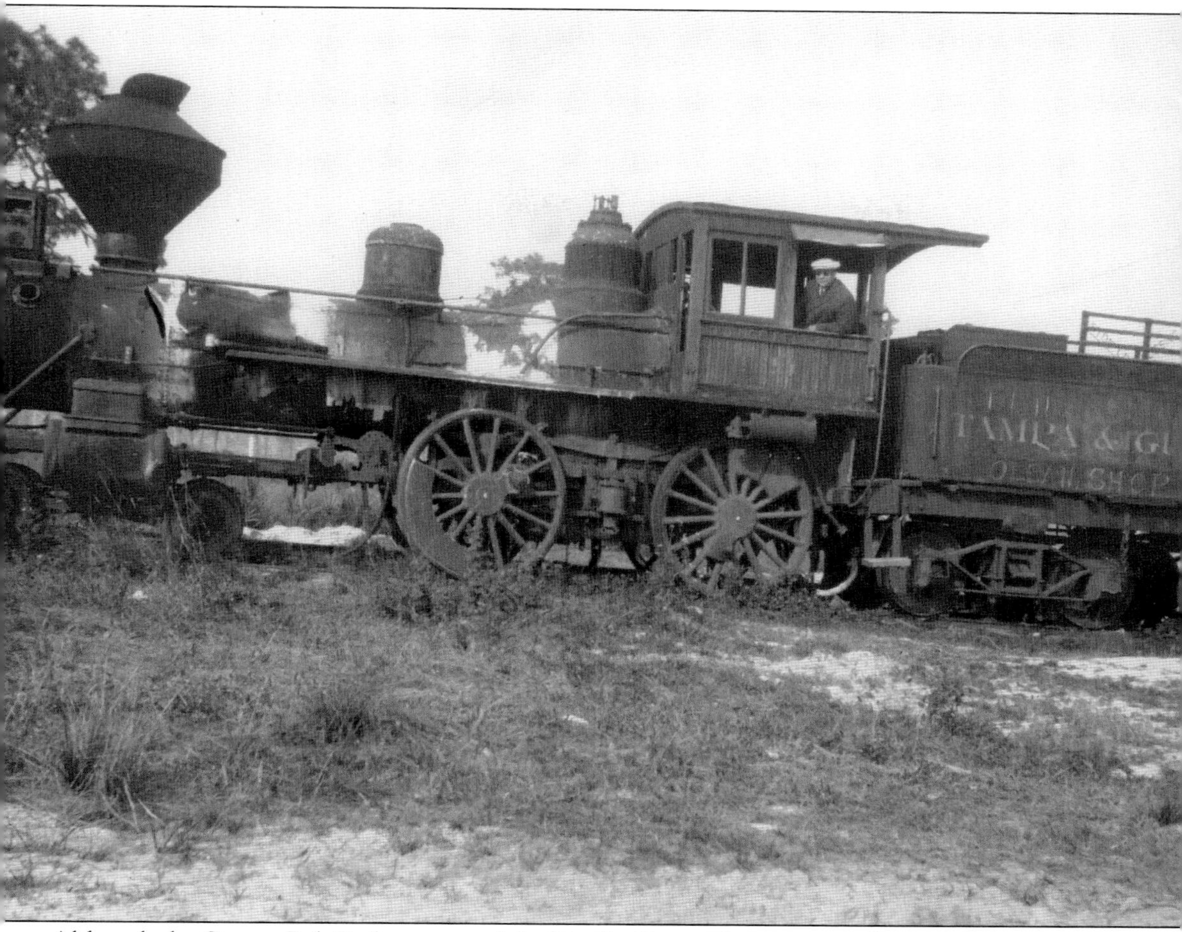

Although the Orange Belt Railway opened the Pinellas Peninsula to more settlers, residents soon clamored for better service. After 1900, as part of Atlantic Coast Line Railroad system, regular service to distant cities was supplemented with shorter runs, such as the twice-daily *Toonerville Trolley* train that ran between St. Petersburg and Tarpon Springs. An early version of commuter rail, the slow-moving *Toonerville* often stopped in the countryside wherever passengers flagged it down. Connections between the Pinellas Peninsula and Tampa remained sporadic until the Tampa and Gulf Coast Railway offered its inaugural service between Tampa and Tarpon Springs in March 1910. By mid-April 1914, the line introduced regular passenger service to Clearwater as crews finished their work on the rails southward to Largo. The Tampa and Gulf Coast Railroad later merged into the Seaboard Air Line (SAL) system. (HV.)

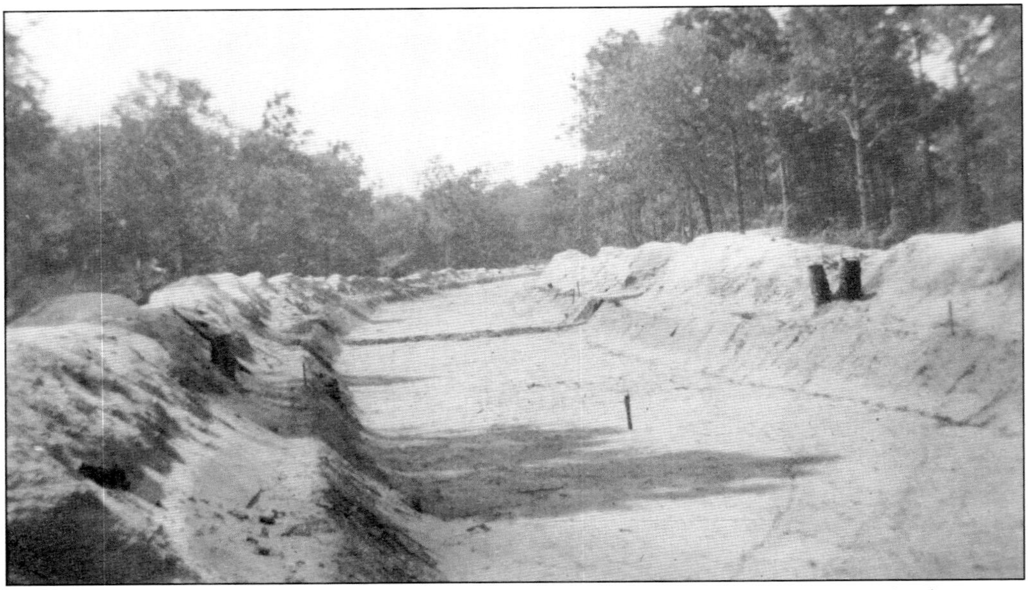

Locomotives from Tampa and the Gulf Coast began service to Largo by June 1914. At that time, crews had already started to lay the roadbed between Largo and Long Bayou along the present-day path of the Pinellas Trail. A wooden bridge crossed Long Bayou near Bay Pines, and the railroad's path continued through the Tyrone area and entered St. Petersburg. In September 1914, the 44-mile line came to an end in downtown St. Petersburg. The image above shows the grading of the path in Oakhurst near the present-day Seminole City Park. The first train to run through Oakhurst appears in the 1914 image below. In 1990, a 5-mile segment of this route between John S. Taylor Park in Largo and Seminole City Park became the first section of the Pinellas Trail, a rails-to-rails recreational path that spans from St. Petersburg to Tarpon Springs. (Both, HV.)

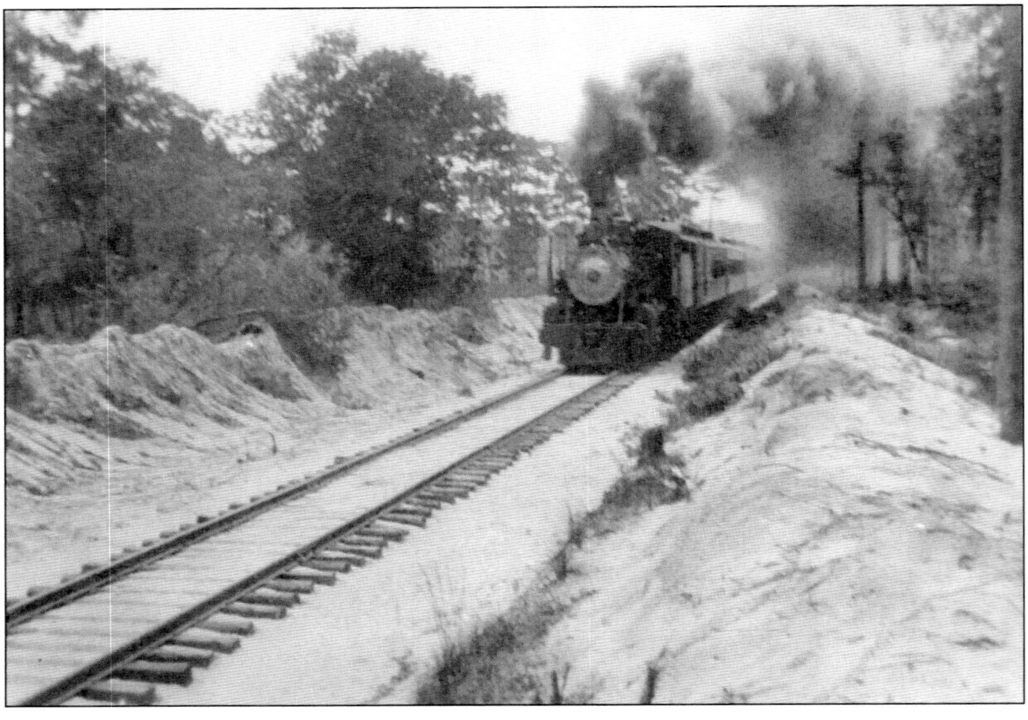

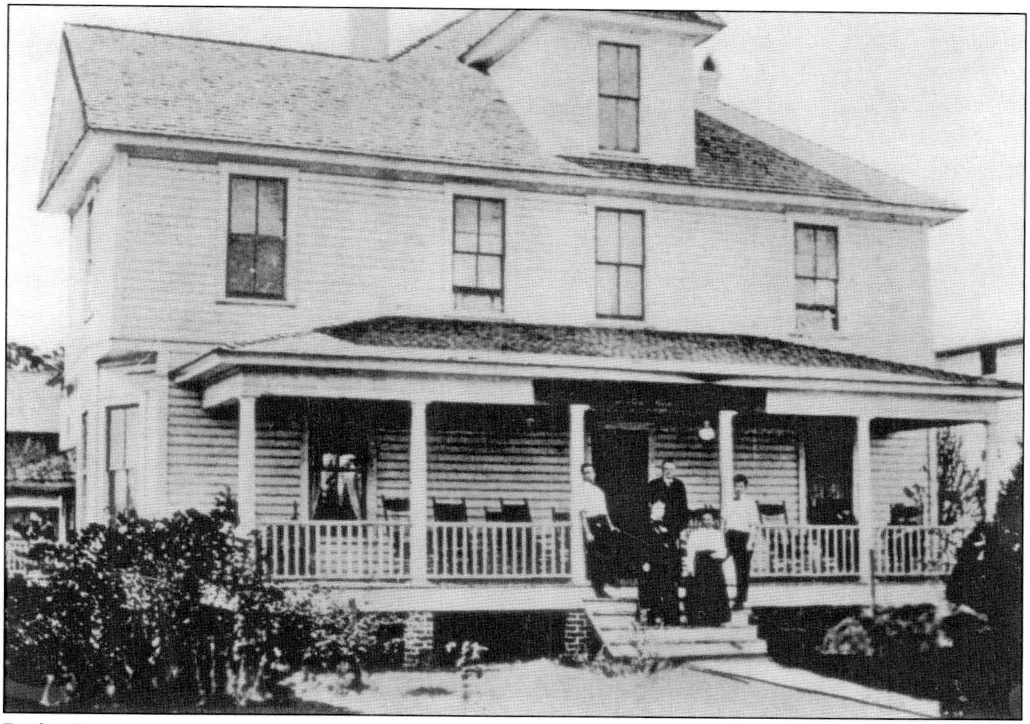

Rufus Fain McMullen and his wife, Georgia, provided the land alongside Bay Drive and First Street for the train depot. A small portion of one of their homes sat on property that became the site of Largo's first hotel. Built along Railroad Avenue and Jackson Street (now First Avenue Southwest) by feed store proprietor Francis Marion Campbell, the Largo Hotel, shown above, hosted monthly dances and became the preferred residence for single men and women in the area. Georgia McMullen operated the hotel for many years. Just a few steps away on First Avenue Southwest, Louis Steele Johnson's drugstore also included rooms as the Hotel Pinellas, below. A well dug on Johnson's property in 1912 provided the first piped water to homes nearby, and later to the 1914 school. (Both, HV.)

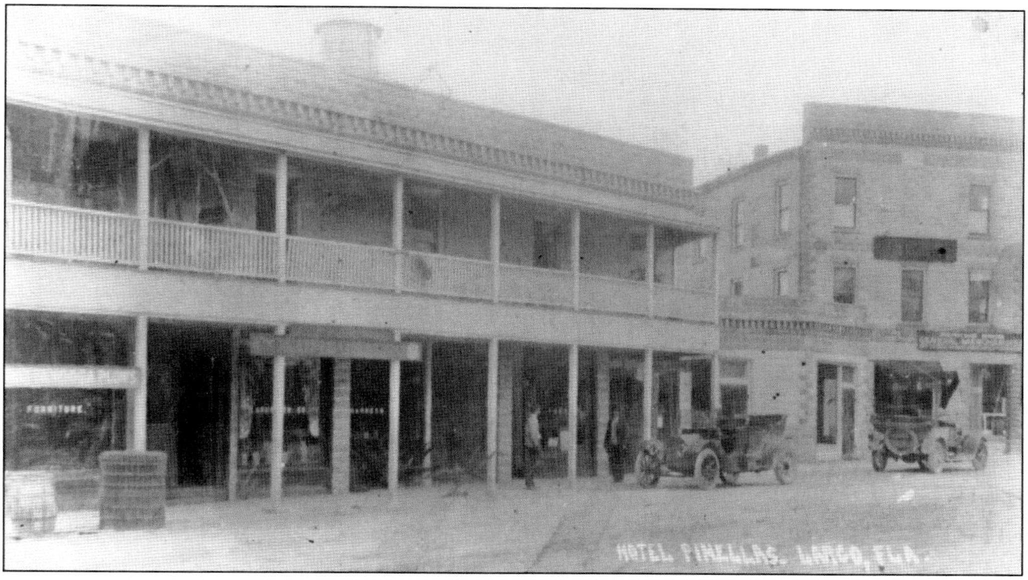

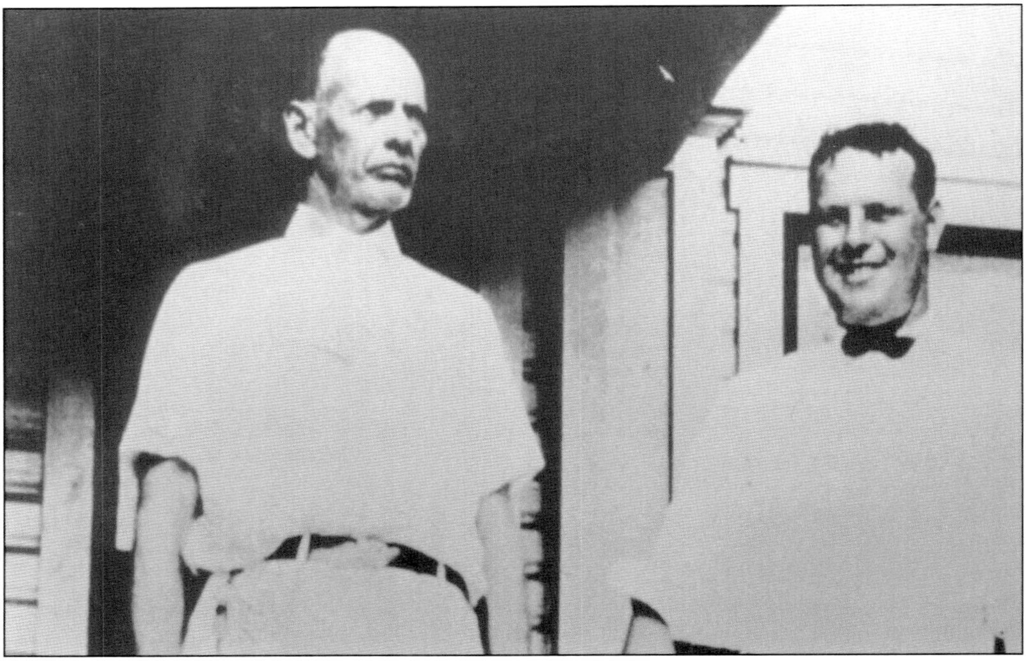

Capt. Charles Wharton Johnson's sons shaped Largo's early political and business climate. Louis Steele Johnson, shown at left above in a photograph from the mid-1920s, served as an early druggist and won election in 1907 as the second mayor of Largo; after his term of office came to an end, he oversaw construction of the Johnson Building that opened across the street from the railroad depot in 1911. George Ward Johnson, shown below in his store in the early 1910s, managed the Farmers' Alliance Exchange, an important source of goods and provisions for many of the region's farmers. Both Louis and George also married members of other pioneer families: Louis exchanged vows with Lottie McMullen, and George wed Agnes Taylor, daughter of William and Frances Kilgore Taylor. (Both, HV.)

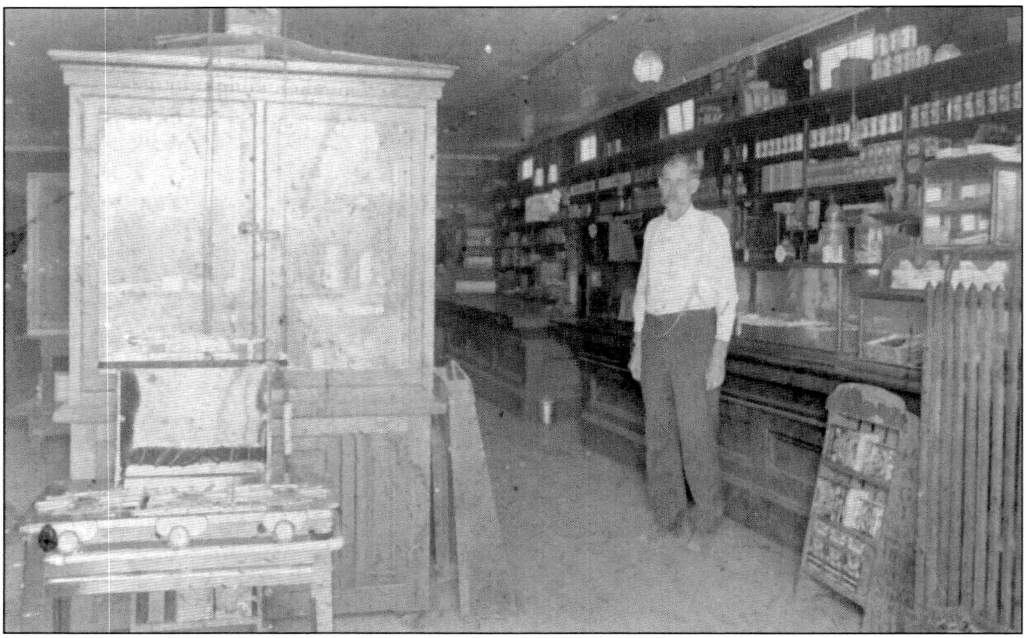

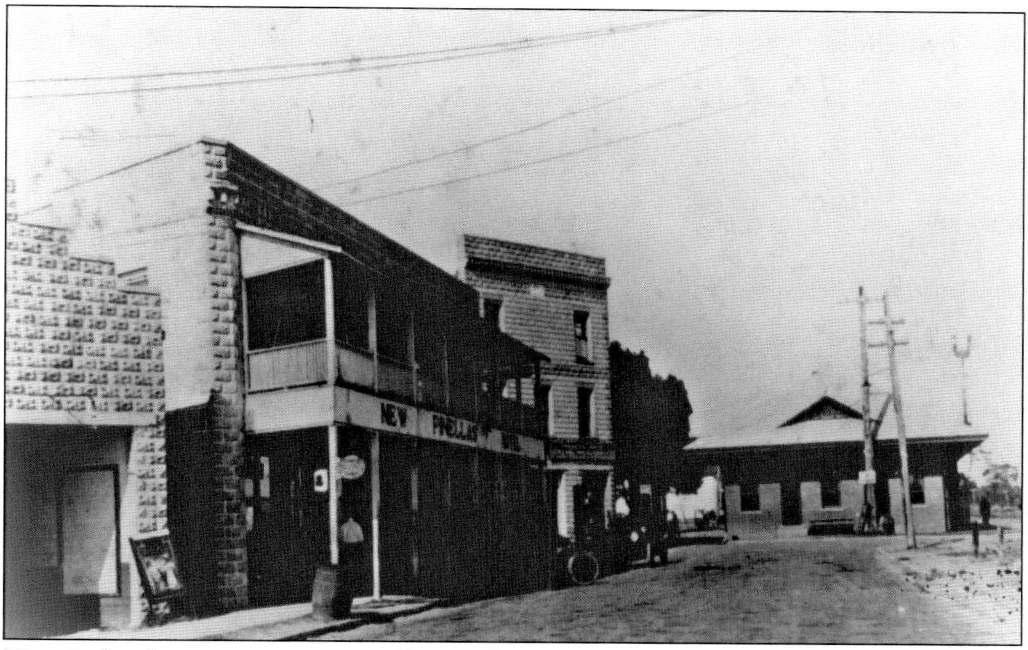

Historical and contemporary views offer a stark contrast in the development around the railroad station. The image above looks northwest along Railroad Avenue during the 1910s. Largo's first movie palace, the Savoy Theatre, appears on the left, next to Louis Johnson's New Pinellas Hotel, with its drug, furniture, and hardware stores. Johnson's structure adjoined John Stancil Taylor's three-story office building, the largest structure of its kind in the growing city when completed in 1909. The terminal appears on the right side of Railroad Avenue, with the tracks to the right of it. By comparison, the October 2010 image below shows First Street Southwest after it had turned into a one-way corridor, allowing eastbound traffic on Bay Drive to merge southbound onto Seminole Boulevard. The terminal would have sat just beyond the truck parked on the grass. (Above, HV; below, author.)

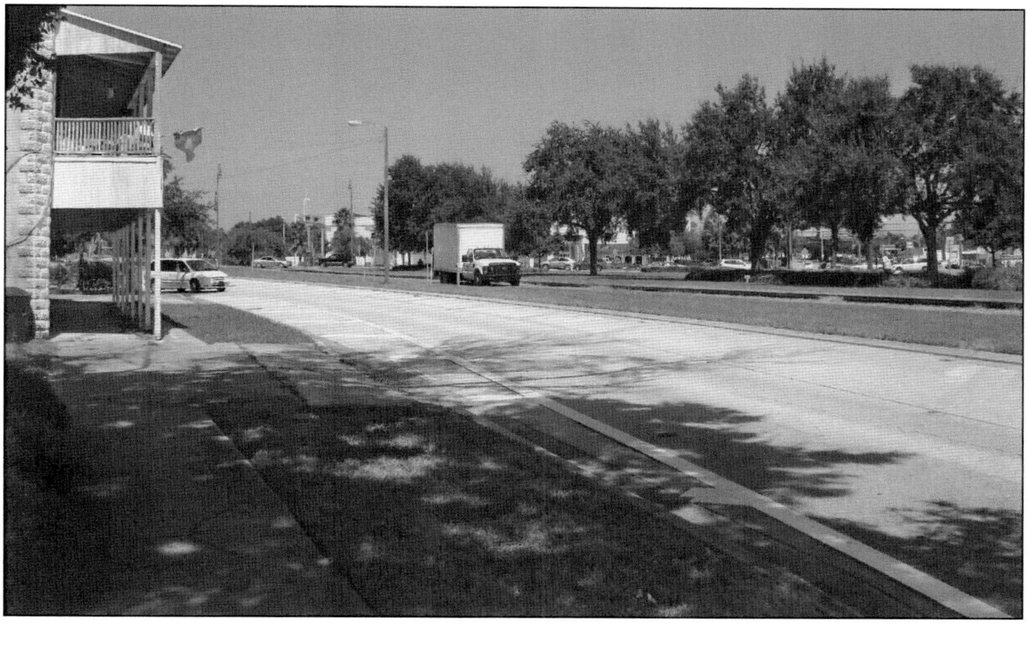

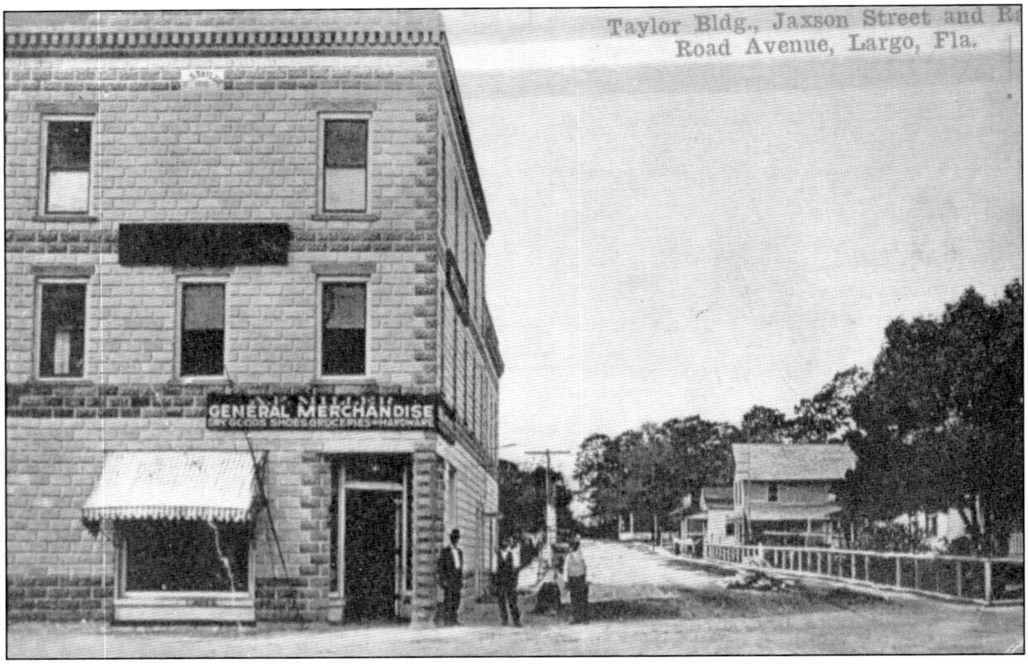

Two other views from near the Atlantic Coast Line Railroad depot reveal a bustling community. The image above shows the Taylor Building looking west from the depot at First Avenue Southwest. Below, a converted tour car transported people on the arduous and sandy roads between St. Petersburg and northern Pinellas. Fortunately, brick pavement had replaced the dirt path along Railroad Avenue by the time these well-dressed folks passed through Largo. The City Market served as a grocery store. Between the market and Johnson's pharmacy, hidden by the vehicle, a barbershop had also opened. The Perkins Brothers General Merchandise store operated out of the Taylor Building on the right. The dispenser along the sidewalk in front of the car was a gasoline pump that sold the Polarine brand of fuel. (Both, HV.)

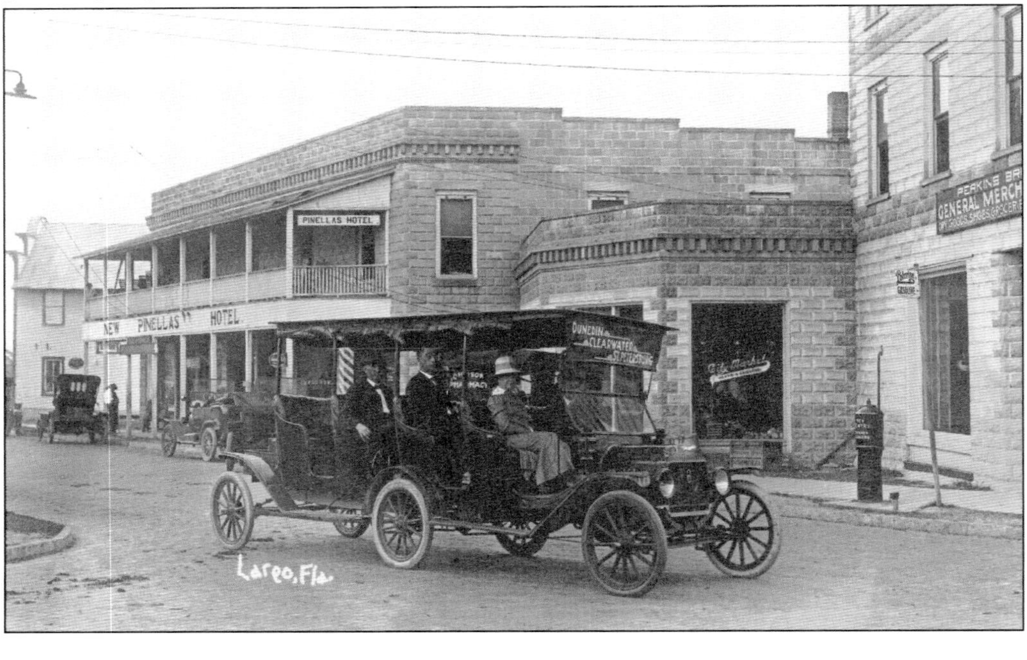

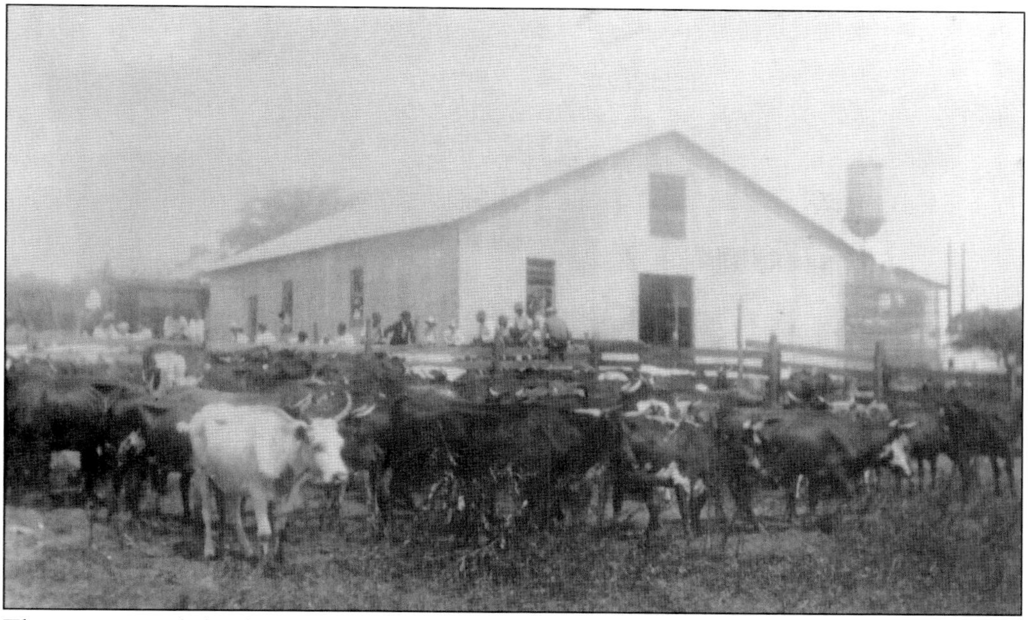

The area around the depot and near the intersection of Bay Drive with Seminole Boulevard/ Missouri Avenue bustled with activity long before the rush hours of today. The photograph above, taken sometime around 1905, faces northwest along the busy intersection as local farmers herded scrub cattle toward the depot and prepared to ship them to northern markets. An earlier wooden version of the feed store existed before John Gainey replaced it with the structure built for Francis Marion Campbell, which included thick rusticated blocks and heart of pine for floorboards. The image below looks south toward the Taylor Building before many of the roads had brick pavement. The railroad depot appears on the left side of the picture. (Both, HV.)

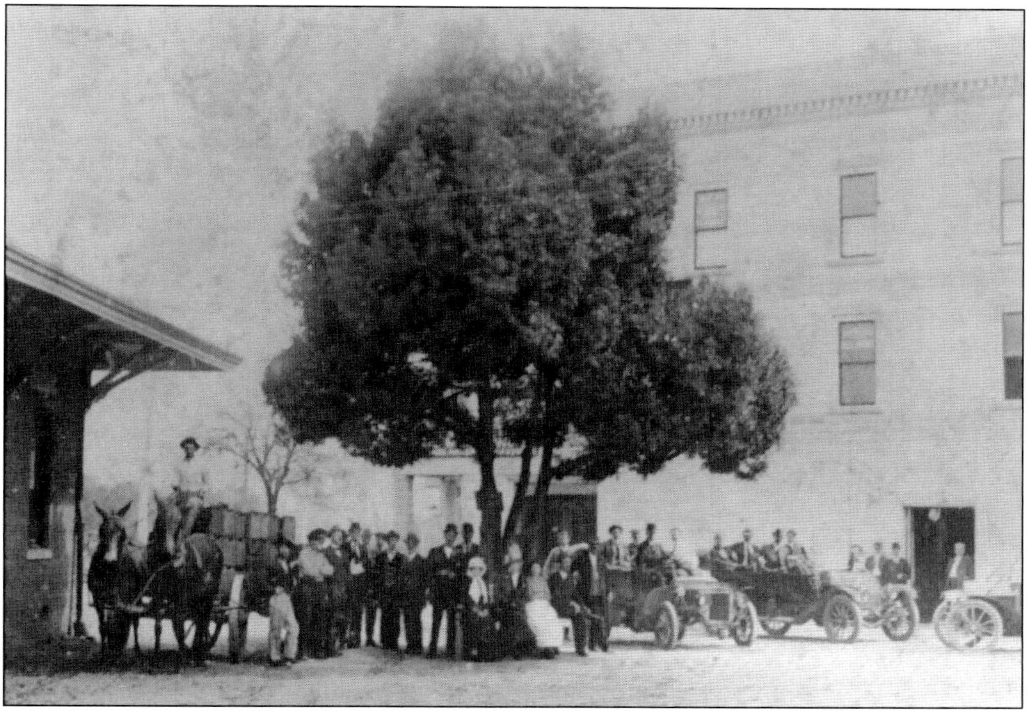

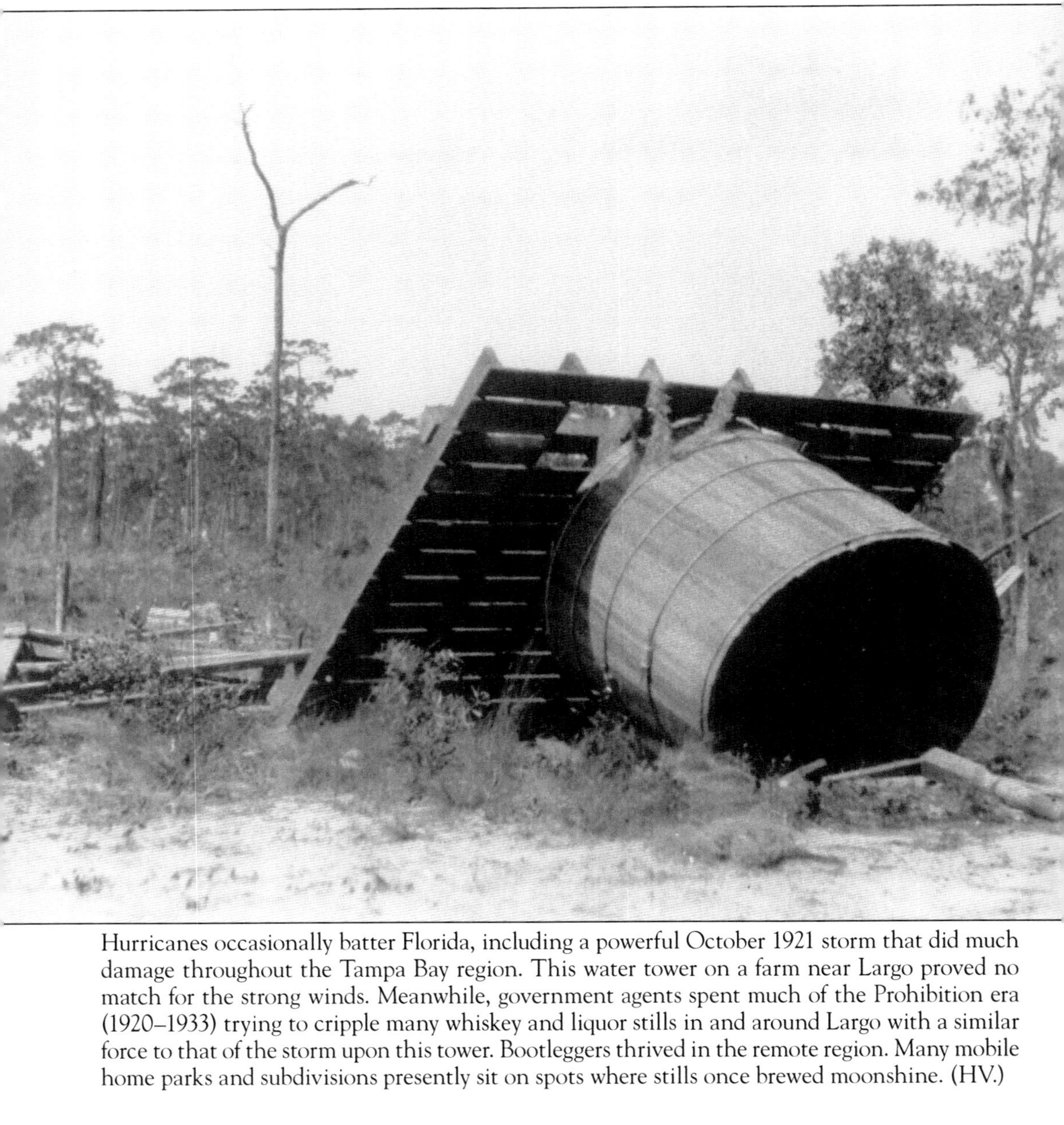

Hurricanes occasionally batter Florida, including a powerful October 1921 storm that did much damage throughout the Tampa Bay region. This water tower on a farm near Largo proved no match for the strong winds. Meanwhile, government agents spent much of the Prohibition era (1920–1933) trying to cripple many whiskey and liquor stills in and around Largo with a similar force to that of the storm upon this tower. Bootleggers thrived in the remote region. Many mobile home parks and subdivisions presently sit on spots where stills once brewed moonshine. (HV.)

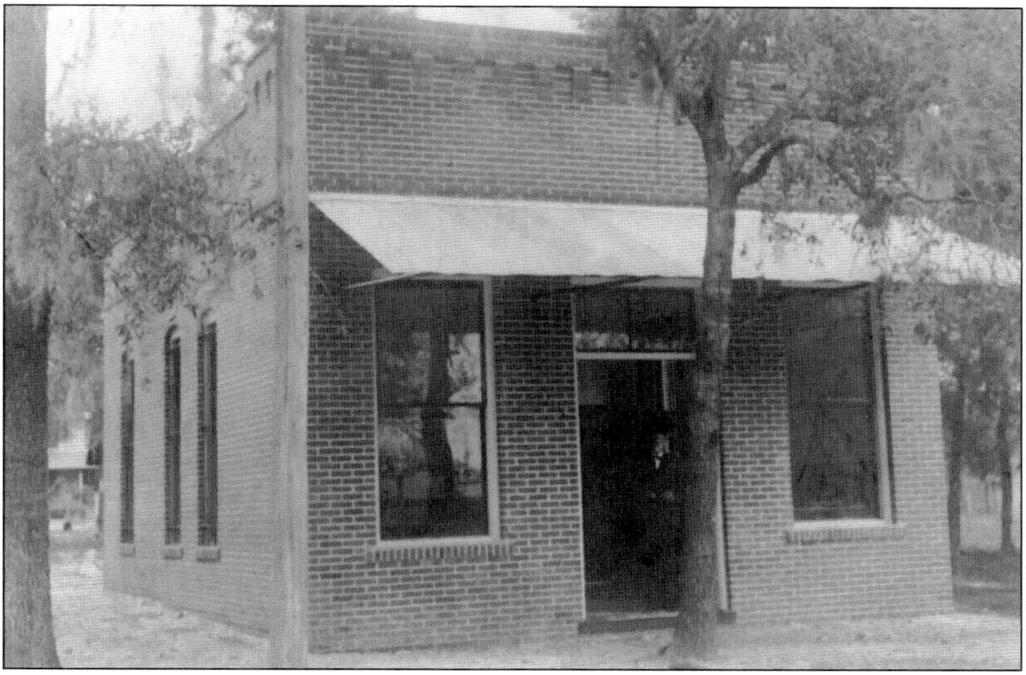

The Bank of Largo, above, was chartered in October 1907. It sat on the corner of First Avenue Southwest and Second Street until its demolition in July 1975. Before it opened, those lacking cash or needing credit had to travel to Clearwater or St. Petersburg. The name of the bank changed during the years, and the structure briefly had other uses, such as a lookout tower during World War II (after the addition of a second floor), as well as a Masonic lodge. Below, J. R. Lovering (center, in the white jacket) stands outside the town's first drugstore in this image from about 1910. He came to Largo after retiring as a physician. Lovering's apothecary faced the railroad tracks near the center of the town. (Both, HV.)

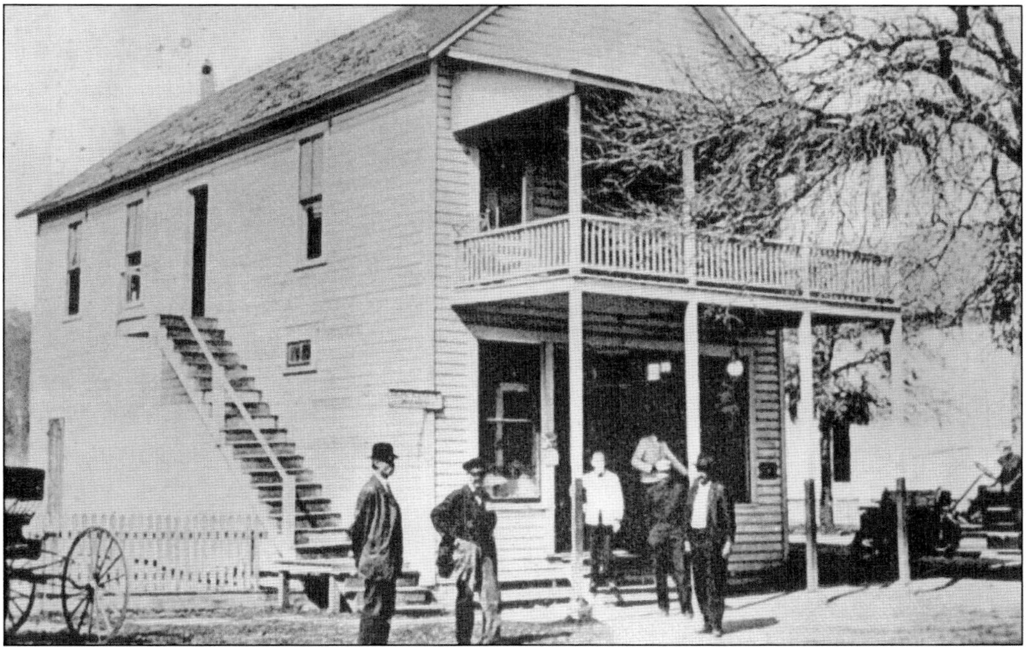

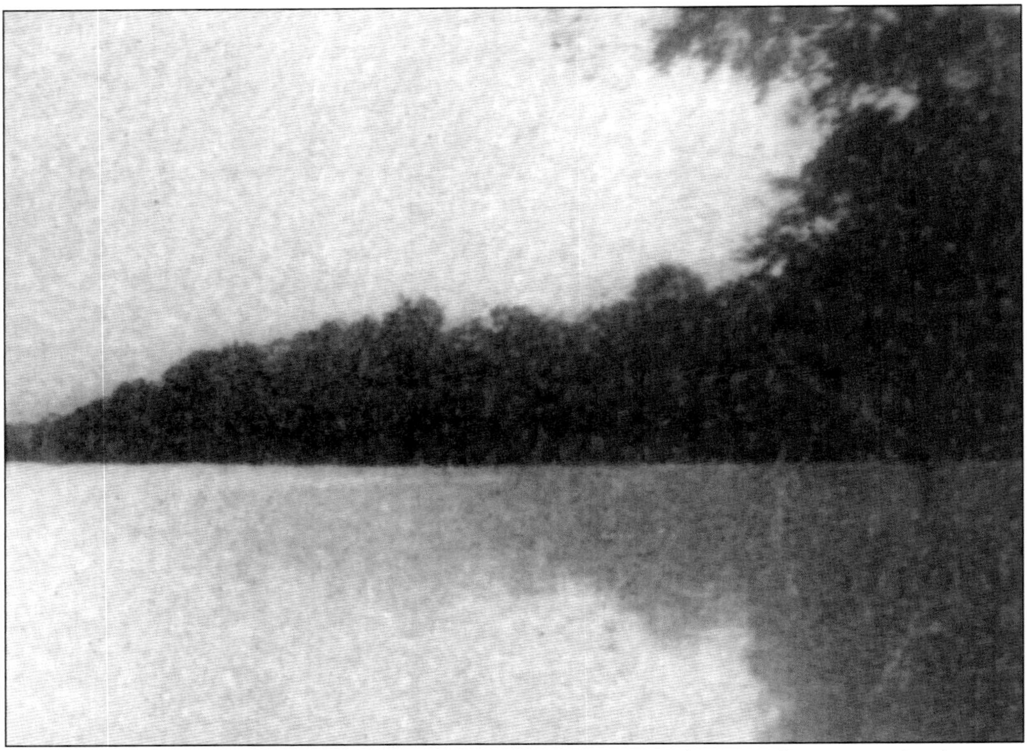

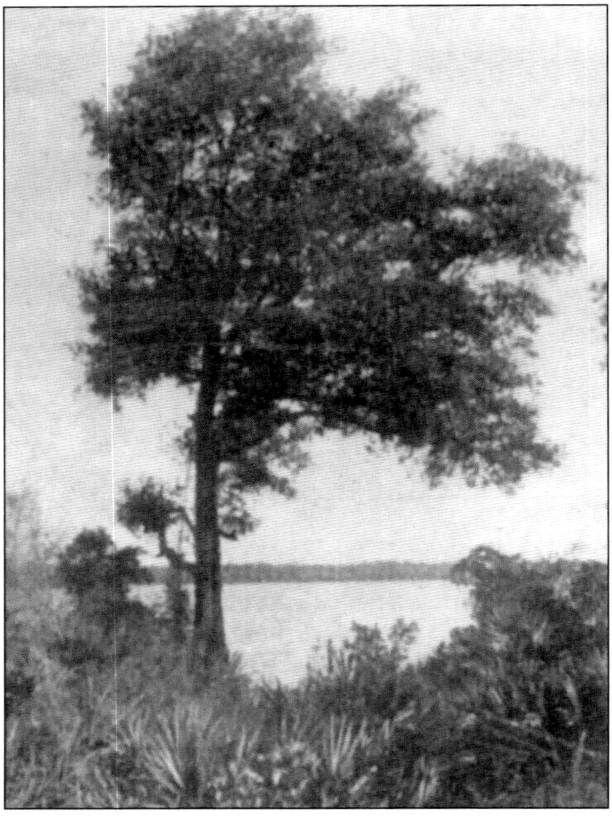

As the town began to take shape with its growing agricultural productivity, some residents started to question how Lake Largo fit into the picture. Although newspapers once touted the 500-acre lake site as an attractive venue near the "golden grapefruit gardens" of central Pinellas, by the mid-1910s, others viewed the lake as a location that seemed ripe for development, but without the need of enduring wet ankles. In late 1915, authorities sold bonds to fund the Lake Largo–Cross Bayou Drainage Project. Through a network of drainage basins, canals, and other modifications to the land, engineers hoped to remove most of the lake and convert the rich, mucky soil into cropland. Soon thereafter, farmers harvested a bounty of crops from the reclaimed land of the former lake. Few photographs of Lake Largo exist. (Both, HV.)

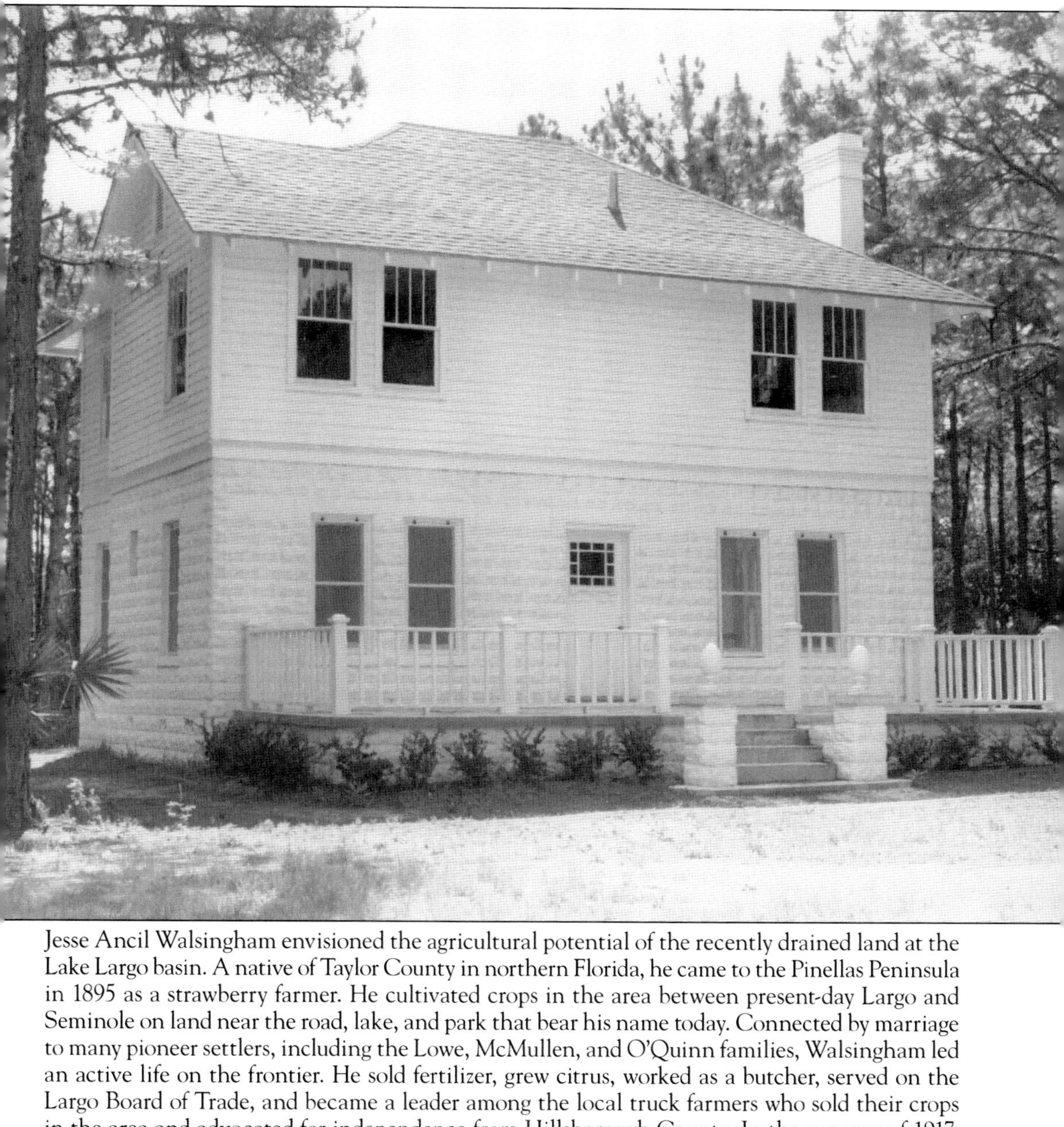

Jesse Ancil Walsingham envisioned the agricultural potential of the recently drained land at the Lake Largo basin. A native of Taylor County in northern Florida, he came to the Pinellas Peninsula in 1895 as a strawberry farmer. He cultivated crops in the area between present-day Largo and Seminole on land near the road, lake, and park that bear his name today. Connected by marriage to many pioneer settlers, including the Lowe, McMullen, and O'Quinn families, Walsingham led an active life on the frontier. He sold fertilizer, grew citrus, worked as a butcher, served on the Largo Board of Trade, and became a leader among the local truck farmers who sold their crops in the area and advocated for independence from Hillsborough County. In the summer of 1917, he became the president of the newly organized Largo Truck Growers' Association. Two years earlier, Jesse and his wife, the former Mary O'Quinn, had moved into this house along Ridge Road, between Ulmerton and Walsingham Roads. This image shows the structure shortly after it moved to Heritage Village in June 1984. (HV.)

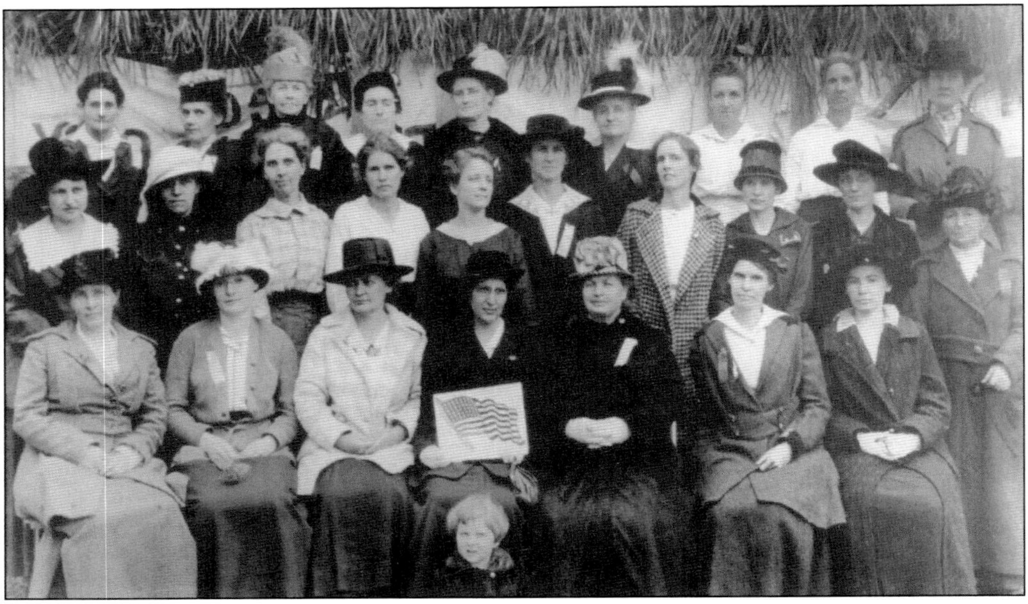

The Largo Woman's Club led the movement for the creation of an annual county fair. Although many of the businessmen in the community initially seemed indifferent, Jesse Ancil Walsingham supported the idea, as did his wife, Mary Adona O'Quinn Walsingham. Working with the Woman's Club, Ancil became vice president of the Fair Association in 1918. When the county commission became the primary financial supporter a decade later, that body hired Jesse Ancil as the first general manager of the Pinellas County Fair, a post he held into the 1930s. Above, members of the Largo Woman's Club pose in a group picture during the period after they had launched the city's first public library and as they planned to start the fair. Below, some of these ladies gathered for a photograph at the fair in the early 1940s. (Both, HV.)

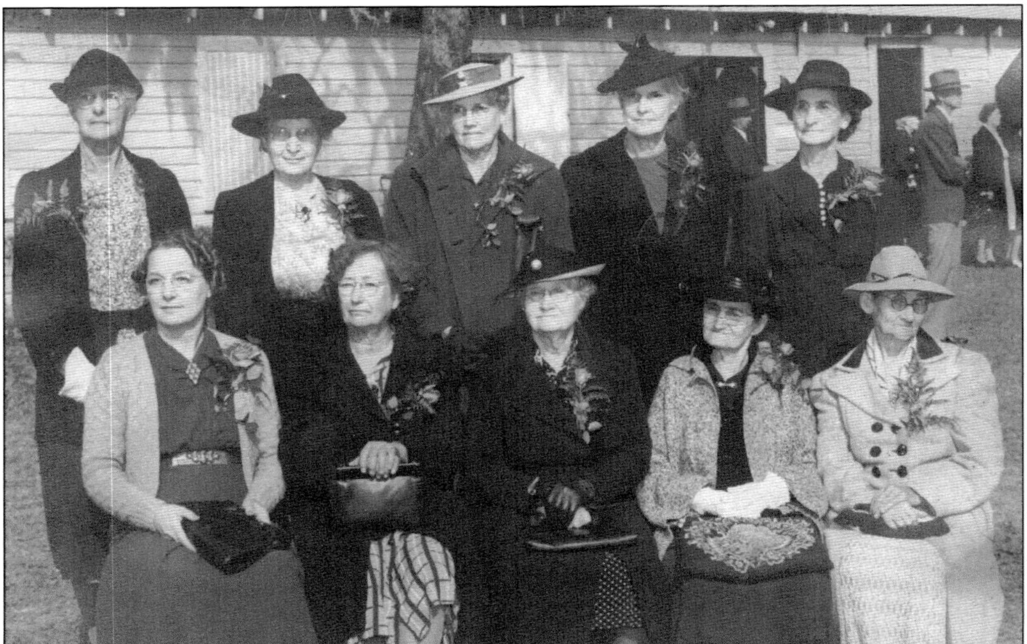

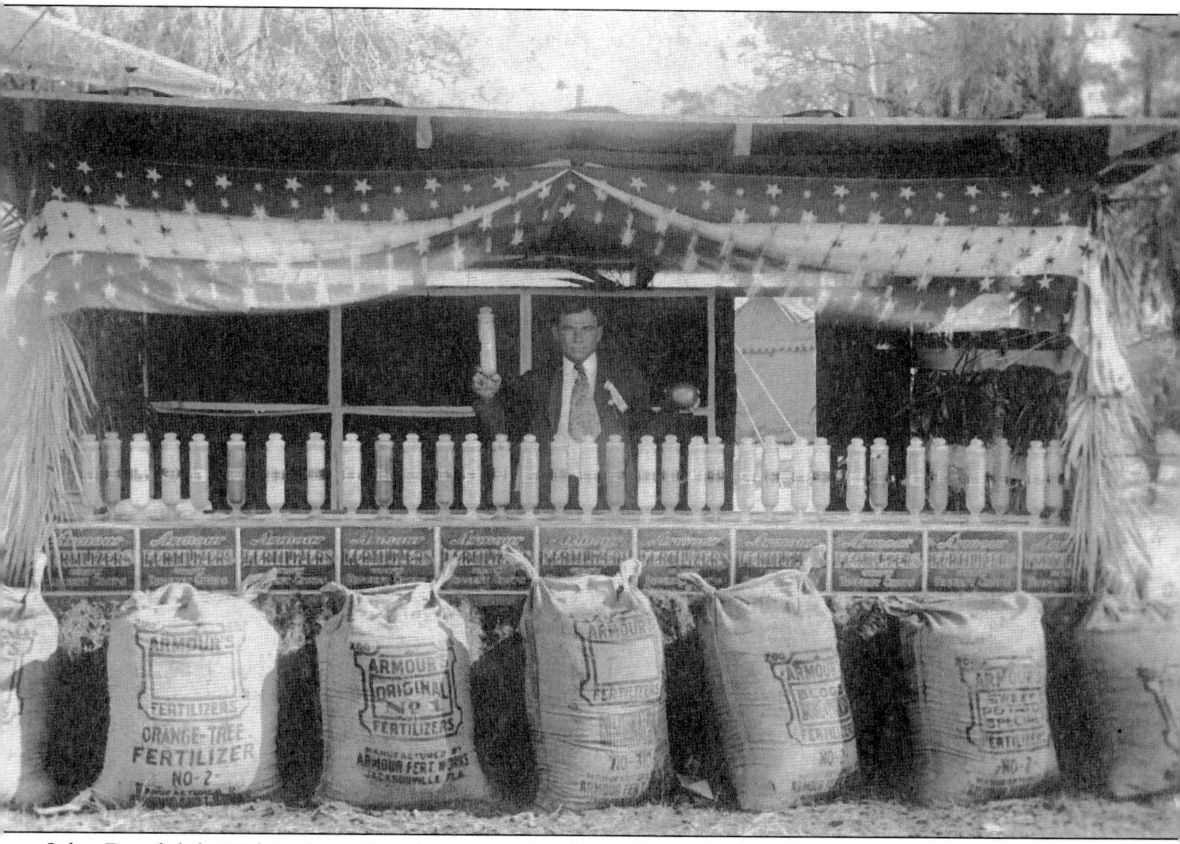

John Randolph Walsingham, Jesse's younger brother, also settled in the Largo area by 1899. He soon married a member of the pioneer Meares family of Anona and settled on a plot of land near Eighth Avenue Southwest and Ridge Road, near the present-day post office. Here Walsingham welcomed visitors to his display booth at the 1921 Pinellas County Fair. (HV.)

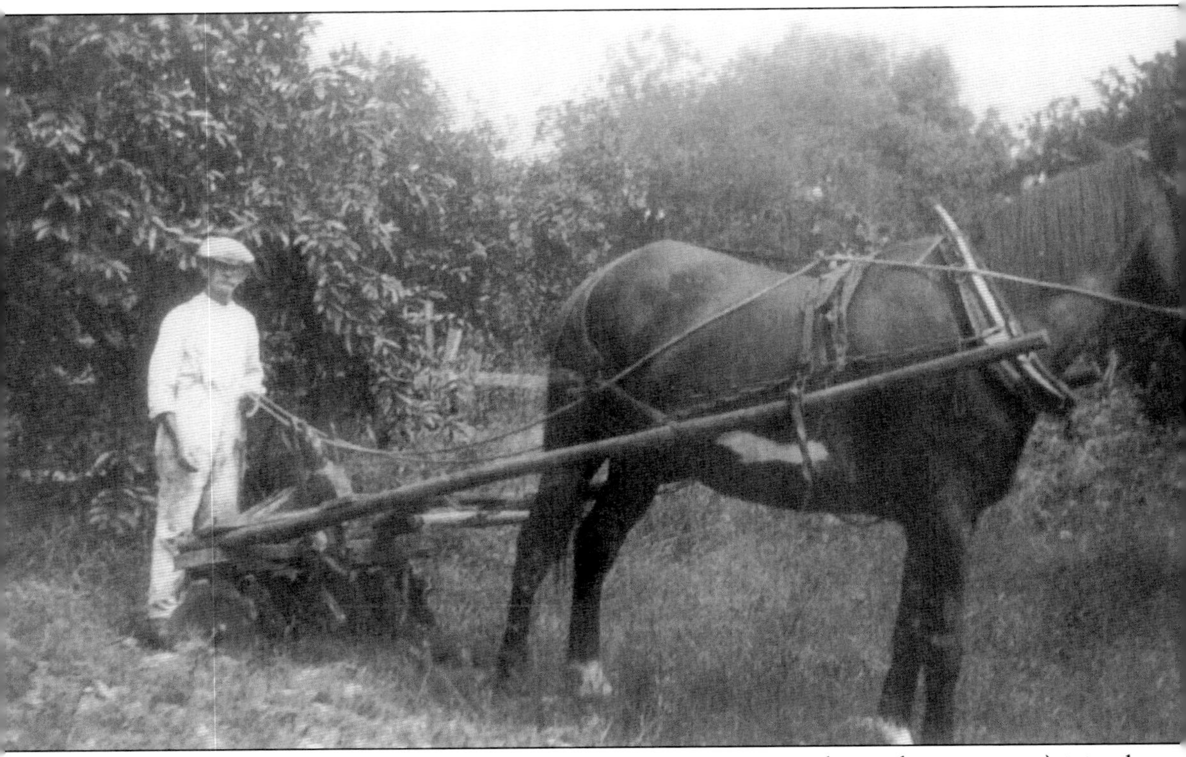

Dr. Bob McMullen (shown above in his later years operating a horse-drawn tractor) joined other farmers in Largo who considered the drainage of Lake Largo a beneficial act. At a time not far removed from Gov. Napoleon Bonaparte Broward's plan to drain the Everglades in the first decade of the 1900s, the March 29, 1918, issue of the *Largo Sentinel* also celebrated the transition of the lakebed into a big plantation: "While it was a pleasing picture before the drainage work . . . it is now a much more pleasing picture when one looks out over the hammock lands now in cultivation . . . This large tract of reclaimed land shows what drainage is worth to that section of the county, which has always been considered practically worthless." Today most of the former lakebed is valued not for the crops yielded, but instead for the buildings and (ironically) swimming pools sitting upon it. (HV.)

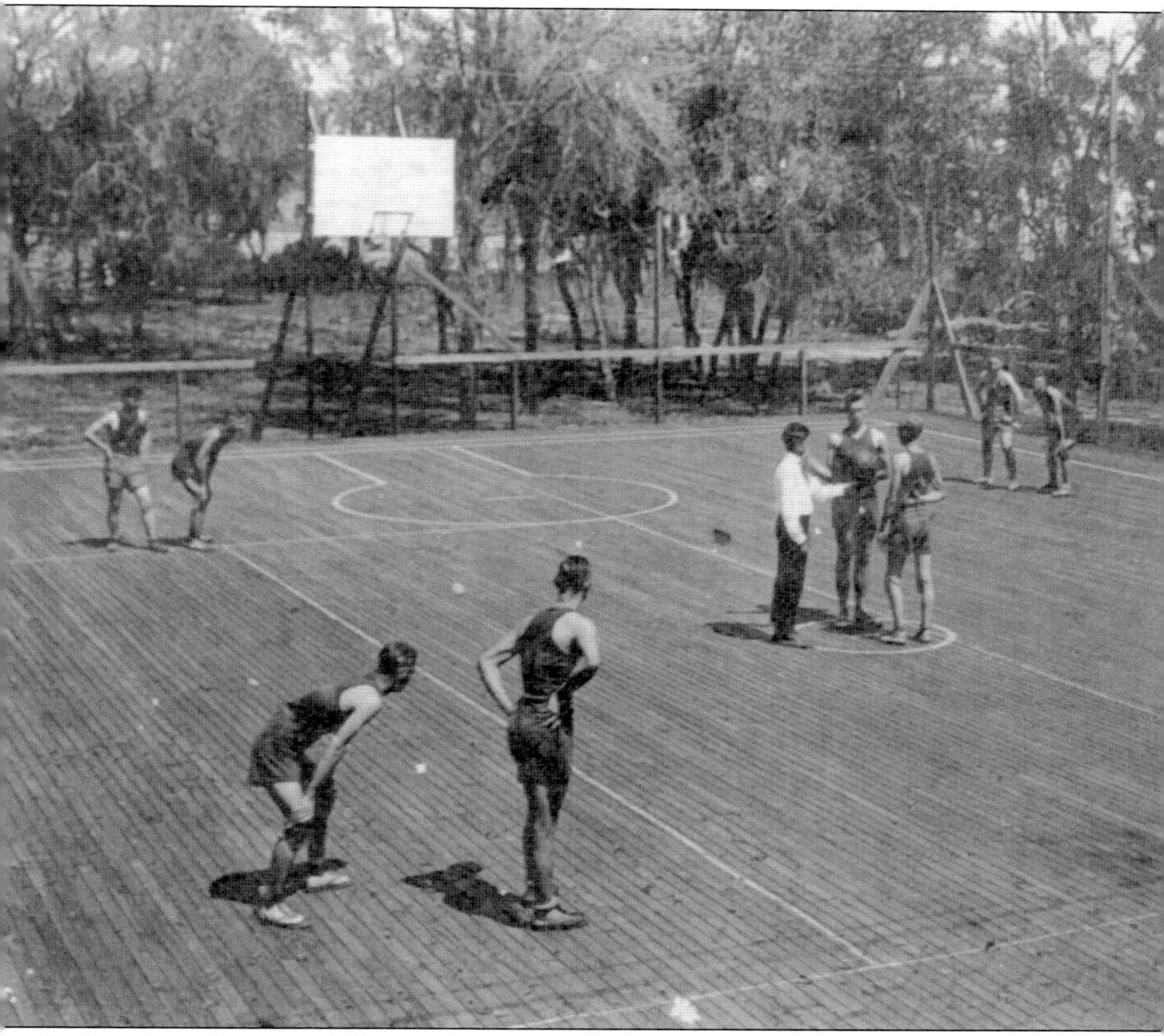

In Largo's rural setting, children and teenagers often spent hours assisting their parents by performing their daily regimen of chores. Such responsibilities, however, did not mean that life was all work without any play. Outdoor recreational activities brought friends together from homes in the city and farms in the surrounding countryside. Swimming, exploring the woods, participating in cane-grinding parties, attending church or picnic outings, and singing or playing musical instruments kept young people busy at a time when radio was in its infancy and computers and televisions did not exist. Competitive sporting contests also attracted crowds. This photograph shows one of the popular gathering places in the mid-1920s, a basketball court in Largo made of wooden boards. (HV.)

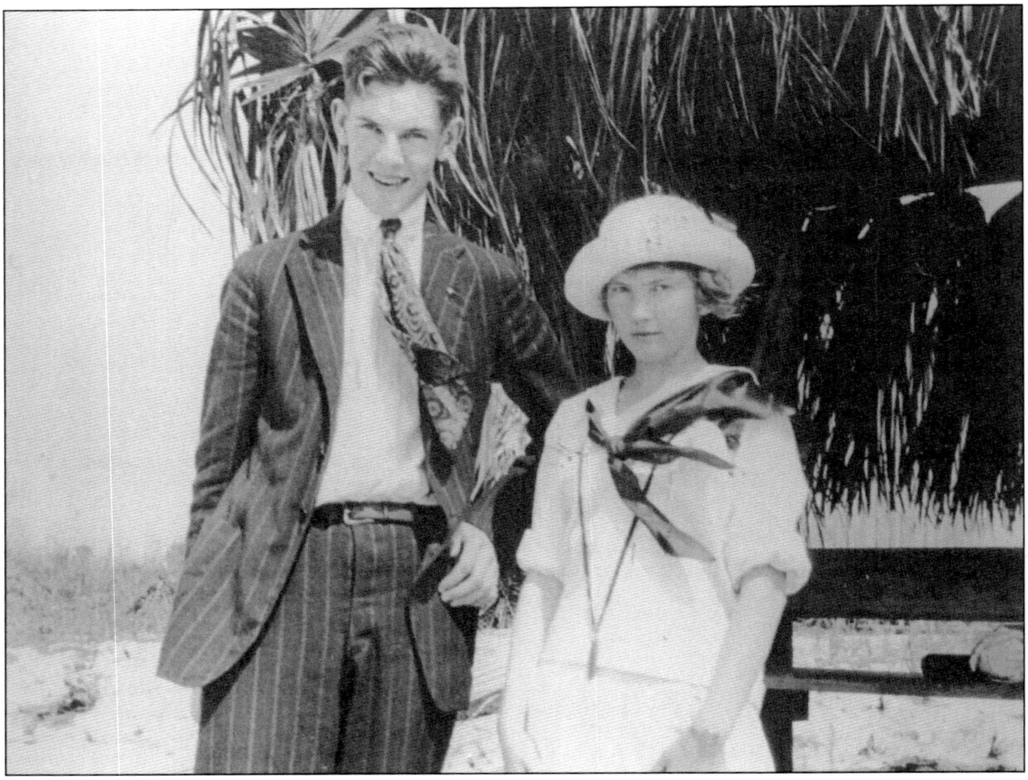

Water may have disappeared from the land east of Largo, but that did not stop early residents from enjoying recreational gatherings along the Gulf of Mexico. Above, Largo High School students Lenox Grey and Blanche LeBaron attend a school-sponsored outing in the late 1910s. (HV.)

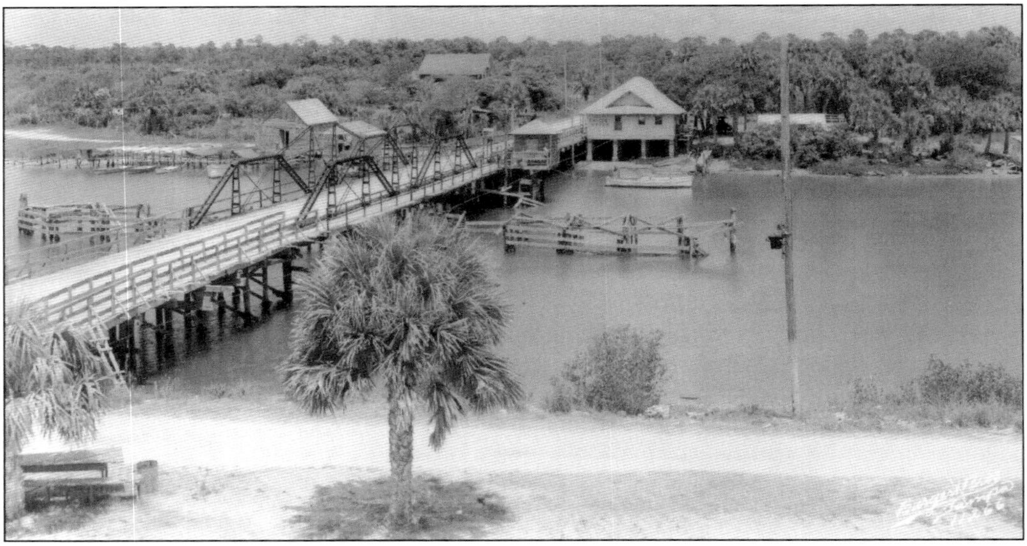

The opening of the first bridge to Indian Rocks in November 1916 spurred development along Sand Key, Anona, and Largo. Erected and managed by members of the McMullen and Hardage families, the bridge required a toll of 15¢ for cars and 25¢ for trucks. A Largo school band played at the opening ceremonies. This May 1924 photograph looks east toward Anona and 113th Avenue on the mainland. (THPL.)

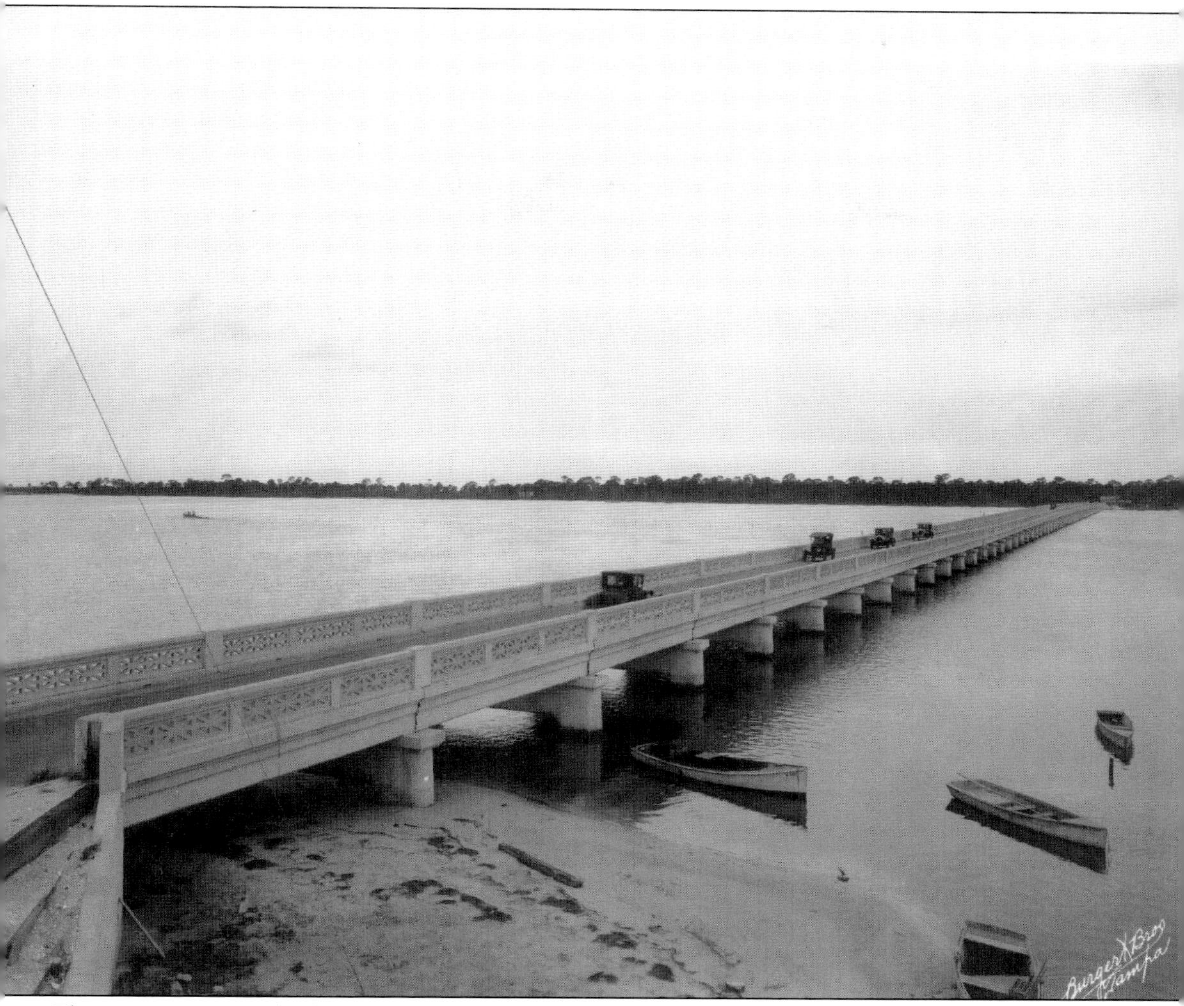

The narrow concrete bridge in this August 1926 photograph connected western St. Petersburg with the Seminole/Largo area at Long Bayou and present-day Bay Pines from 1924 until a replacement span opened in 1966. Bridges on this site played an important role in Largo's development and Pinellas County's history. This span replaced earlier rickety wooden structures. The first bridge, erected in 1910–1911, collapsed shortly after it opened when a man and his team of mules hauling wood reached the midpoint. Their weight caused the poorly constructed concrete pilings to tumble. Angry residents of the Pinellas Peninsula, then a part of western Hillsborough County, demanded answers from the distant county seat in Tampa. Indifference from the other side of Tampa Bay helped to garner support for the movement to create Pinellas County in 1912. A wooden replacement span built in 1914 washed away during the October 1921 hurricane. Bridges across Long Bayou shortened the distance between Largo and lower Pinellas, allowing farmers to transport commodities into St. Petersburg while that city's real estate developers brought investors to Largo in search of inexpensive acreage. (THPL.)

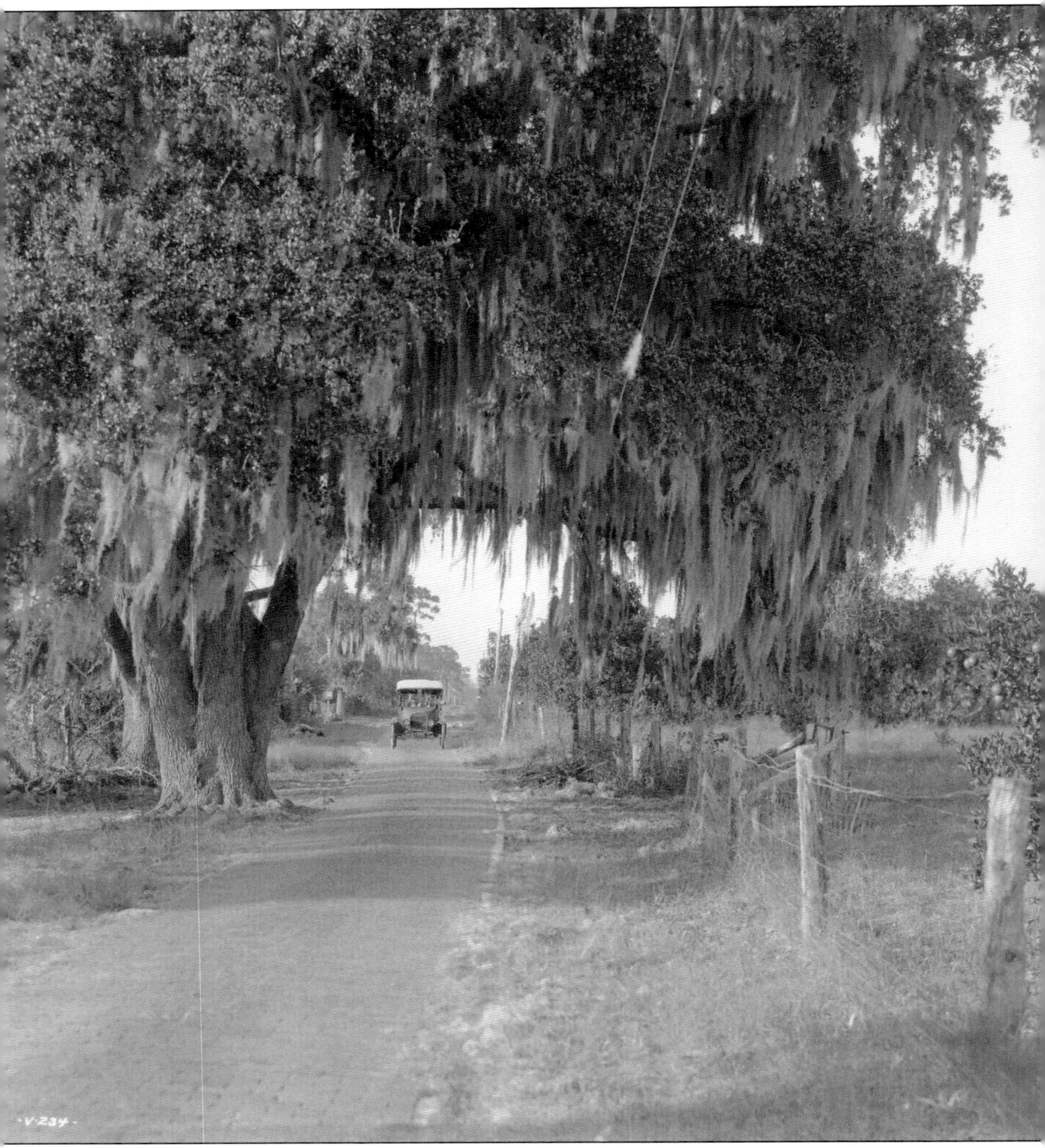

Almost 40 years after the beginning of the national Good Roads Movement, this 1920 portrait of a couple traveling in their automobile along a single-lane brick street in Largo recaptures the way that drivers navigated paved and unpaved paths between distant communities in Pinellas County. During the land boom of the 1920s, the larger cities of Clearwater and St. Petersburg embarked upon aggressive road widening and improvement projects. However, fewer dollars flowed to Largo and the other smaller towns that missed the frenzied real estate speculation occurring elsewhere in the region. Brick roads such as this provided truck farmers and those driving vehicles with citrus and cattle with a quick and easy way to get their products to larger markets in the region. (THPL.)

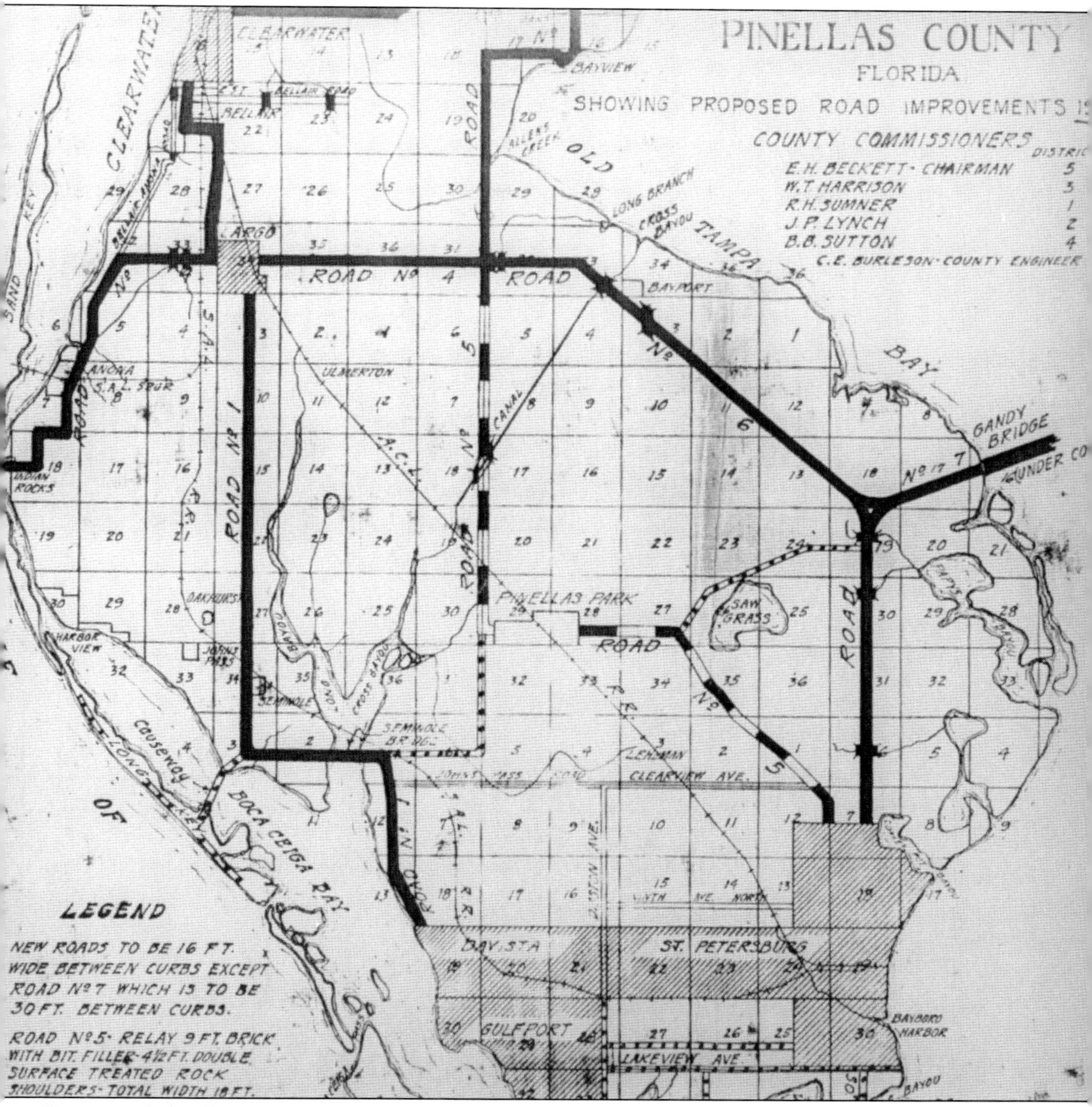

Better roads finally connected Pinellas communities after officials developed plans for an ambitious network of improved highways. Road No. 1 on this map followed the present path of Missouri Avenue/Seminole Boulevard, across the Seminole Bridge, then along Park Street southward toward western St. Petersburg (the Davista area). Road No. 4 ran east from the city along Bay Drive beyond present-day U.S. Route 19, where it met Road No. 6. Now Roosevelt Boulevard, Road No. 6 was a southeastern extension intended to provide a direct connection from Largo to the first bridge built across Tampa Bay, the Gandy Bridge (opened in 1924). Another major road project called for improvements to the northern extension of Ridge Road (now Clearwater-Largo Road) beyond Belleair and into Clearwater. Workers also planned to widen Bay Drive west from Largo to Indian Rocks Road, along a path that reached the Indian Rocks Bridge near the Narrows. (HV.)

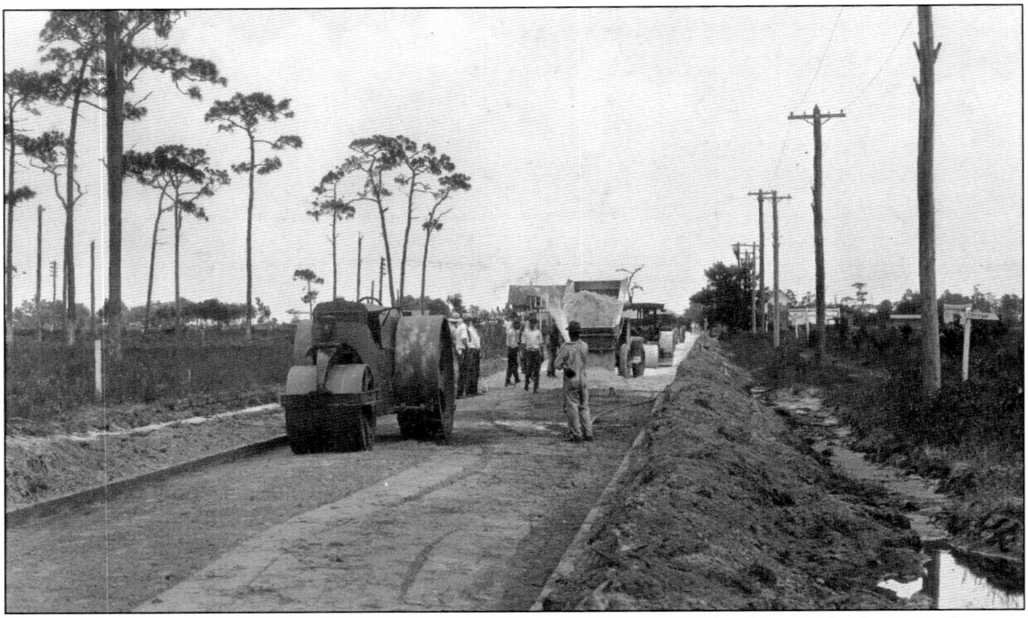

New roads are being carved into the countryside in the photograph above, which shows Rosery Road near Missouri Avenue and the new Highland Park development. On land once homesteaded by Daniel McMullen's family, rock trucks deposited the base of the pavement. By early 1925, agents for the Bayview Investment Company touted Highland Park as a neighborhood near three of the county's fastest growing cities—Largo, Belleair, and Clearwater—complete with paved roads, sidewalks, and other amenities. During the height of the real estate boom, they offered daily tours from St. Petersburg to the area near Highland Avenue, "less than an hour's ride over excellent boulevards." An advertisement from March 1925 appears below. Much of Highland Park became part of Largo after voters approved an annexation referendum in November 1955. (Both, HV.)

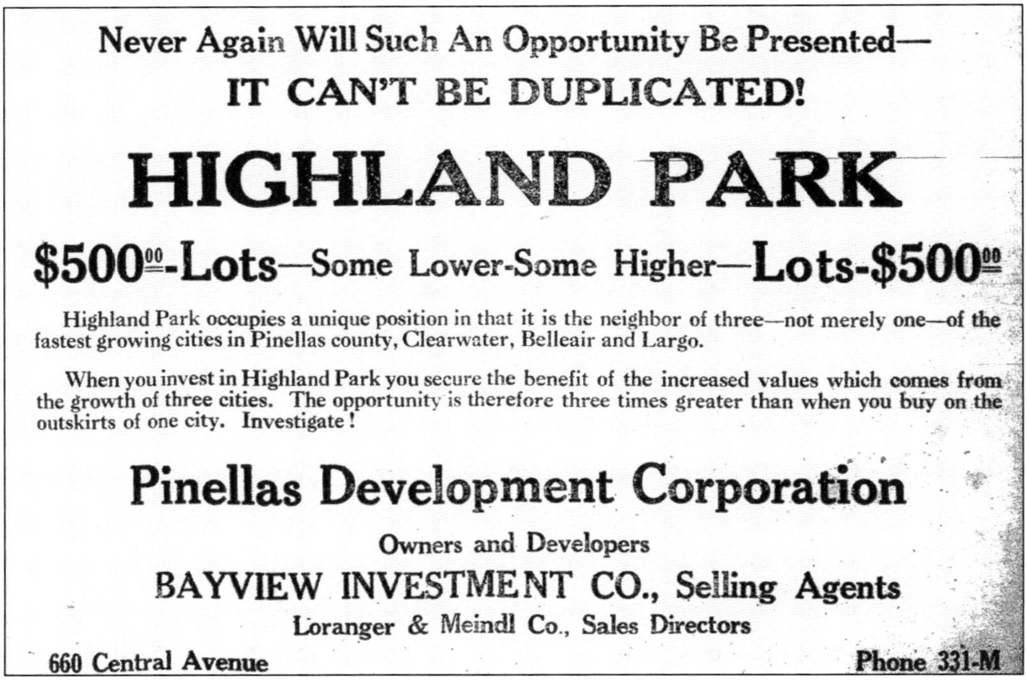

Never Again Will Such An Opportunity Be Presented—

IT CAN'T BE DUPLICATED!

HIGHLAND PARK

$500.00-Lots—Some Lower-Some Higher—Lots-$500.00

Highland Park occupies a unique position in that it is the neighbor of three—not merely one—of the fastest growing cities in Pinellas county, Clearwater, Belleair and Largo.

When you invest in Highland Park you secure the benefit of the increased values which comes from the growth of three cities. The opportunity is therefore three times greater than when you buy on the outskirts of one city. Investigate!

Pinellas Development Corporation

Owners and Developers

BAYVIEW INVESTMENT CO., Selling Agents

Loranger & Meindl Co., Sales Directors

660 Central Avenue Phone 331-M

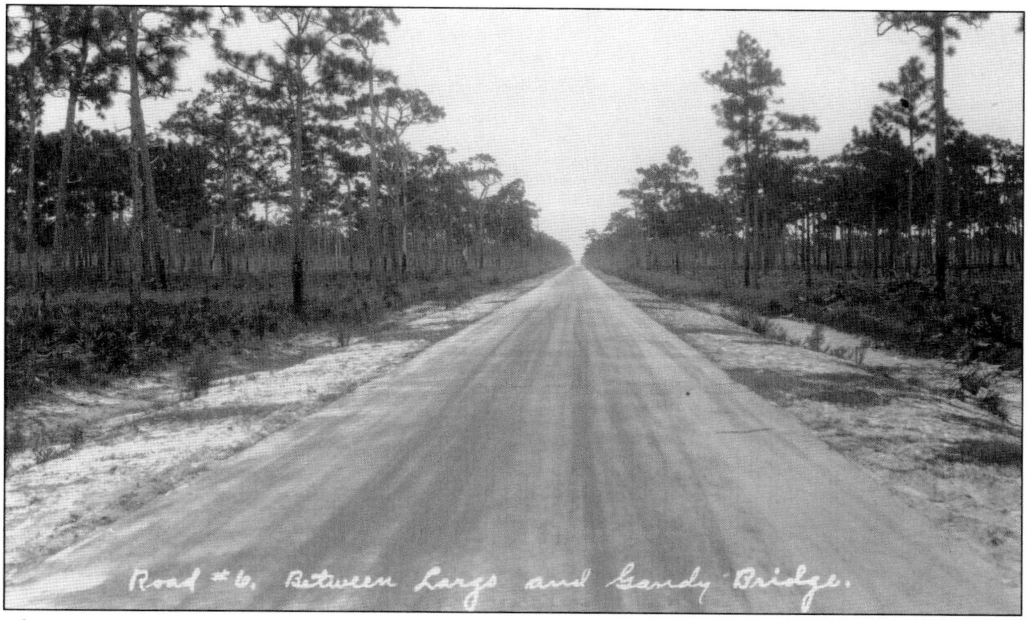

The improved road network between Largo and other areas expanded the acreage that farmers placed under cultivation in the short term and later fostered residential and commercial developments. The image above showing County Road No. 6 during the mid-1920s bears no resemblance to the busy stretch of Roosevelt Boulevard it is today. Within 30 years, pines disappeared from this roadway along the route between St. Petersburg-Clearwater International Airport and Gandy Boulevard in northeastern St. Petersburg. In the picture below, workers surveyed the path of County Road No. 3 in the Oakhurst section between Largo and Indian Rocks. Similar to the way that crews in mountainous areas blasted away portions of the rocky terrain with dynamite, road crews in the largely uninhabited area of Oakhurst detonated explosives to remove large oak trees obstructing their path. (Both, HV.)

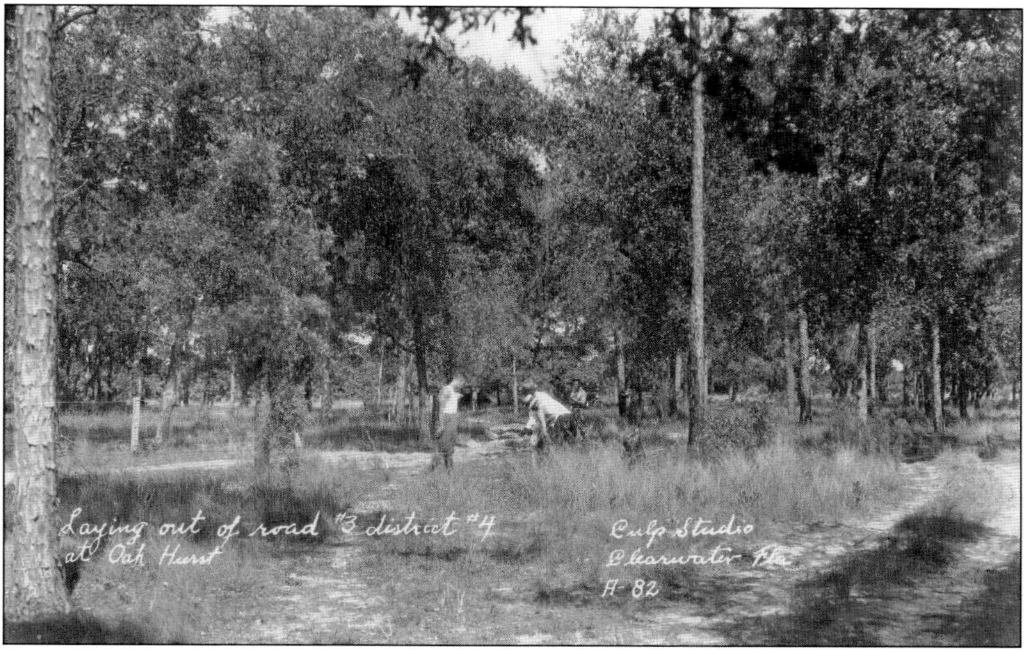

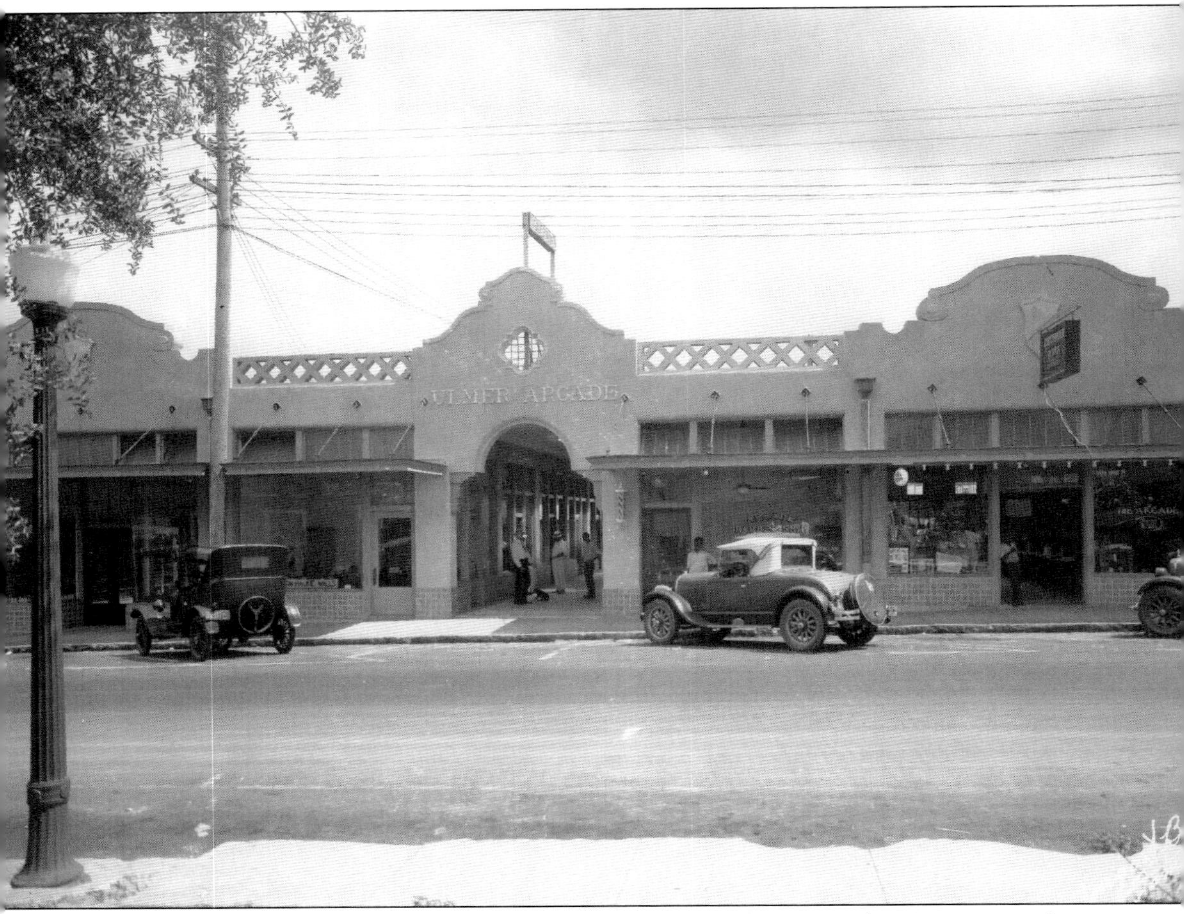

Located at Bay Drive and Railroad Avenue, the Ulmer Arcade, M. W. Ulmer's commercial center, had expanded from a single small building to a complex of stores by the time a photographer captured this image in June 1926. The Ulmer Arcade also served as a de facto community center, hosting events such as school PTA fund-raisers in the late 1920s and Red Cross war relief drives in the spring of 1940, more than a year before America entered World War II. The Ulmer family sold the arcade in July 1941, and it changed hands a few times during the next three decades. An October 1971 newspaper article described this once-bustling plaza as "worn and shabby . . . virtually abandoned . . . and covered with dust and the grime of half a century." Condemned shortly thereafter, the arcade suffered catastrophic damage in a December 1973 fire and was later demolished. (THPL.)

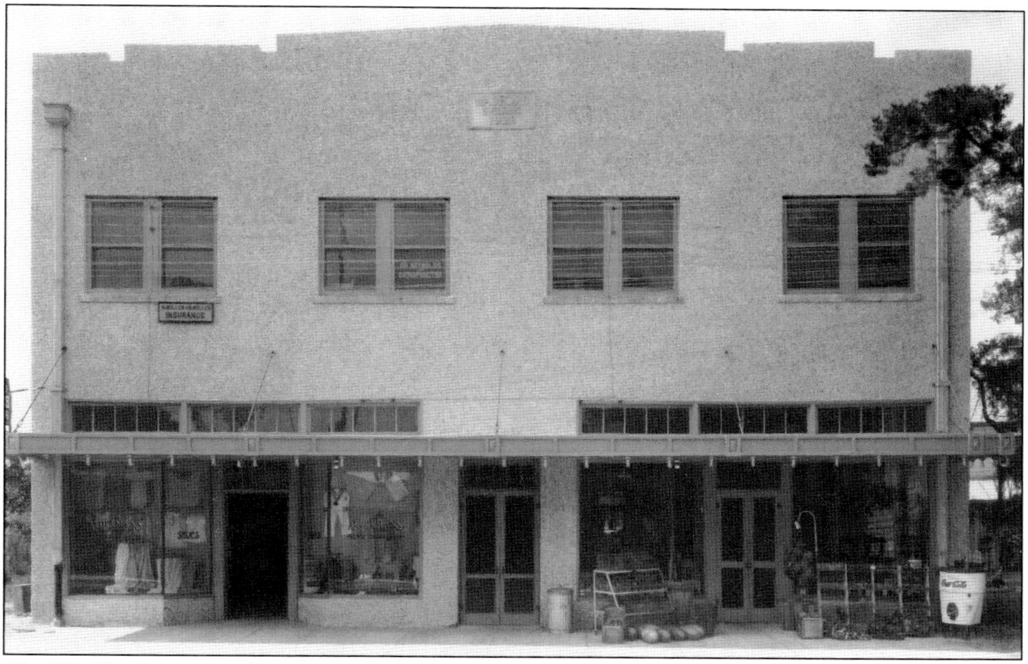

The Wadfords operated a grocery (at right) on the ground floor of this building across the street from the arcade. This picture from July 1926 shows the structure shortly after it opened. A dry goods and clothing store shared space on the first floor, with the McMullen insurance agency and a chiropractor on the second floor. The Wadfords later expanded their grocery and rented apartments upstairs. (THPL.)

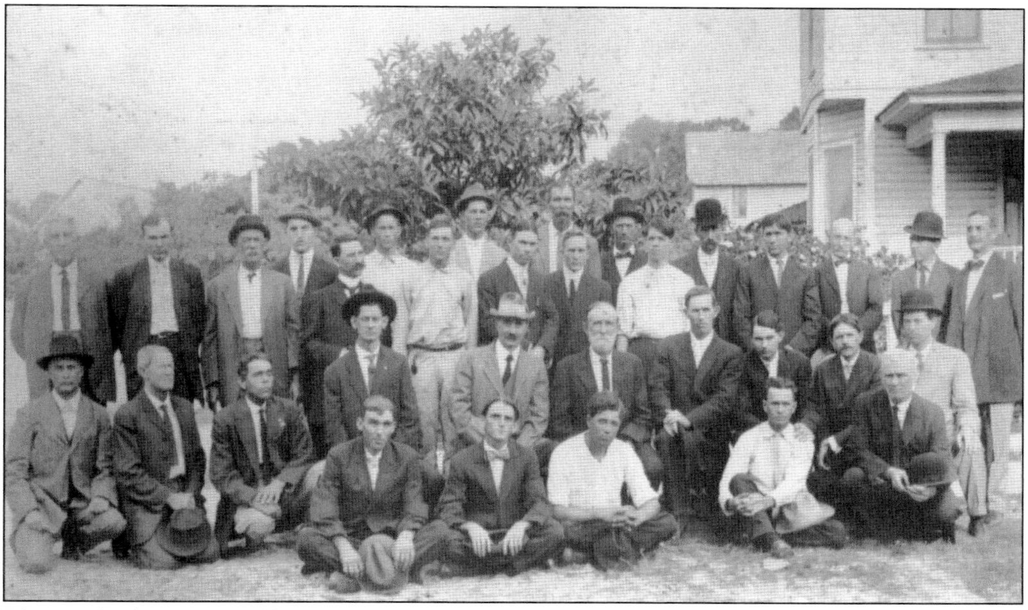

The Methodist men's Bible class gathered in 1912. At that time, the flock worshipped in a small building located east of the town park (Ulmer Park) with plans for a more elaborate structure under way. Notable members of the community, including Henry Kilgore, Dr. Bethel McMullen, and Eli McMullen, appear in this picture outside of F. M. Campbell's home near the railroad depot. (HV.)

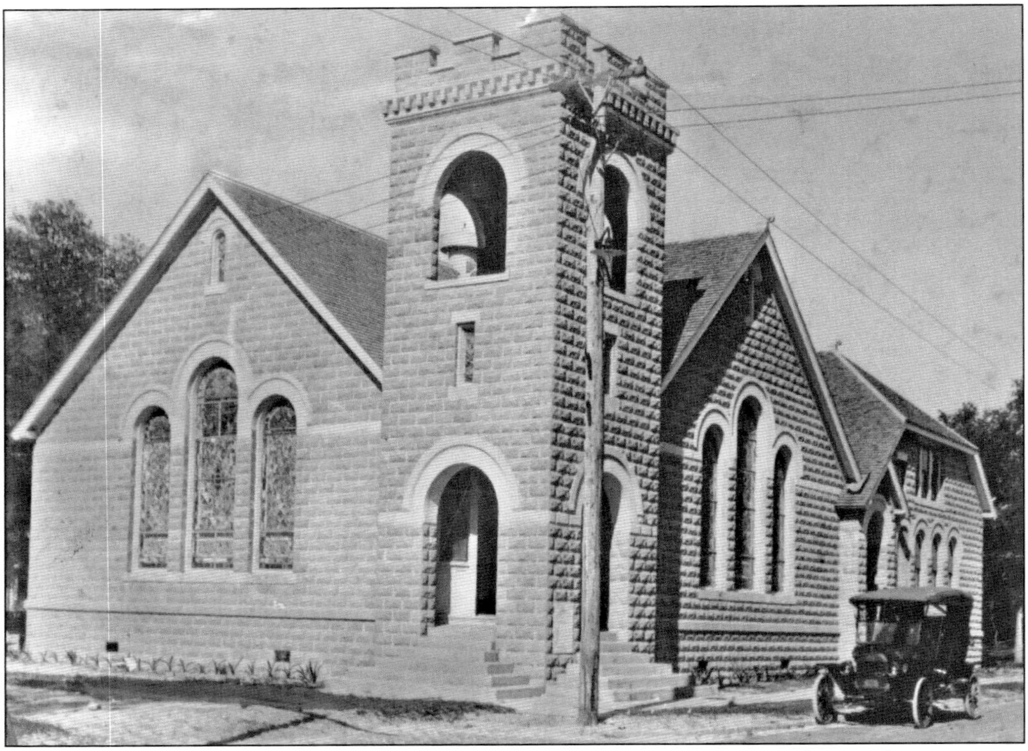

The First Methodist Church moved into this Romanesque structure at the northwest corner of Fourth Street and First Avenue Southwest in 1913. The image above reveals the church as it appeared shortly after opening in 1913. By June 1926, the church had a large cross that illuminated at night. Attendance increased rapidly after World War II, prompting the church's members to expand the facility. In 1962, they acquired a parcel one block south of this building, between First Avenue Southwest and Cleveland Avenue. A new sanctuary rose on the new site in 1963–1964. Plans to demolish the older church in the early 1970s upset some of the members. They gathered blocks and wood scraps from the site of this building when it met the wrecking ball. (Above, HV; below, THPL.)

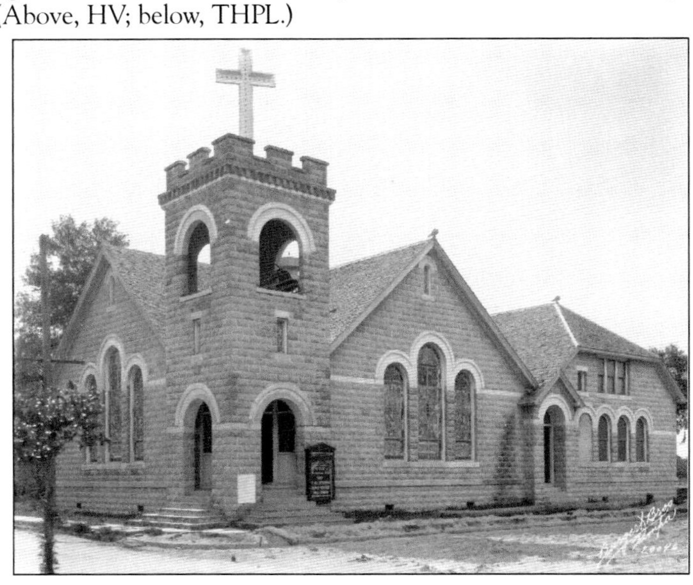

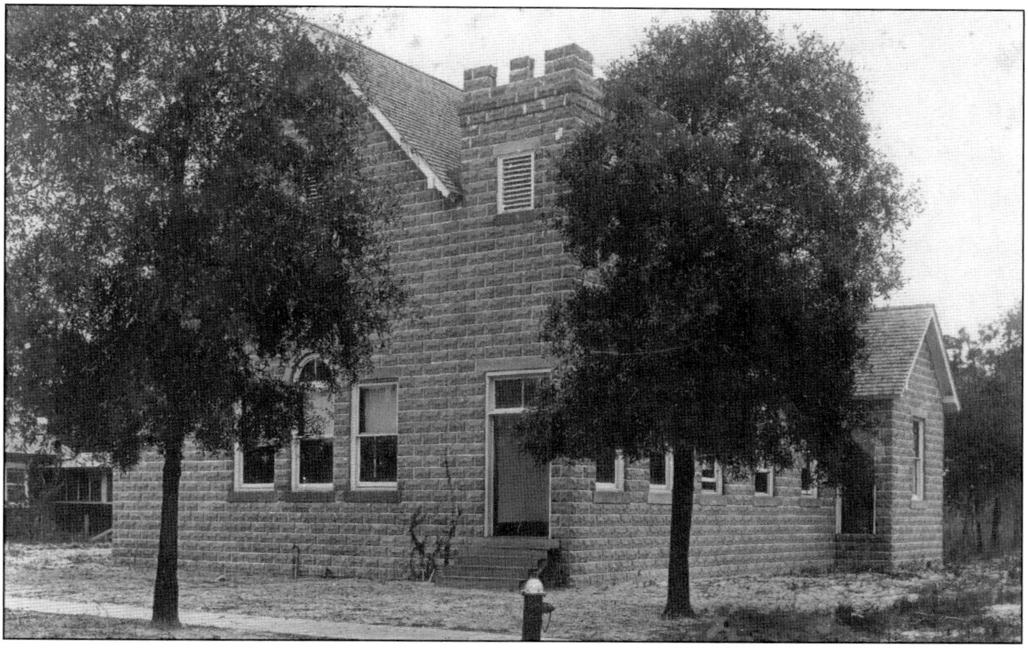

Built in 1912, this structure at the intersection of Sixth Street and First Avenue Southwest served as the home of Largo's First Baptist Church until 1967. After that, the church moved to a site now used by the School Board of Pinellas County, and later to Eighth Avenue Southeast, near Largo Middle School. The 1912 sanctuary, shown in this 1918 image, still stands today. (HV.)

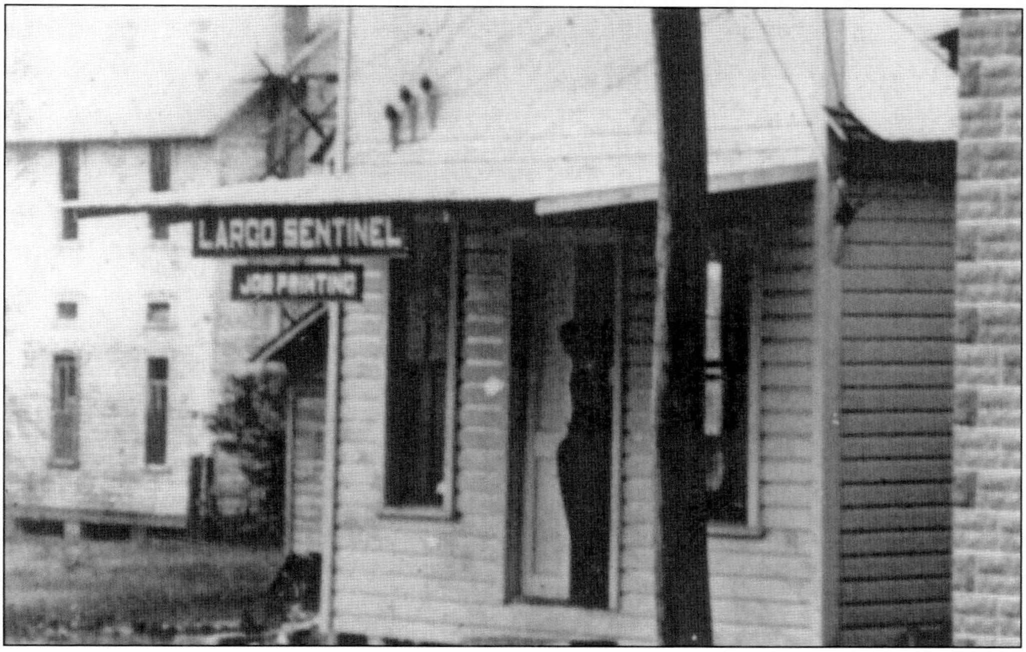

While religious institutions spread the word to their flock, the *Largo Sentinel* offered a weekly pulpit for issues facing the community. The first issue appeared in January 1912, the month that Pinellas County gained its independence. The *Sentinel* became a supportive voice for the community, especially during the 29 years J. Stanley Pecarek owned the paper. This view shows the early printing office in 1913. (HV.)

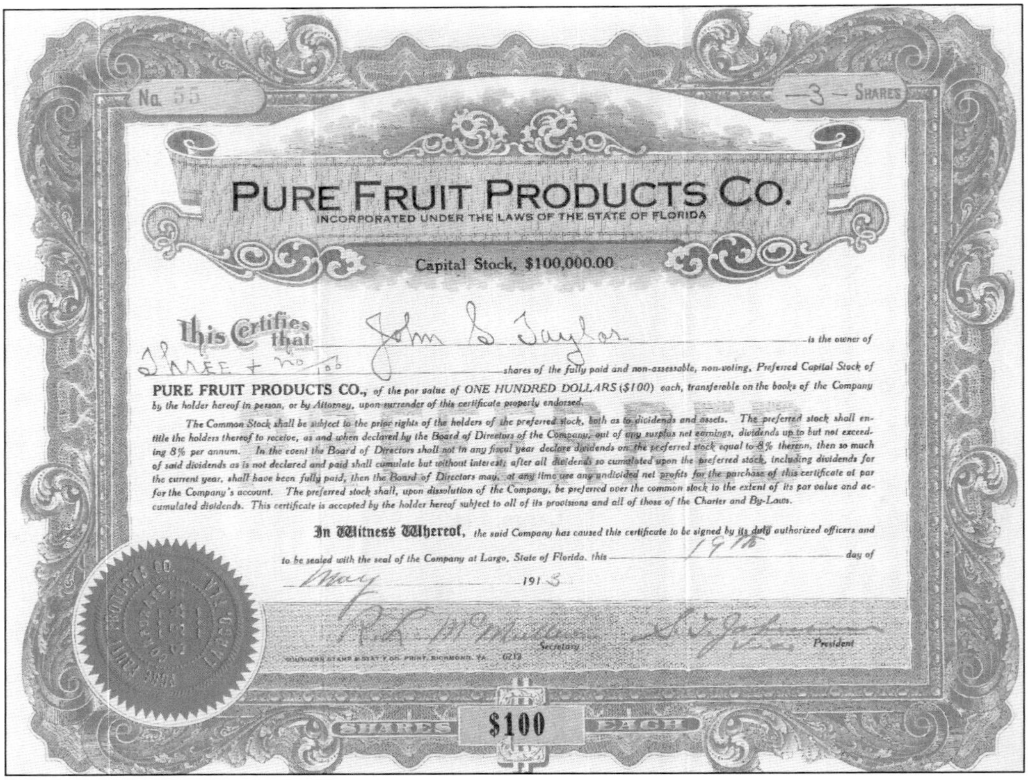

No. 55

—3— SHARES

PURE FRUIT PRODUCTS CO.

INCORPORATED UNDER THE LAWS OF THE STATE OF FLORIDA

Capital Stock, $100,000.00

This Certifies that John S. Taylor is the owner of Three + no/100 shares of the fully paid and non-assessable, non-voting, Preferred Capital Stock of PURE FRUIT PRODUCTS CO., of the par value of ONE HUNDRED DOLLARS ($100) each, transferable on the books of the Company by the holder hereof in person, or by Attorney, upon surrender of this certificate properly endorsed.

The Common Stock shall be subject to the prior rights of the holders of the preferred stock, both as to dividends and assets. The preferred stock shall entitle the holders thereof to receive, as and when declared by the Board of Directors of the Company, out of any surplus net earnings, dividends up to but not exceeding 8% per annum. In the event the Board of Directors shall not in any fiscal year declare dividends on the preferred stock equal to 8% thereon, then so much of said dividends as is not declared and paid shall cumulate but without interest; after all dividends so cumulated upon the preferred stock, including dividends for the current year, shall have been fully paid, then the Board of Directors may, at any time use any undivided net profits for the purchase of this certificate at par for the Company's account. The preferred stock shall, upon dissolution of the Company, be preferred over the common stock to the extent of its par value and accumulated dividends. This certificate is accepted by the holder hereof subject to all of its provisions and all of those of the Charter and By-Laws.

In Witness Whereof, the said Company has caused this certificate to be signed by its duly authorized officers and to be sealed with the seal of the Company at Largo, State of Florida, this 19th day of May 1913

R. L. McMullen, Secretary

S. T. Johnson, Vice President

SHARES $100 EACH

As citrus groves increased in size and value, investors enjoyed a variety of business partnerships that supported the industry. Robert Lee "Dr. Bob" McMullen served as secretary for the Pure Fruit Products Company and signed this stock certificate issued to John S. Taylor. A bountiful harvest of citrus with the Hi-Stepper label at Taylor's packinghouse illustrates the importance of these facilities to the local economy. (Both, John S. Taylor Collection, HV.)

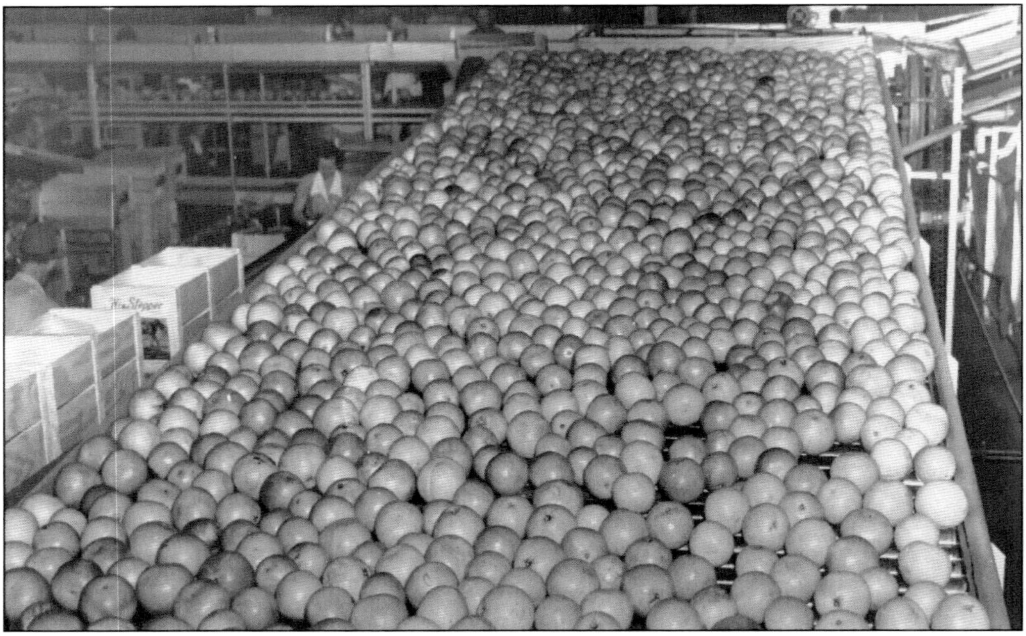

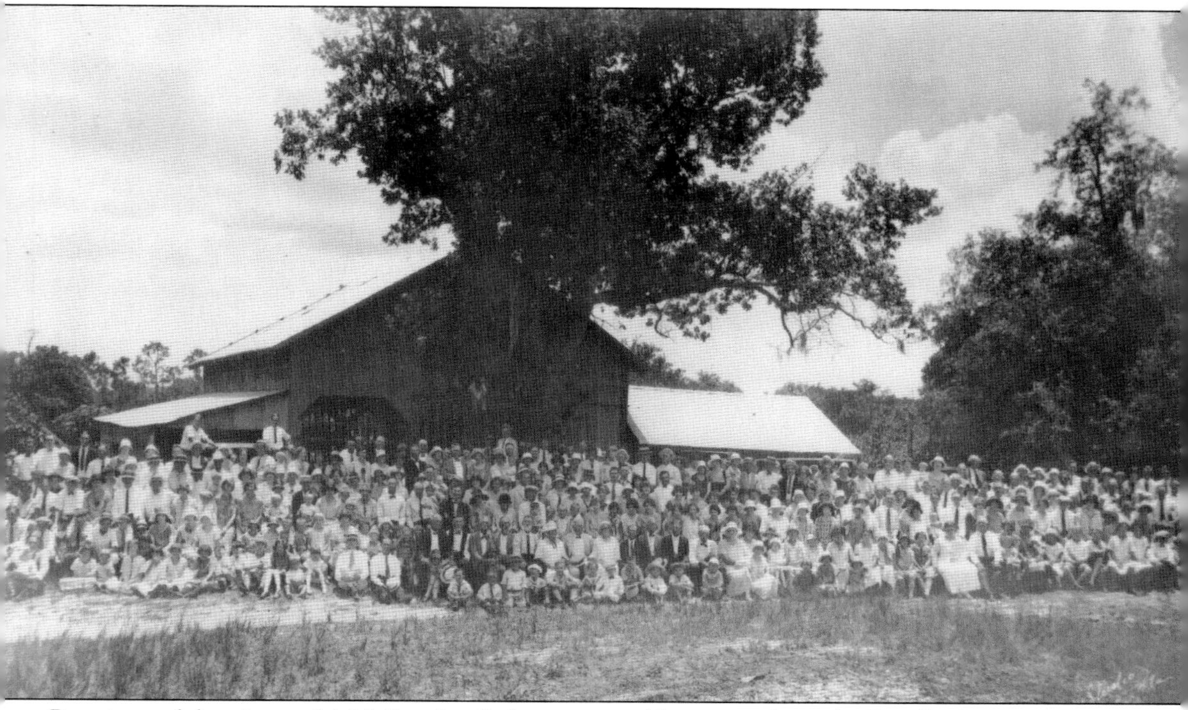

Reunions of the pioneer McMullen family became notable events along the Pinellas Peninsula. Hundreds of descendants of the seven McMullen brothers gathered at family homesteads, the county fairgrounds in Largo, or other destinations. This image captures a July 4, 1925, assembly on the land homesteaded by Uncle Dan McMullen and Margaret Ann Campbell McMullen in the late 1860s. The site was near Missouri Avenue and Rosery Road in present-day Largo. (HV.)

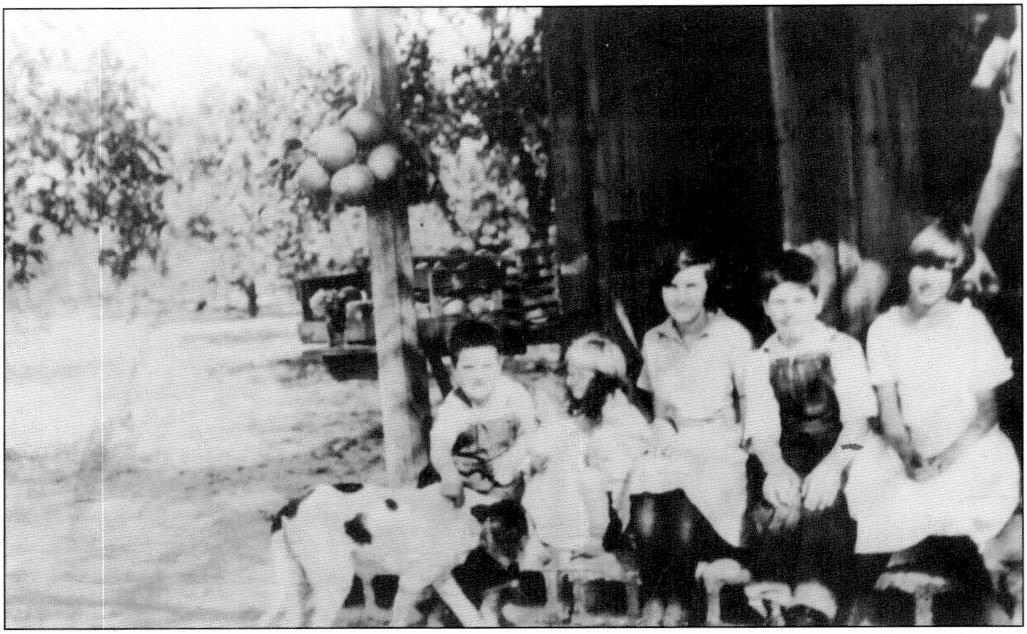

David Ulmer moved his family from the Palm Harbor area to a site on Seminole Boulevard 3 miles south of Bay Drive near Orange Lake Village and Walsingham Road. His wife operated a roadside fruit stand there by the time this photograph was taken in 1928. In 1931, daughter Audrey (center) became the first Miss Largo. (HV.)

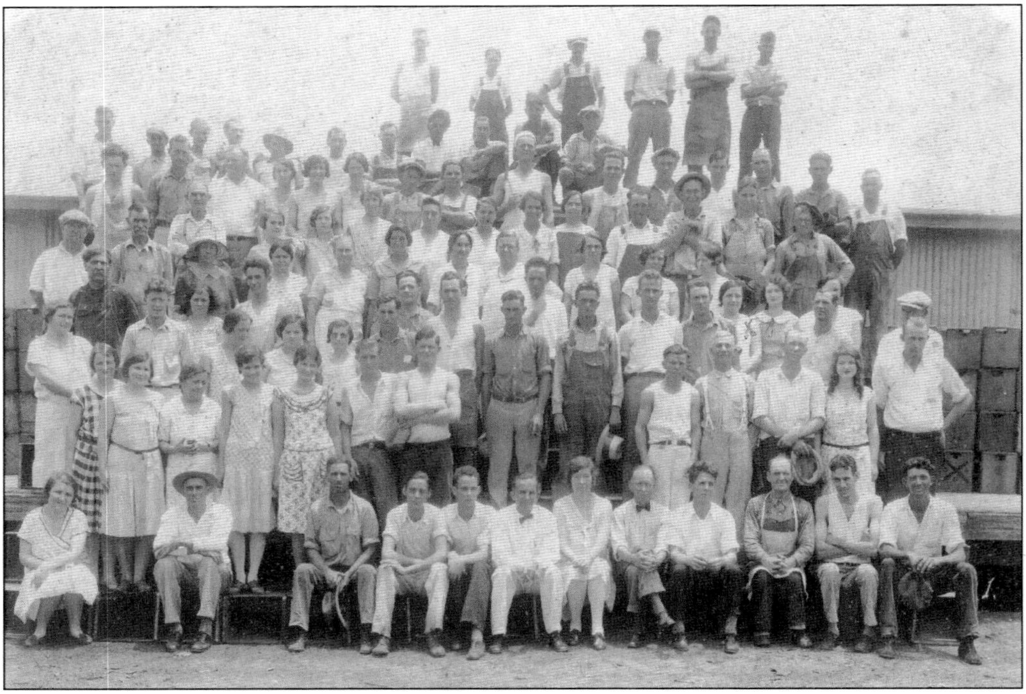

Although Florida's economy suffered after the land boom came to an end, farming and citrus operations in Largo cushioned the blow. By the time members of the Citrus City Growers Association gathered for this group photograph to commemorate the end of the spring 1929 harvesting season, real estate speculation had stalled in Pinellas. (HV.)

Three

The Fair City Midway Through Its History 1930–1954

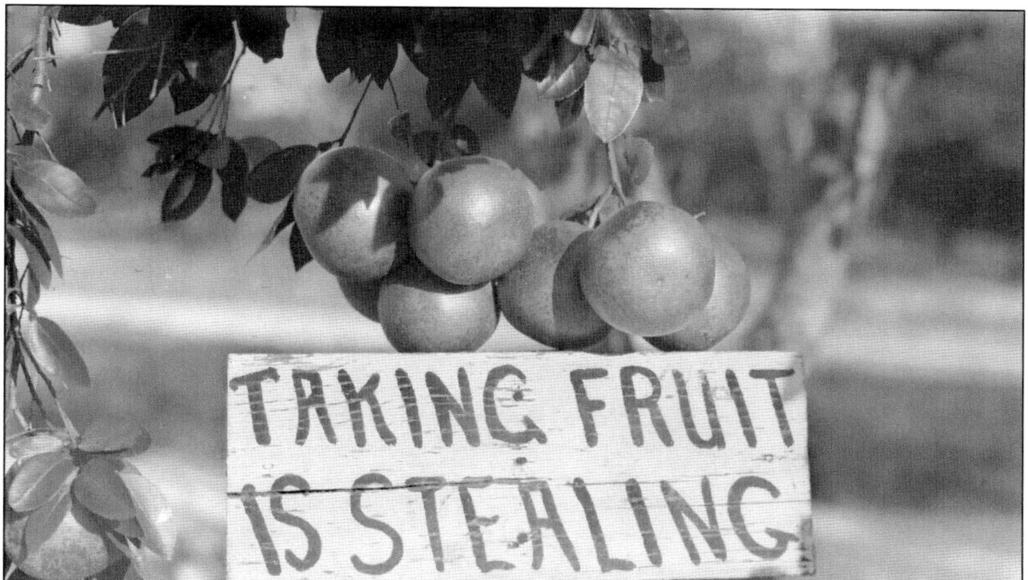

The Great Depression gripped Florida earlier than most of the nation. The frenzied speculation that transformed Tampa, St. Petersburg, Miami, Coral Gables, Palm Beach, and Sarasota into boomtowns after World War I bypassed most of the rural settlements in the Sunshine State. Although Largo's farmers enjoyed prosperous times as they brought their crops to nearby markets during the early 1920s, the land boom's demise by late 1926 left the state's economy in a poor condition. By the late 1920s, grove owners in rural areas had to protect their crops from hungry thieves who wanted to take a bite out of their diminishing profits. (USFSP.)

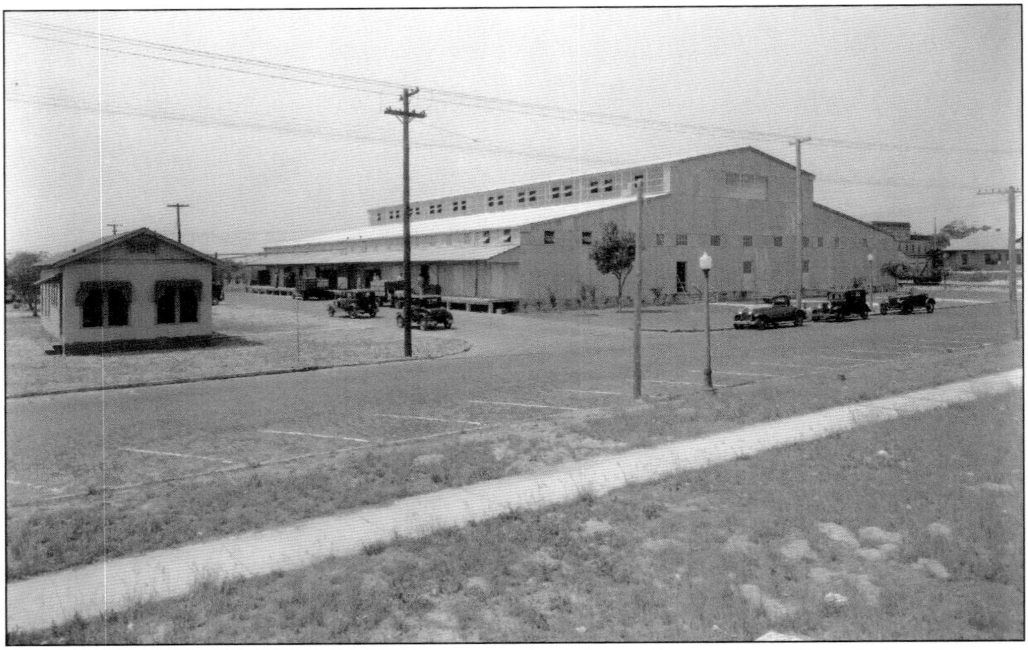

Although Florida's economic downturn extinguished the real estate boom long before the stock market collapsed in October 1929, the demand for citrus products from the groves surrounding Largo remained strong. An explosion at John S. Taylor's packinghouse during the spring 1931 harvesting season threatened Largo's financial health. On April 1, a fire started within the wooden factory, most likely fueled by chemicals used to color the fruit. Flames quickly consumed the factory, as well as stacks of wooden boxes and containers full of citrus. Taylor immediately launched plans to replace the factory with a new and improved structure. The image above, taken by the Burgert Brothers firm, shows the new factory in April 1932. The image below, from the Taylor family collection, offers a view along East Bay Drive in 1935. (Above, THPL; below, John S. Taylor Collection, HV.)

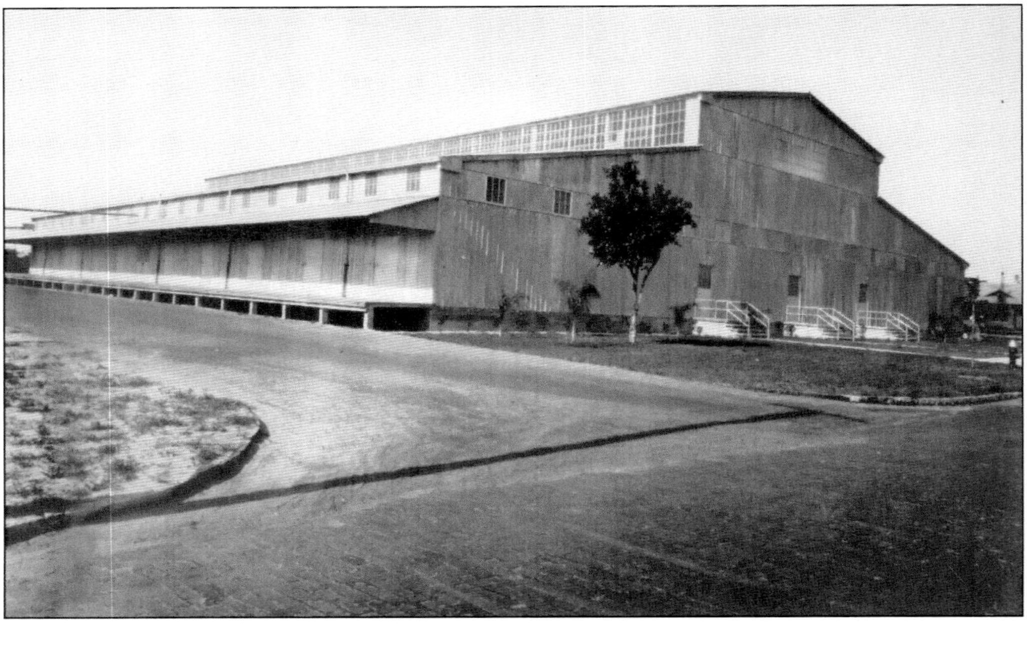

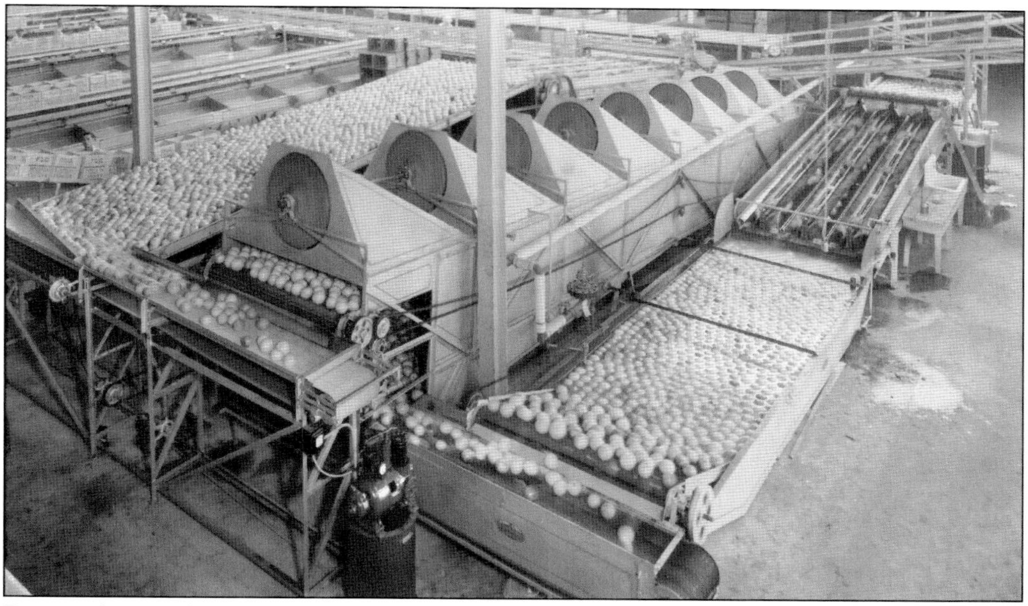

During the April 1931 fire, nearby residents rushed to the scene, hoping to save the factory and the jobs it brought to Largo. The only part of the factory spared was a small office with the company's business records. While crews built the new plant with a cement base and steel walls to replace the wooden packinghouse that burnt to the ground, Taylor's employees worked at other facilities to fulfill orders, such as the Kilgore packinghouse in Clearwater. Taylor invested about $85,000 in this new facility, with nearly $50,000 of that amount set aside for improved machinery. New washing and polishing machines and an extensive conveyor belt system appear in these April 1932 photographs taken as the employees resumed operations at their new Largo facility. (Both, THPL.)

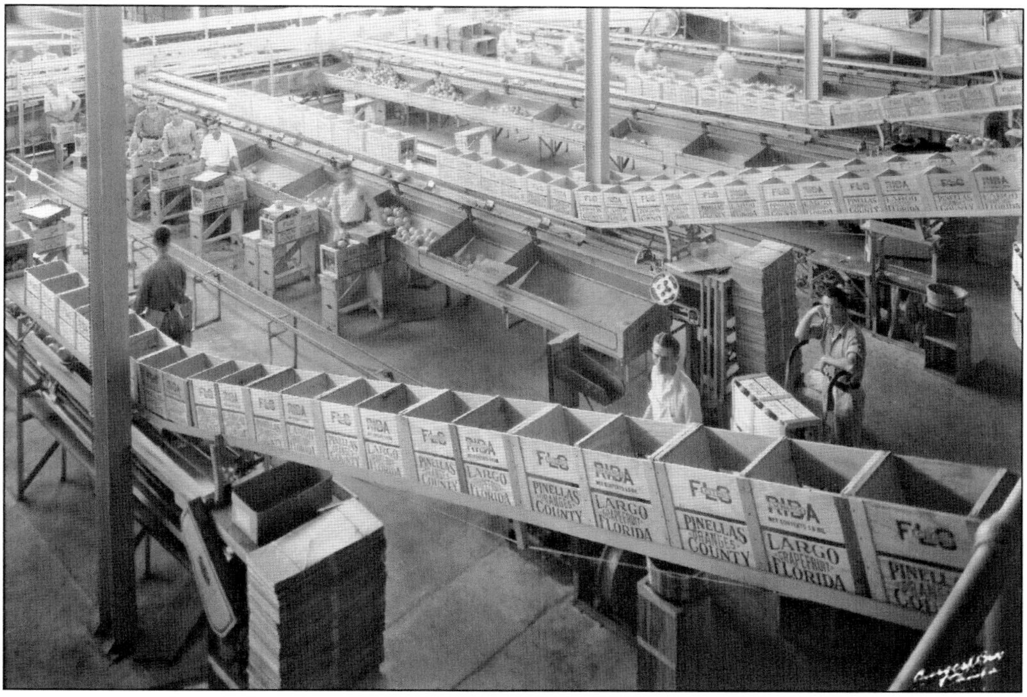

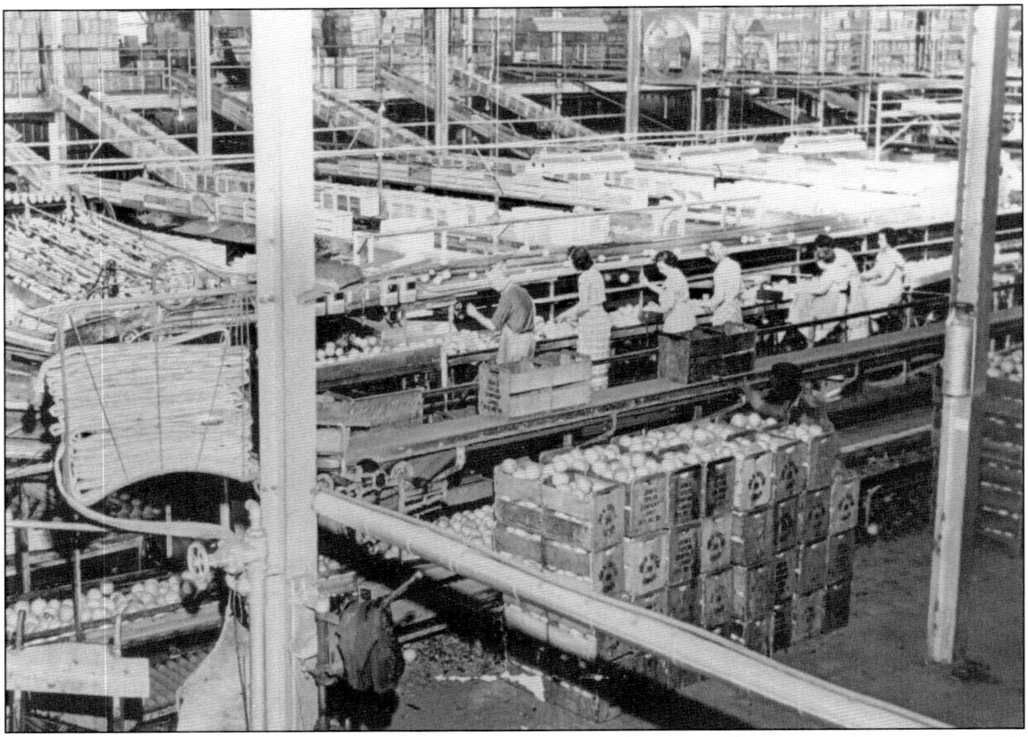

Improvements at John S. Taylor's newly constructed packinghouse, such as a complex conveyor belt system and fruit sorting stations, allowed workers to expedite orders at the height of the shipping season during the mid-1930s. The factory provided jobs to women and African Americans at a time when the stagnant economy offered few alternatives. (HV.)

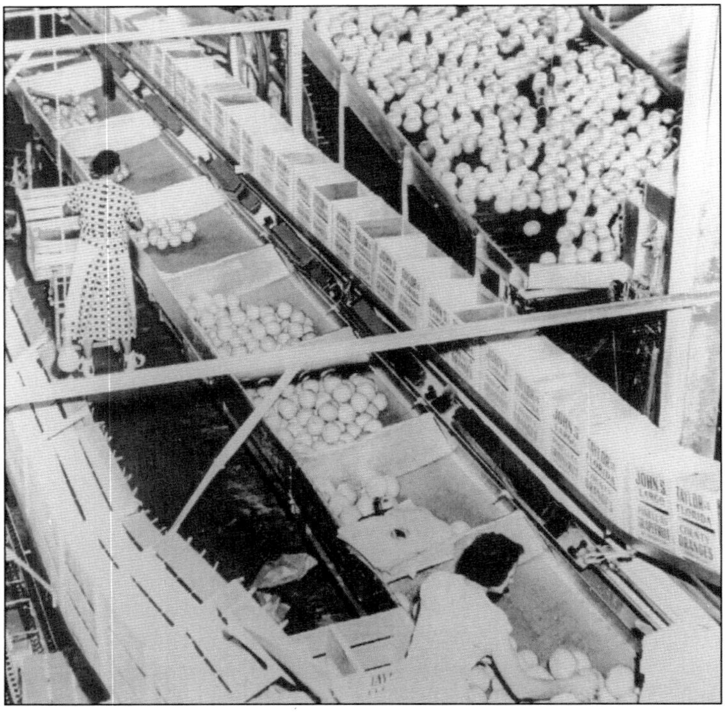

Two employees inspect grapefruit as the machine on the right cleans, polishes, and sorts the fruit. The loud machines and dedicated workers at the Taylor packinghouse kept the economy humming during the lean years of the Great Depression. John S. Taylor's crates were proudly branded with both "Largo" and "Pinellas County" so that those receiving these delicious products knew of their origin. (HV.)

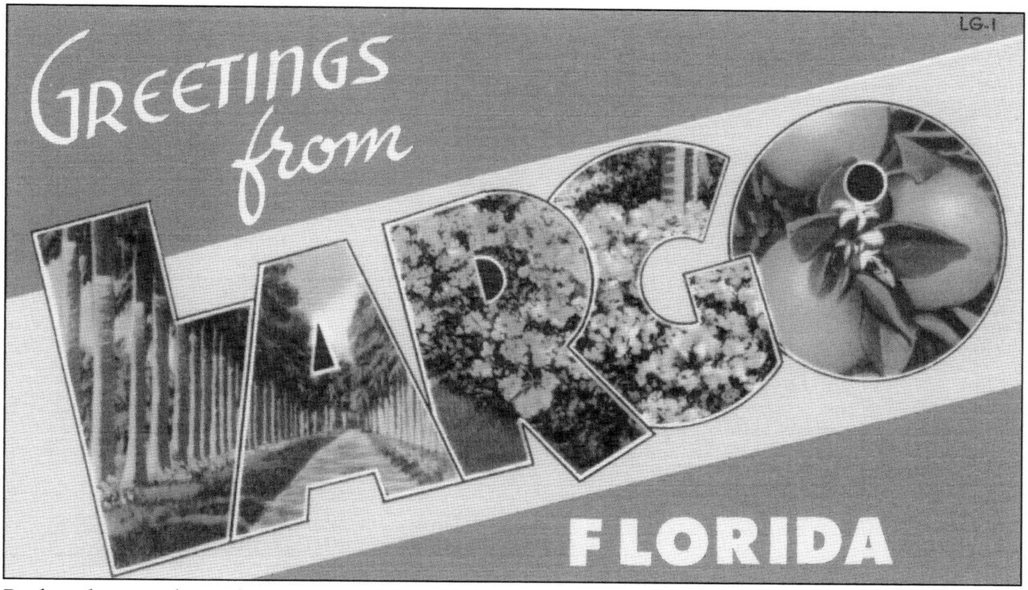

Packinghouses throughout peninsular Florida created colorful labels as a way to brand their fruit and showcase their communities. Workers affixed these iconic labels to the wooden crates before they shipped the fruit to distant venues. John S. Taylor's brands included Black Diamond (a premium label for his highest quality fruit) and Sunny Florida. Wood shortages during World War II compelled many citrus packing facilities to replace labeled crates with the preprinted cardboard containers still found in many produce stands today. Taylor's Sunny Florida label appears below. The postcard above from the mid-20th century vividly focuses on agricultural commodities as a way to identify Largo rather than the typical tourist destinations (such as piers, beaches, and fancy hotels) found on postcards for other Florida cities. (Both, HV.)

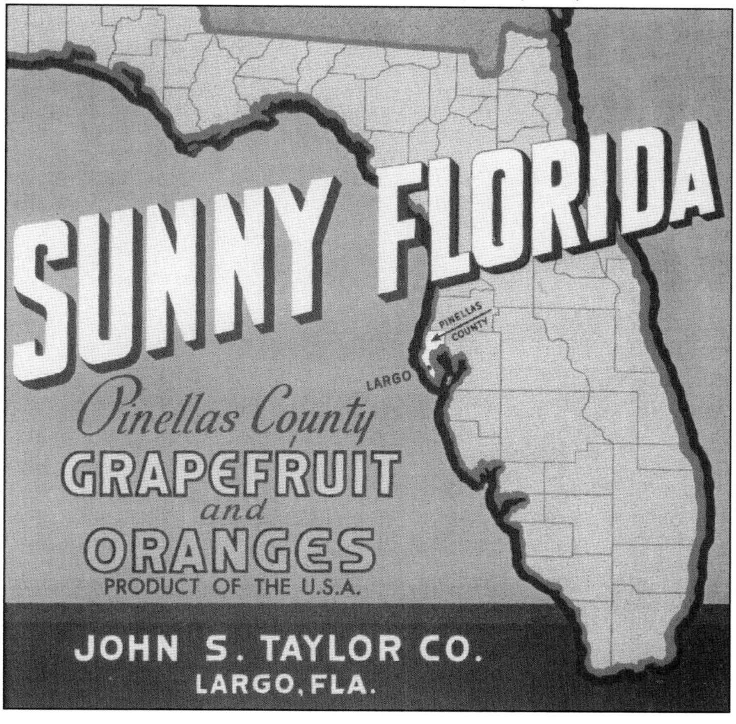

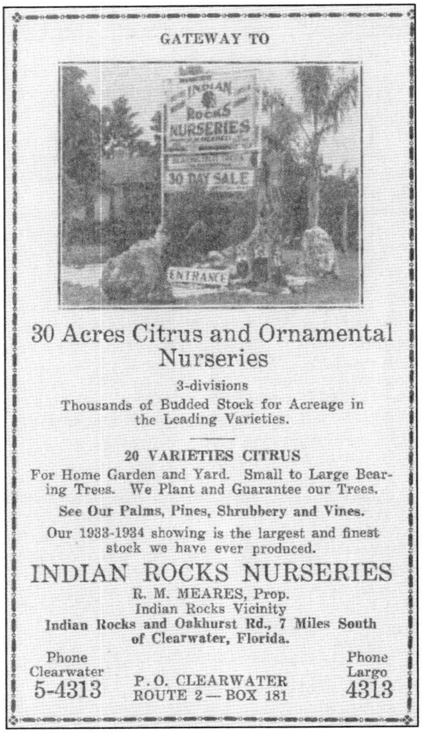

The advertisement for the Indian Rocks Nursery at left appeared in the program for the 1934 Pinellas County Fair. Members of many pioneer families continued to focus on agricultural endeavors and participate in activities that promoted the fair. A portion from the front page of the 1937 program below lists admission fees and reveals the entryway arch at the fairgrounds during the 20th annual exposition of the fair. (Both, HV.)

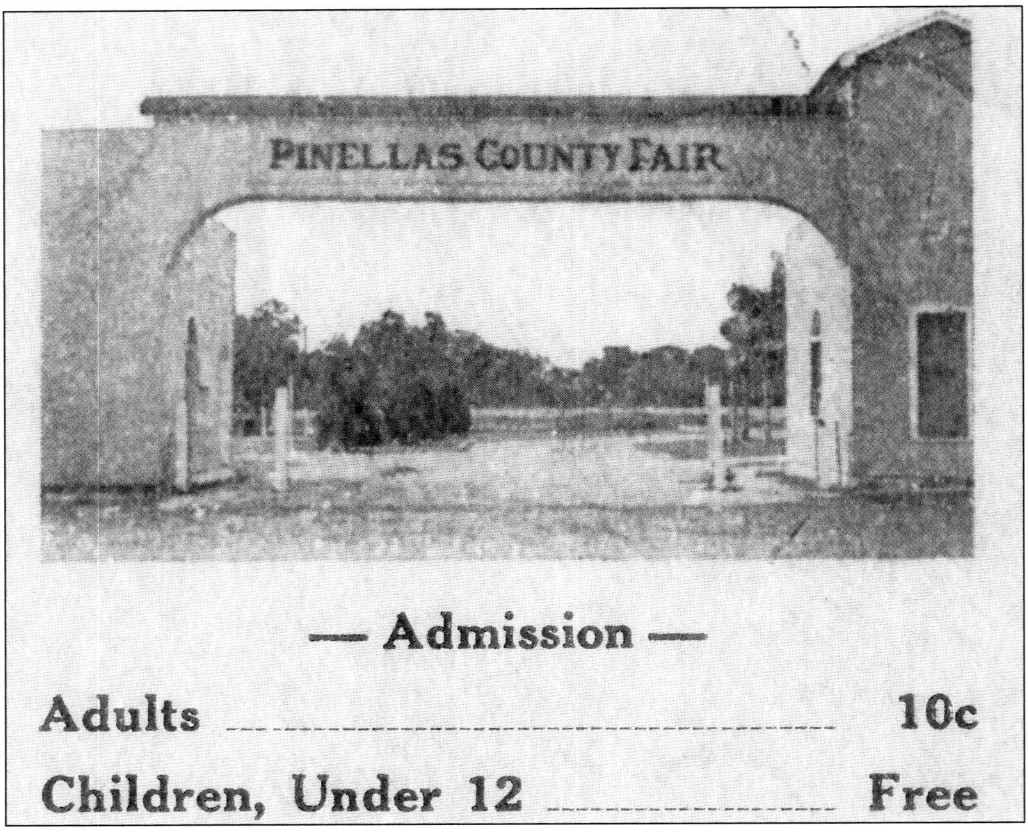

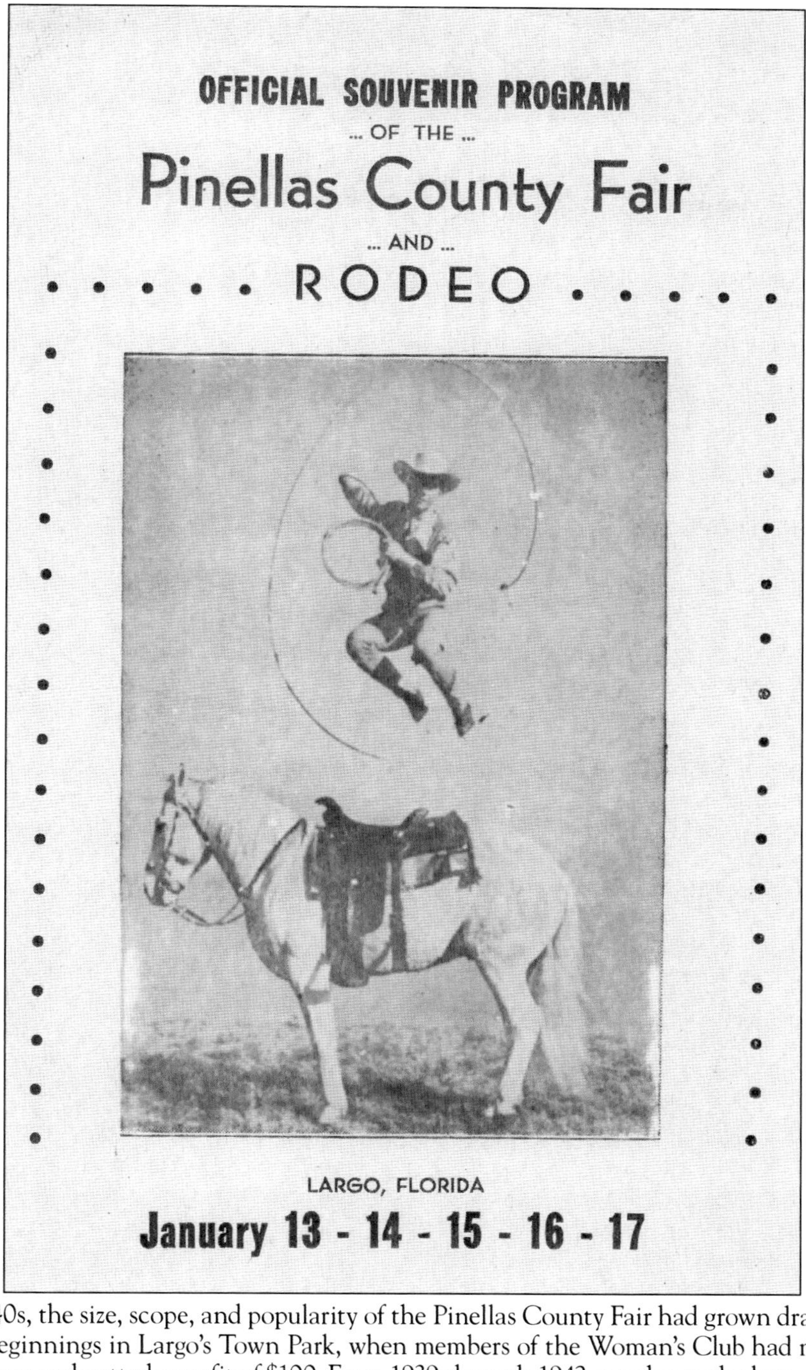

By the 1940s, the size, scope, and popularity of the Pinellas County Fair had grown dramatically since its beginnings in Largo's Town Park, when members of the Woman's Club had made pine needle purses and netted a profit of $100. From 1939 through 1942, a rodeo took place. Although wartime exigencies led to the cancellation of the fair from 1943 through 1945, the fair returned with increased attendance after World War II came to an end. In 1948, organizers launched a horse show that included cash prizes. By the 1950s, the fair proclaimed itself the "Pageant of Pinellas Progress," with more than 10,000 children participating in these annual fairs as musicians, exhibitors, or contestants. Schoolchildren throughout Pinellas County took field trips during the weeklong gatherings, although white and nonwhite children often attended on separate days. (HV.)

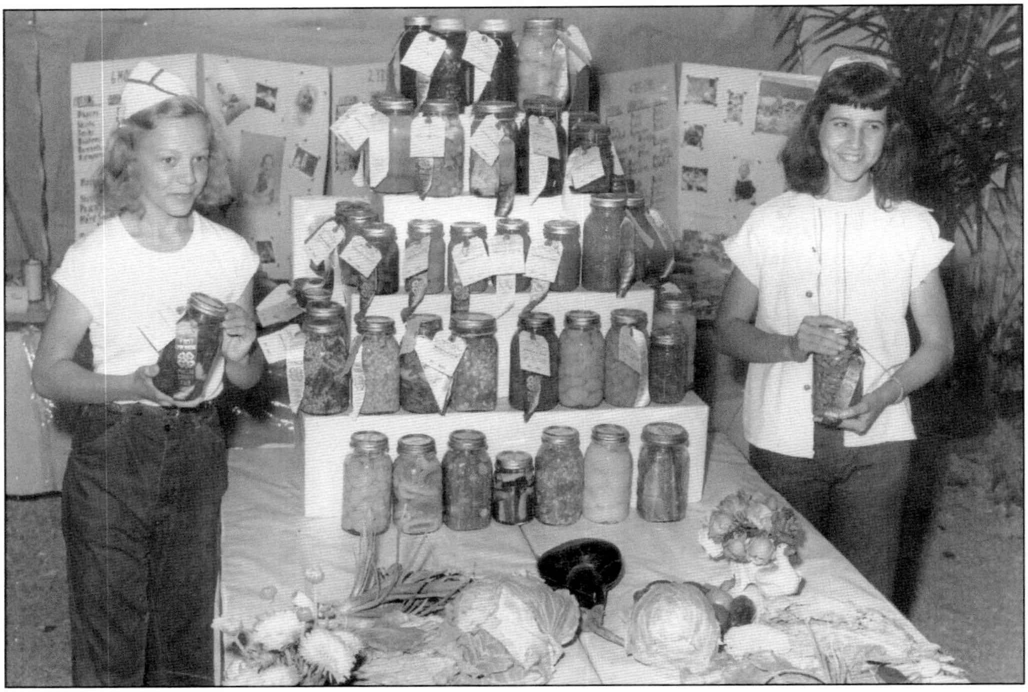

These images from the Pinellas County Fair in 1949 capture the excitement of Pinellas County youngsters when they received awards for their agricultural accomplishments. Above, two girls stand alongside a display for entries for the 4-H competition in canning. Such skills were certainly necessary a few years earlier during World War II, when shortages and rationing restrictions required residents to conserve supplies and encouraged them to plant victory gardens. Below, four girls who earned honors for their poultry pose for a picture. (Both, HV.)

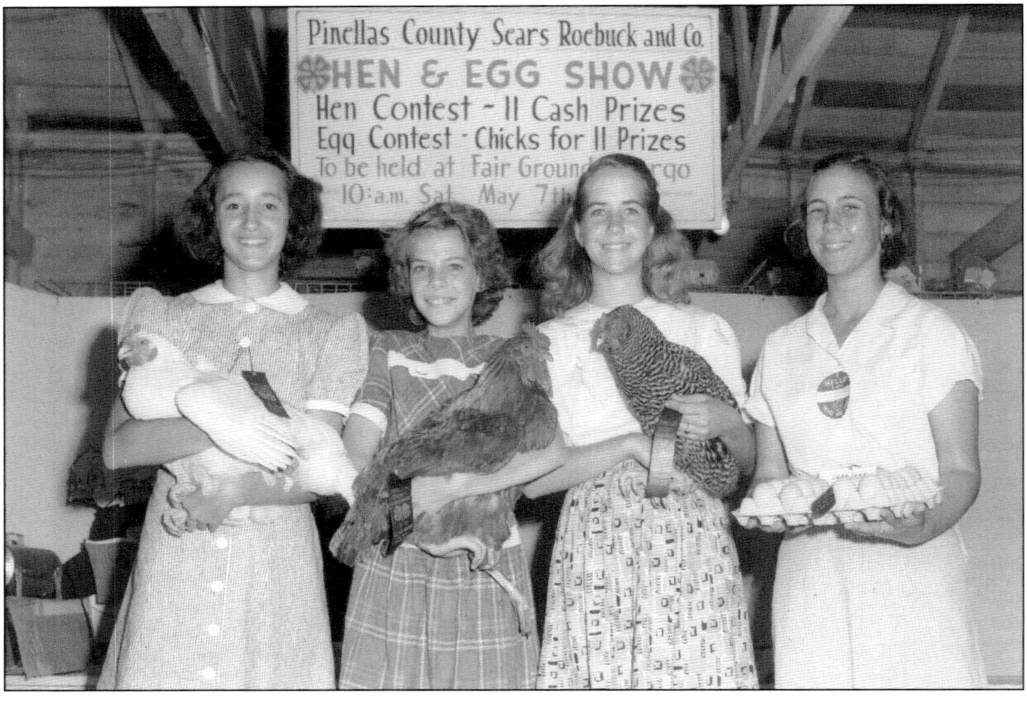

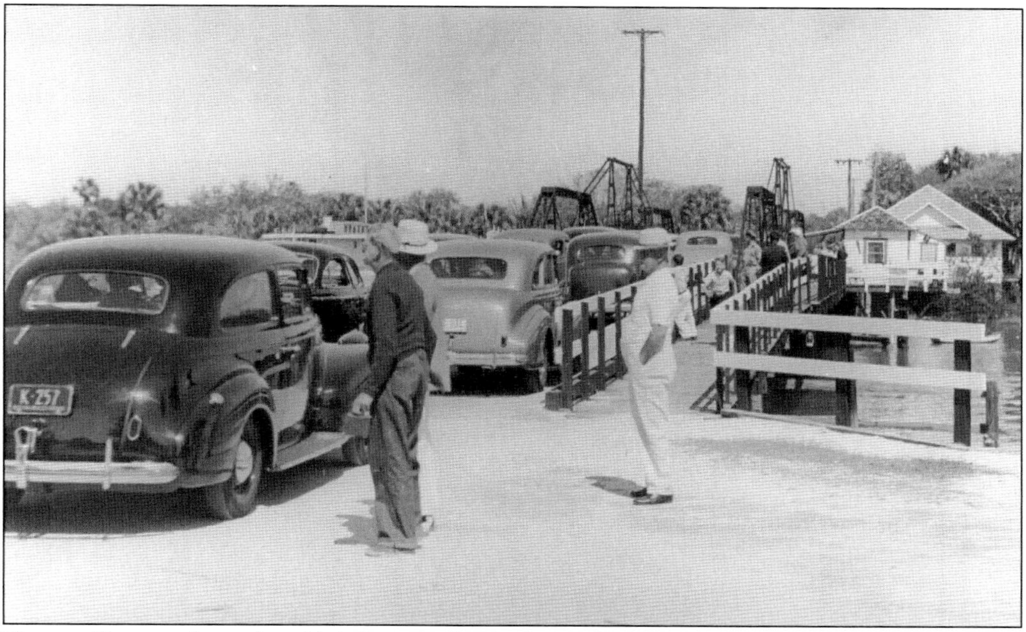

This traffic jam along the old Indian Rocks Bridge took place in 1939, two years after Pinellas County acquired the narrow structure for less than $17,000 and lifted the tolls. Vehicles had to negotiate a two-lane roadway only 15 feet wide, leaving drivers little room for error. A concrete bascule drawbridge along Walsingham Road, less than a mile north of this site, opened with great fanfare in June 1958. (HV.)

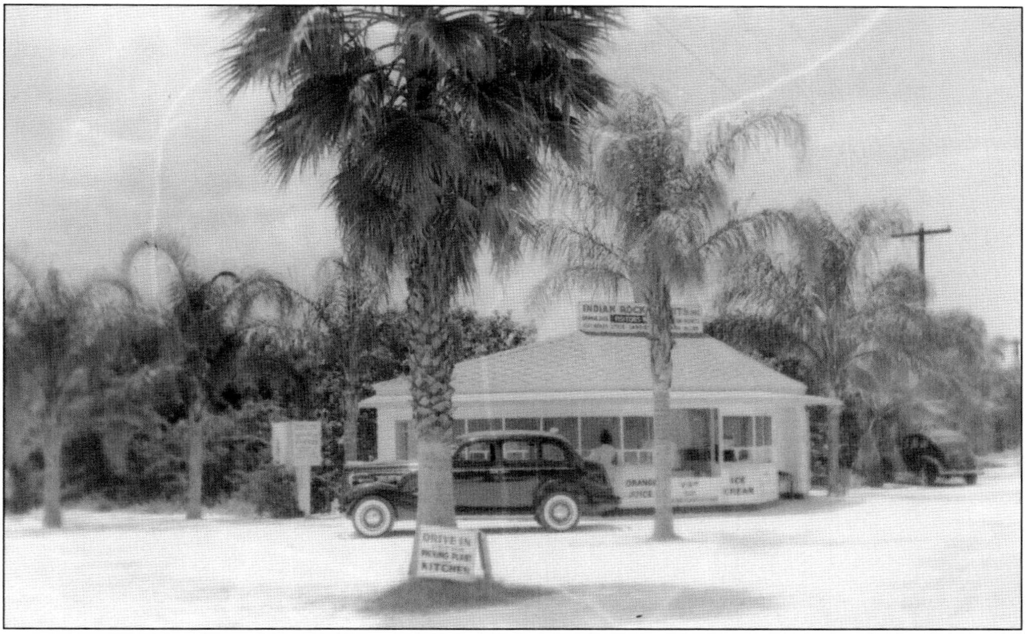

Along the mainland road between Indian Rocks Beach and Largo, vehicles passed by the Indian Rocks Fruit Company, a large grove and packing plant once located in the area where Walsingham Road approached Hamlin Boulevard and Oakhurst/Indian Rocks Road. A popular stopping place for many tourists, the store offered candies, juices, marmalades, and ice cream in addition to a wide variety of packed fruit. (HV.)

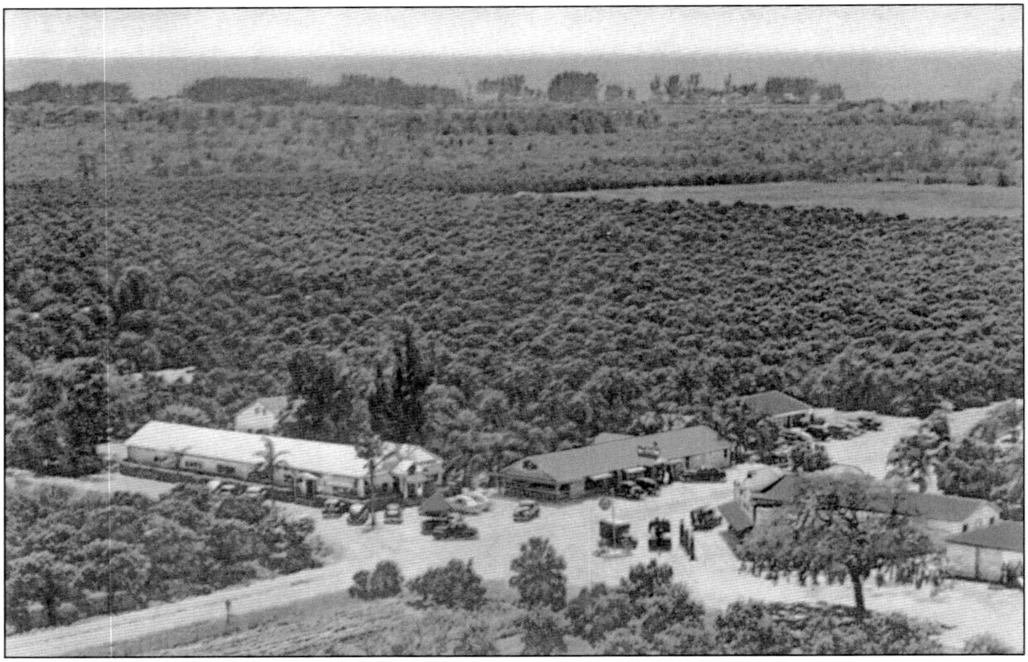

This postcard offers an aerial view of the groves and buildings at and around the Indian Rocks Fruit Company looking northwest toward Anona, Indian Rocks Beach, and the Gulf. After World War II, homes replaced groves at a furious pace. To get a view of this same location approximately a half-century later, compare this image with the aerial photograph on the first page of chapter five. (HV.)

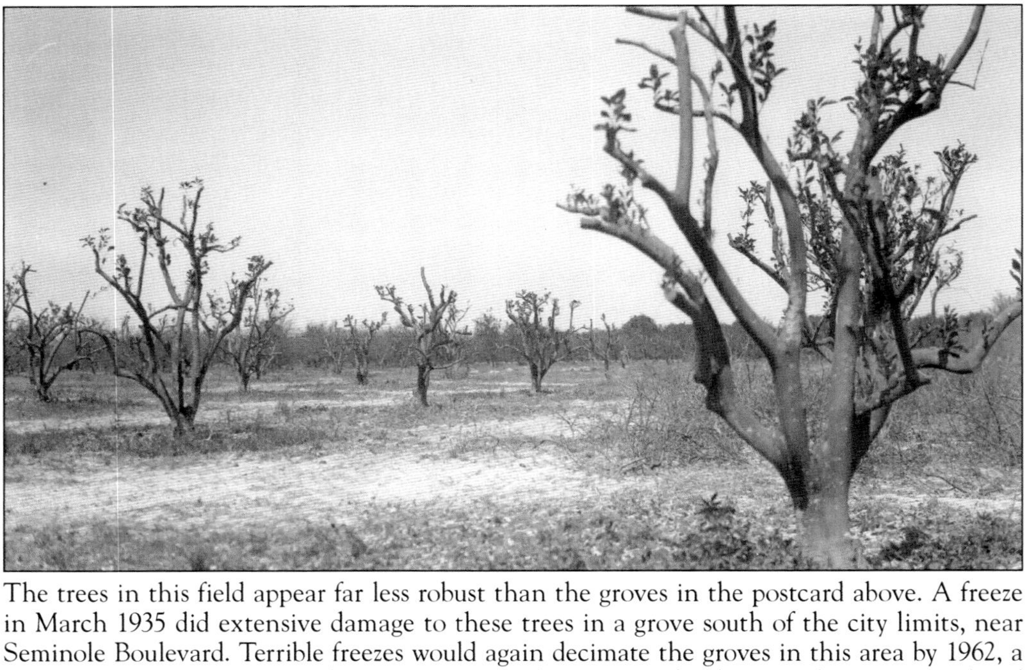

The trees in this field appear far less robust than the groves in the postcard above. A freeze in March 1935 did extensive damage to these trees in a grove south of the city limits, near Seminole Boulevard. Terrible freezes would again decimate the groves in this area by 1962, a year after classes began at nearby Orange Grove Elementary School. Homes have since replaced the groves. (HV.)

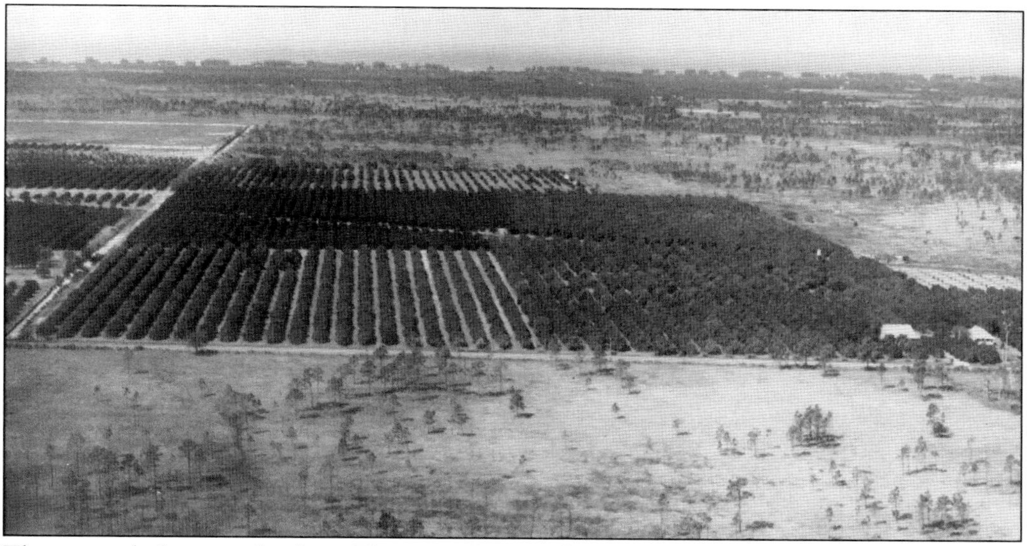

These aerial photographs show Thurston Groves along Ridge Road in the mid-1930s. In the westward view above, the intersection of Ridge Road and 102nd Avenue occupies the lower left corner, with 102nd Avenue passing beyond the former Seaboard Air Line Railroad tracks (now the Pinellas Trail) toward 125th Street. Groves had existed in this area since the McMullens and O'Quinns came to this site shortly after the Civil War. While living near these groves as a young teenager in the 1870s, William A. "Uncle Billy" O'Quinn sometimes encountered bears and panthers. Below, the close-up image shows the main entrance to Thurston Groves along the west side of Ridge Road just north of 102nd Avenue. The Seaboard Air Line Railroad tracks also appear in the upper right corner of the photograph near the smaller trees the Thurstons had just planted. (Both, HV.)

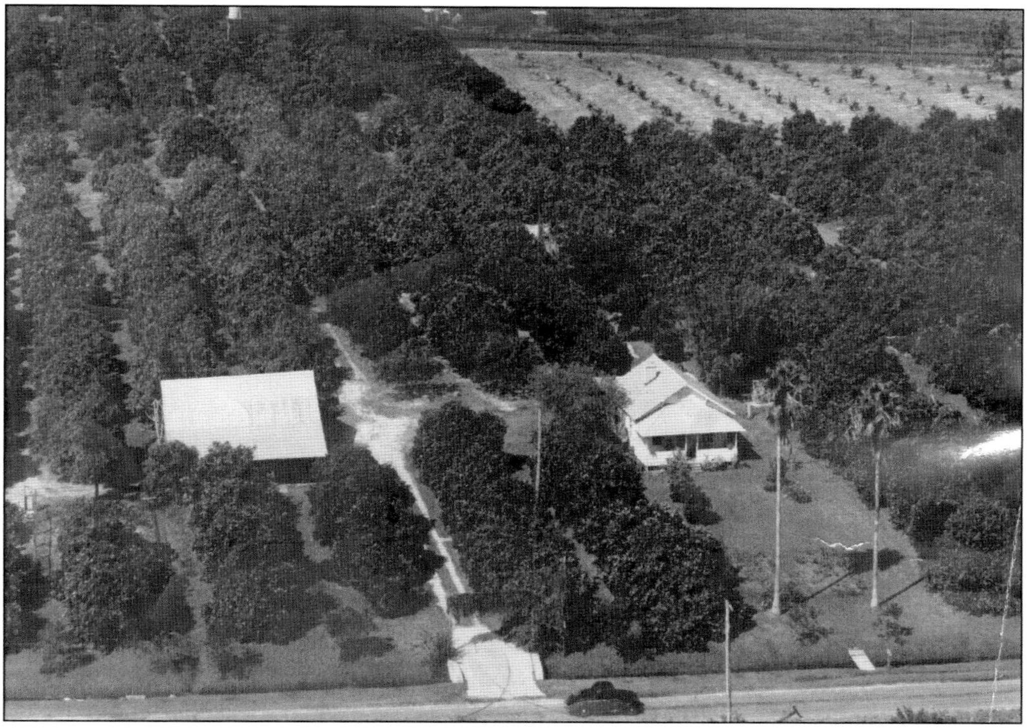

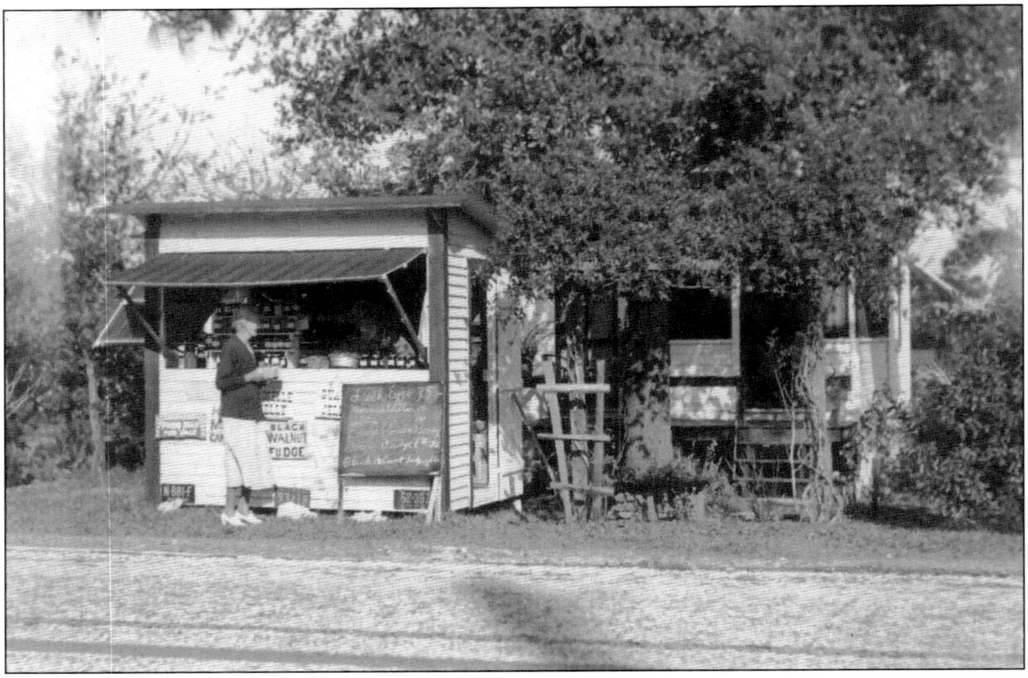

Groves and farms covered much of the landscape south of Largo toward Long Bayou. Although residents had referred to the area as Seminole for many years, it remained a part of unincorporated Pinellas County until voters in a small portion of this land voted to incorporate Seminole as a municipality in 1970. The Enterprise Fruit Stand, above, located along Seminole Boulevard and Eighty-ninth Avenue near the western shore of Lake Seminole, sold a variety of fruits and marmalades, as well as eggs, honey, and assorted fudges. Further down the road, the Orange Bowl's proprietors understood basic marketing. In 1949, a sign over the entrance touted "Plenty of fruit inside (if) too hot outside," while another sign along the building's side encouraged tourists with cameras to follow the arrows if they wanted to take pictures of the citrus. (Both, HV.)

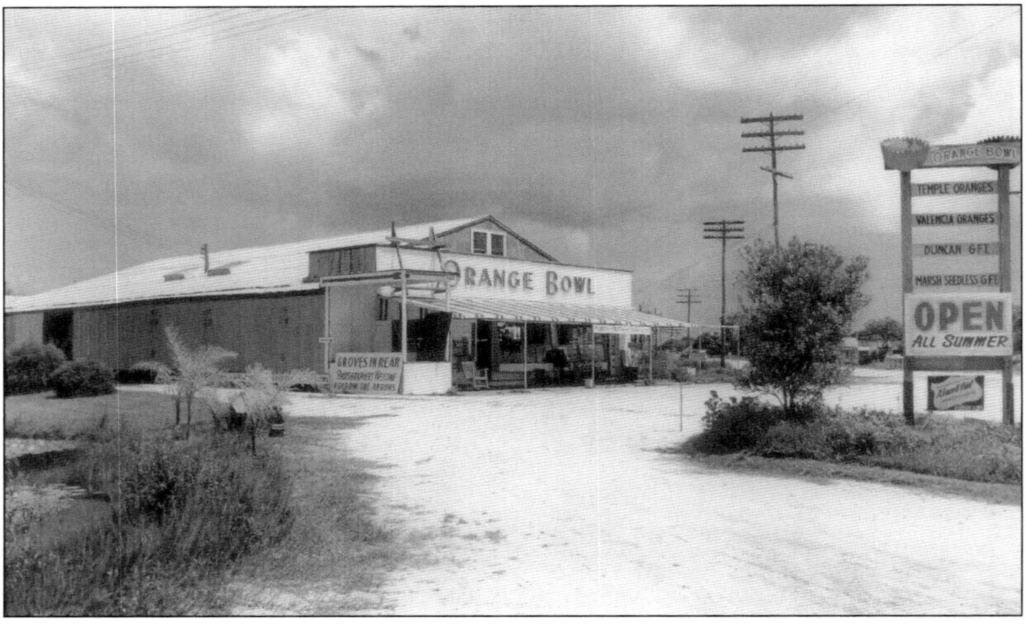

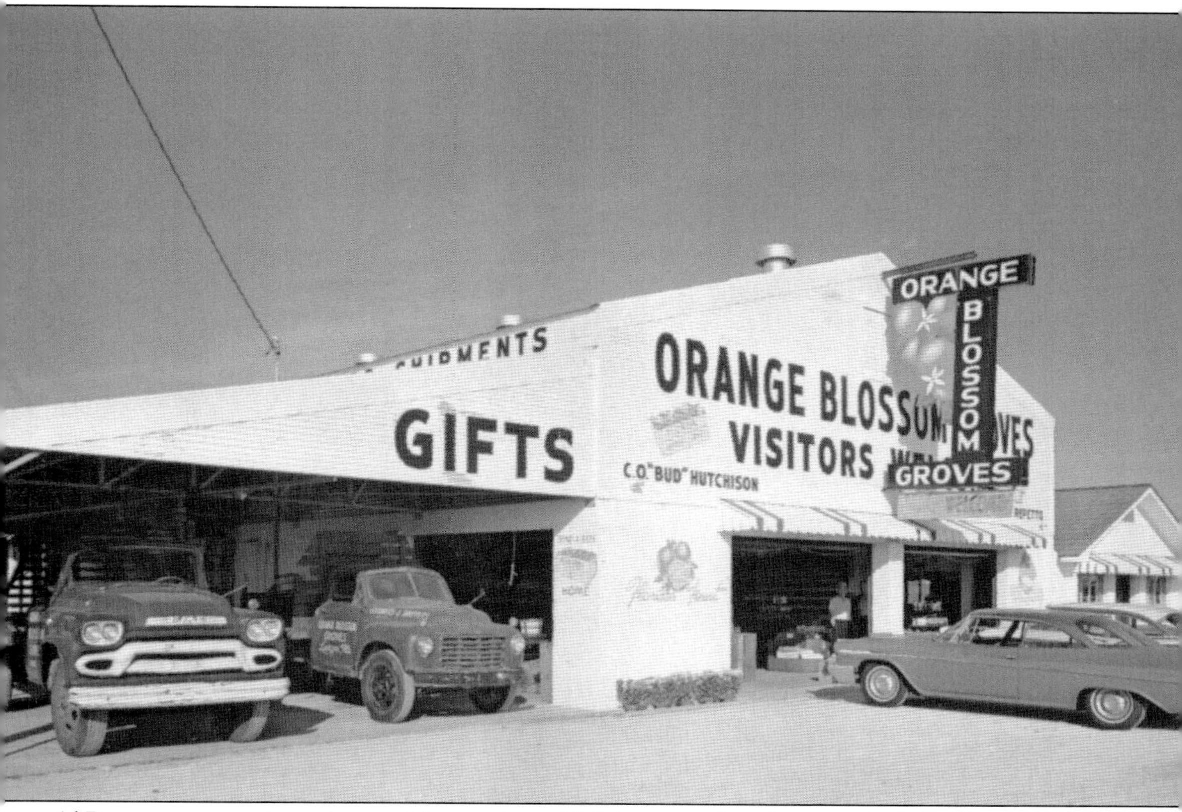

Al Repetto grew up in and around Largo. As a child, he remembered seeing the large citrus trees that had thrived in the area for many years, some of them nearly 40 feet high, with the lowest fruit hanging more than a dozen feet above the ground. After returning from service in the U.S. Navy during World War II, Repetto and his brother-in-law opened Orange Blossom Groves in 1946. Their hand-squeezed juice earned many accolades from locals and tourists alike. Repetto's citrus holdings grew substantially by the 1950s. As newcomers flocked to the region and homes replaced most of the groves, Repetto somehow managed to keep Orange Blossom open, even as subdivisions encroached around his facility on Seminole Boulevard. By 2002, less than 40 acres of groves remained under commercial cultivation in Pinellas County. All of this land belonged to Repetto. (HV.)

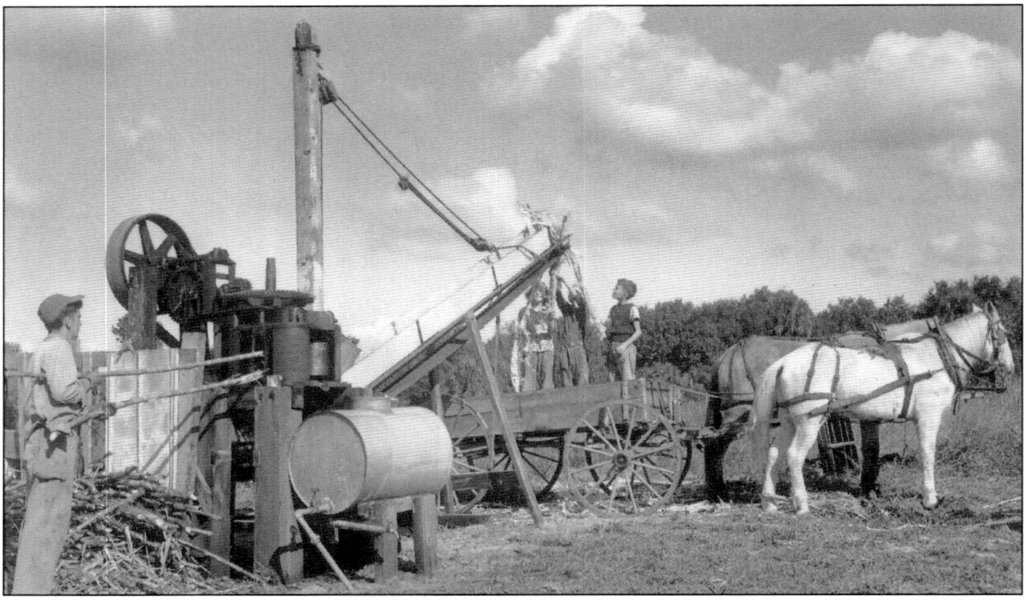

Sugarcane grindings became regular events in the Largo area by the late 1800s. Members of the Lowe, McMullen, and Meares families held candy pullings, which were gatherings where they would boil molasses or sugar cane, stretch the syrup cane byproduct, and cut it into hard candies. These get-togethers often included horseback rides in the country and swimming parties along the Gulf of Mexico. Farmers sometimes used the skimming from the syrup kettles as animal feed, even giving extra helpings of the heavily fermented feed to their hogs so that they could enjoy watching the swine stagger and stumble around the farmstead as part of the festivities. These images from the 1930s show the cane grinding and boiling process on Angus McMullen's farm at Anona. Angus and his son Warren appear in the image below. (Both, HV.)

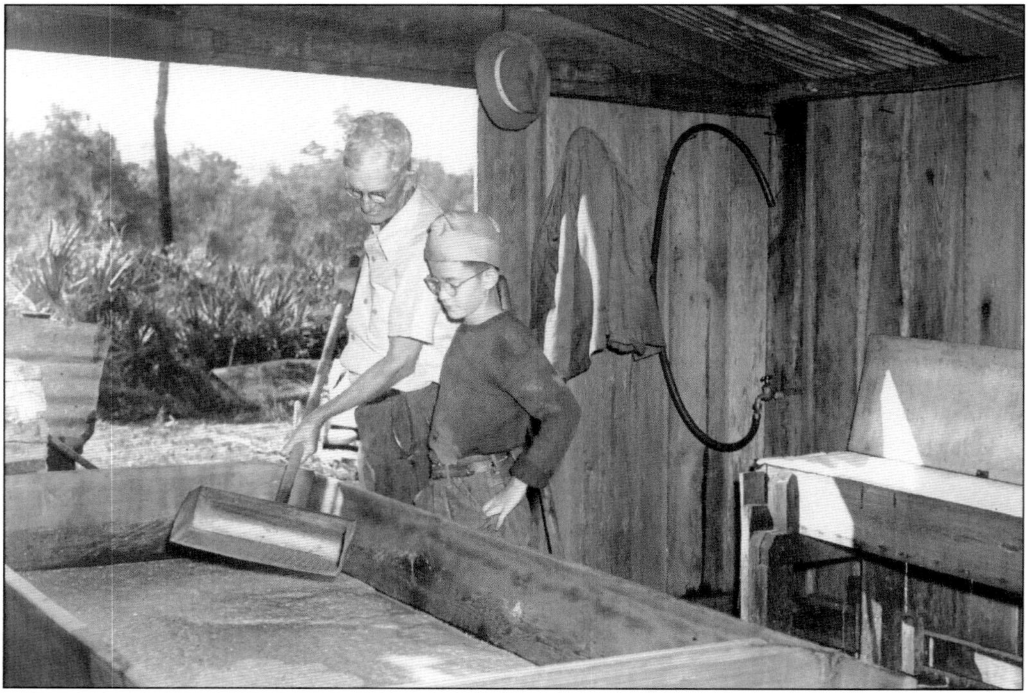

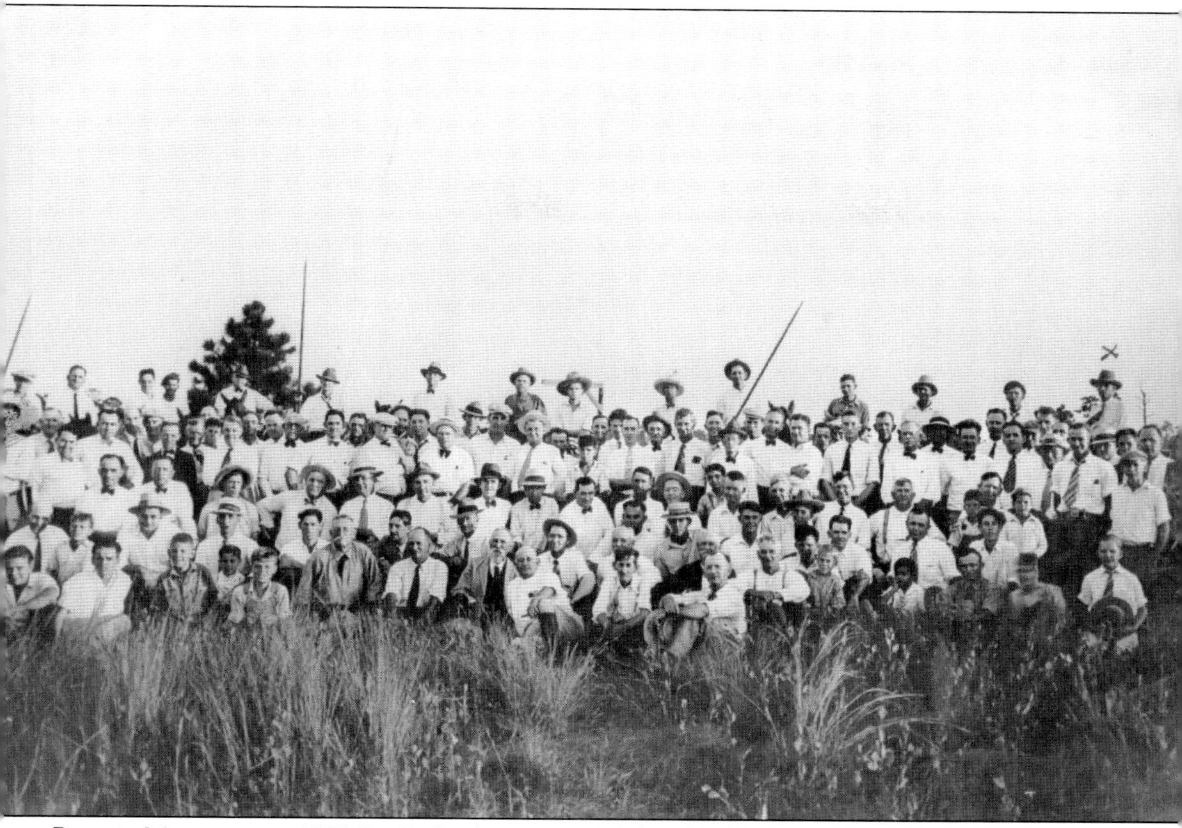

Born in Minnesota in 1895, Jay B. Starkey came with his family to Florida in 1897 and settled in the small village of St. Petersburg in 1900. Starkey bought his first calf at the age of 12. As a teenager and young man, he often traveled with other pioneers much older than him, cowboys such as Will Booth and William and Birt McMullen. After serving in World War I, he left a St. Petersburg post office job in 1922 to become a rancher in central Pinellas. Soon he bought 10 acres south of Largo for a down payment of $50, a horse, and a cow. Before Park Boulevard cut across Long Bayou at Lake Seminole, he forded cattle and horses across those waters in the 1920s. Here Starkey (marked with an "X" at right in this image) joined other friends and workers at the Ulmerton Ranch near Largo. Starkey managed the Ulmerton Ranch at a time when it became the leading producer of pork in Florida. (HV.)

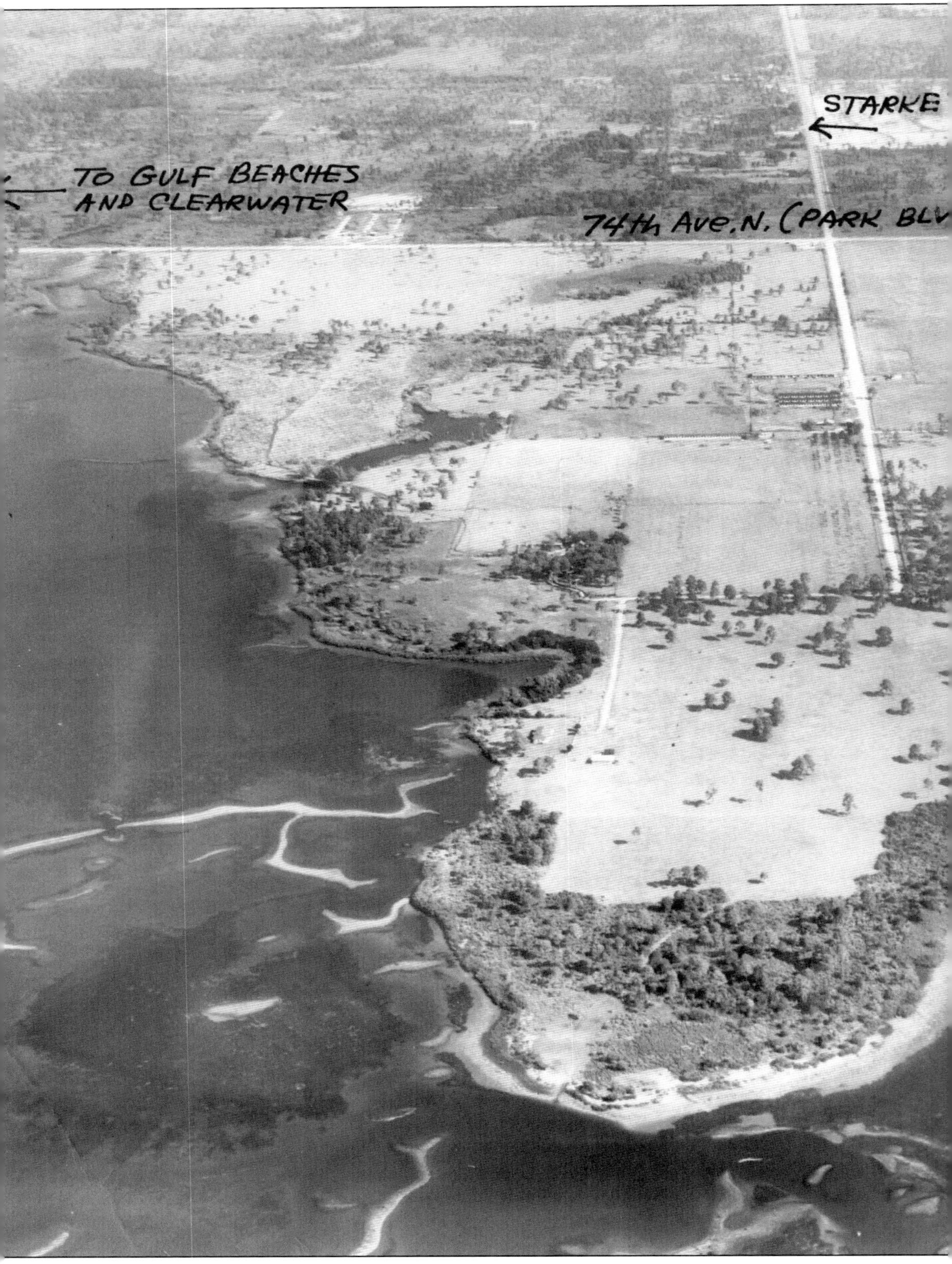
STARKE
TO GULF BEACHES
AND CLEARWATER
74th Ave. N. (PARK BLV

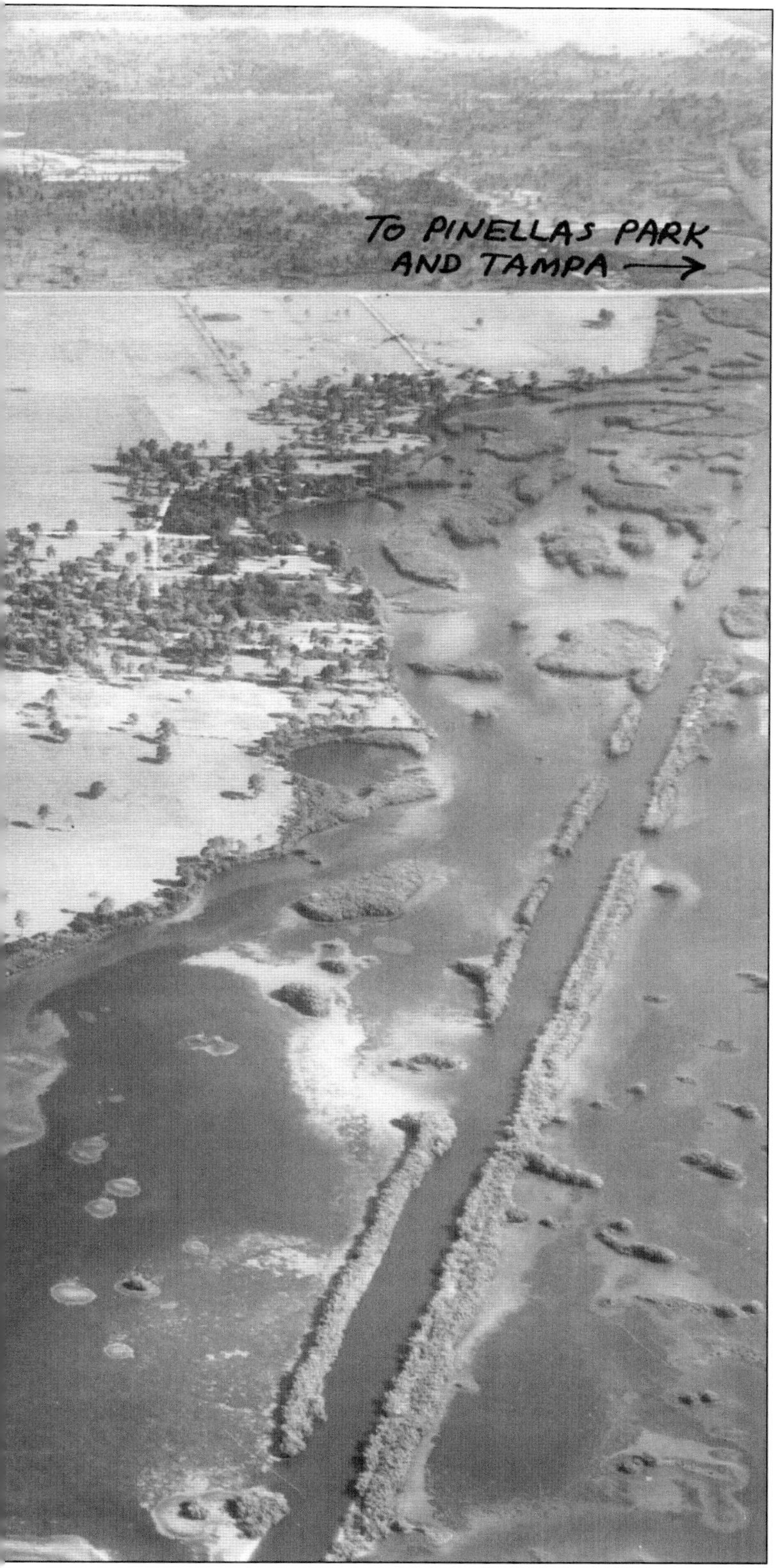

This aerial view faces north at the intersection of Park Boulevard and Starkey Road, probably shortly after engineers constructed a dam along Long Bayou (to the left of the photograph) in the summer of 1949. Built at a cost of $160,000, the dam transformed a saltwater marsh into a freshwater estuary known as Lake Seminole, a great resource used by farmers in Seminole and southern Largo to irrigate crops and groves. At the time of this photograph, Jay B. Starkey and his associates owned much of the acreage along Starkey Road north toward Ulmerton Road. At one point, Starkey herded over 2,000 hogs in this area. Although he initially held out when approached about selling some of his land, by late 1956, he and others began to sell tracts near this intersection. (HV.)

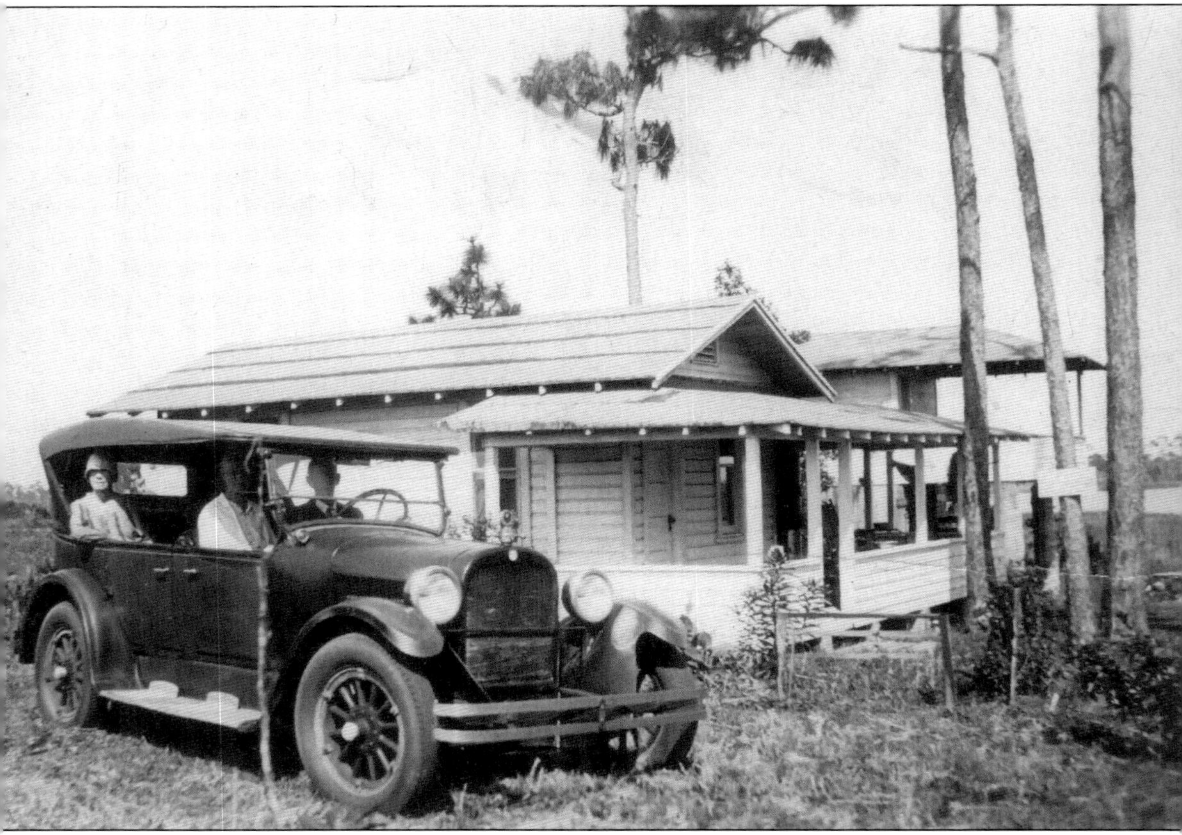

Those living along Florida's waterfront may have enjoyed the views, but they also had to endure the mosquitoes. A concerted effort to control these pests began in September 1930. Virgil C. Almand of the Anti-Mosquito Association led efforts to get nearly 3,000 Pinellas County residents to sign a petition requesting a referendum to create a mosquito control district. Almand and other members of the commission, including developers David Welch (of Madeira Beach) and Thomas Rowe (owner of the Don CeSar Hotel) focused their eradication efforts along the Gulf Beaches and St. Petersburg. Residents living along estuaries in the Largo area continued to suffer through summertime swarms of mosquitoes. The property in this 1930s photograph sat along upper Long Bayou, north of Park Boulevard, before the creation of Lake Seminole as a freshwater reservoir. Nearby cattle farms, small ponds, and humid weather certainly brought the residents many unwanted visitors during the summer months. (HV.)

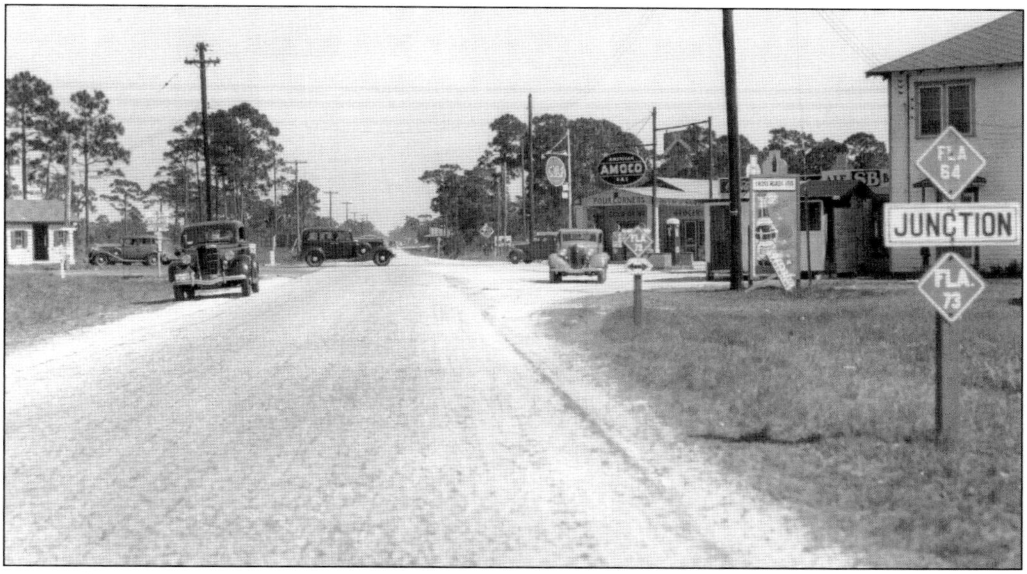

Jay Starkey and the McMullens often herded their cattle past the Four Corners area. Also known for a while as Dutchman's Corner, the intersection of Roosevelt Boulevard and what was known as Haines Road at the time of this 1930s photograph later became a place of great frustration. The picture above shows this intersection looking east toward High Point, long before it became one of the most congested intersections in the region (at the spot where East Bay Drive crosses U.S. Route 19 and becomes Roosevelt Boulevard). By 1989, drivers on U.S. Route 19 benefited from a new overpass. Tri-City Plaza would be on the left. The image below shows early dredging operations in 1949 to create an extension of West Bay Drive across the Intracoastal Waterway to Belleair Beach. This aerial looks northeast from Belleair Beach toward Belleair and Clearwater. (Both, HV.)

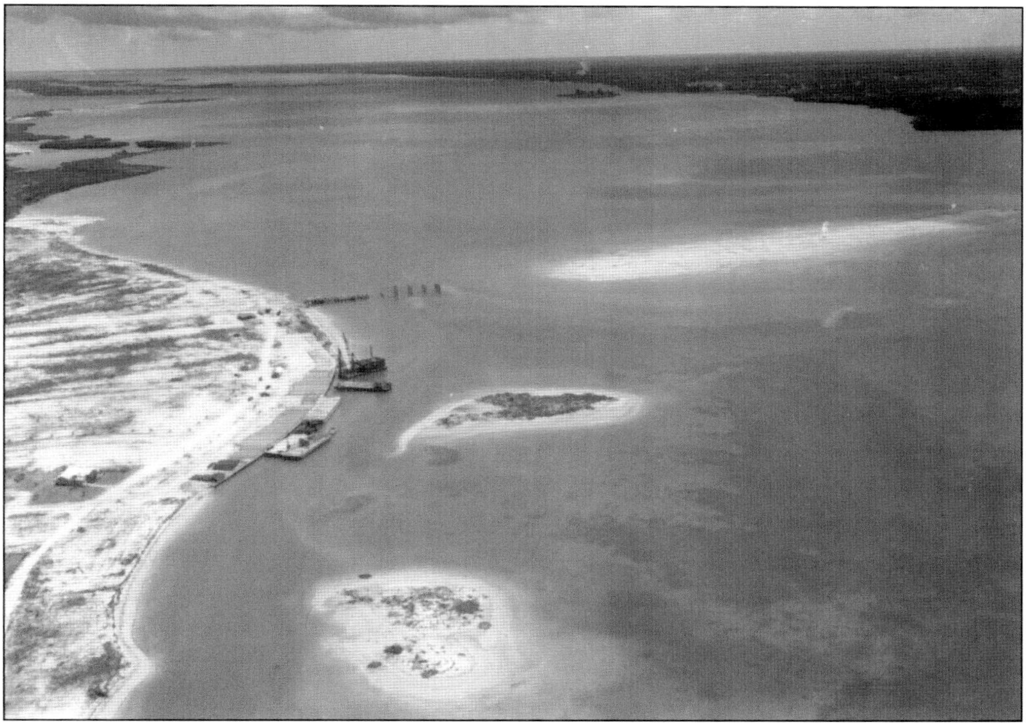

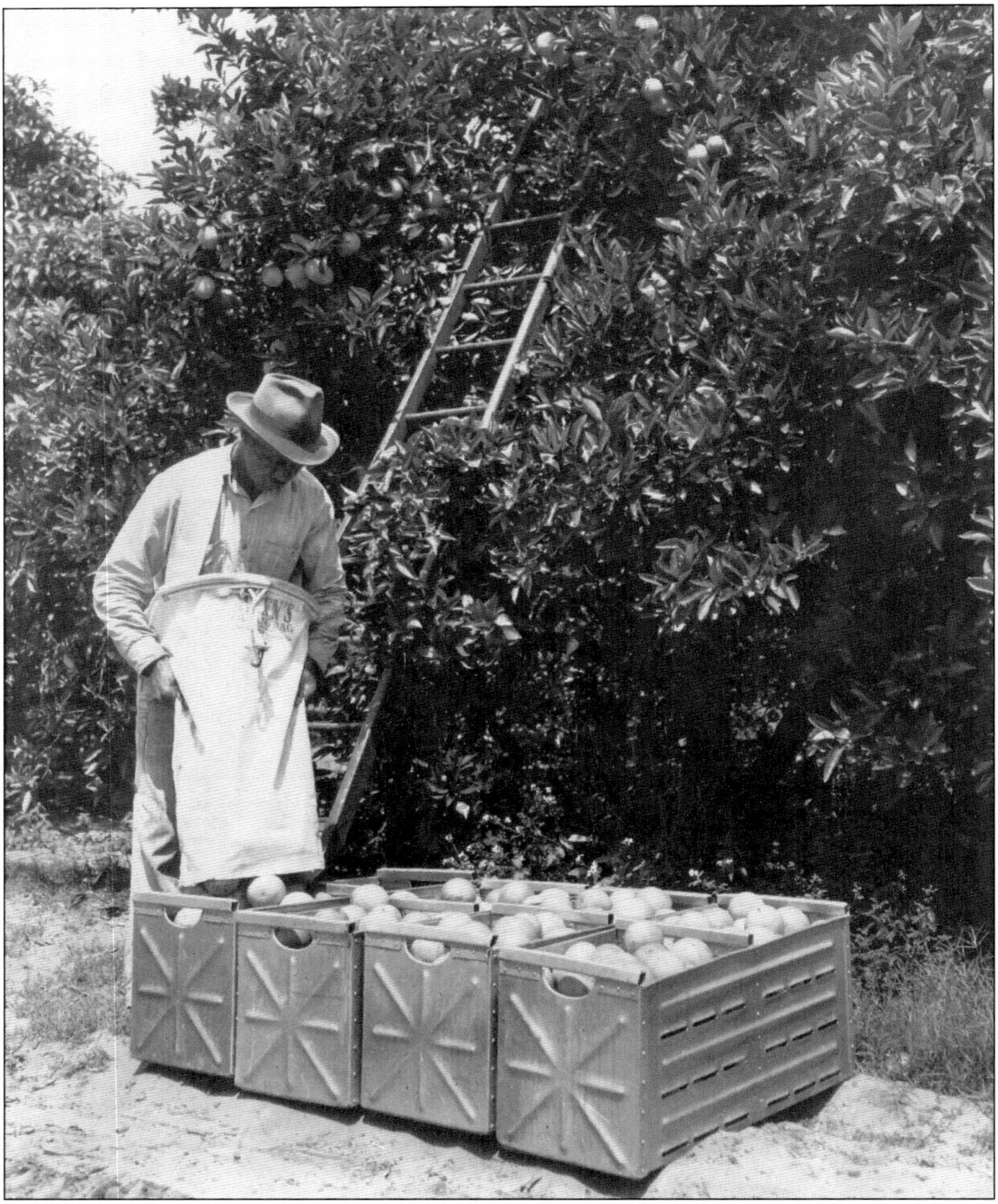

The harvesting of citrus and farm crops required a regular workforce. The worker in this image packed citrus in aluminum crates, a common practice after World War II. African Americans in search of jobs migrated to Largo's small African American "Quarters" settlement in the early 1900s. Located north of Bay Drive at the railroad tracks and near the site of the former livery, this settlement west of Missouri Avenue endured laws and customs that enforced racial segregation. After a fire burned most of the Quarters by 1950, many residents moved to an unincorporated area south of Largo. Some worked on the groves of J. D. Baskin at a point known as Baskin Crossing. Brothers Lloyd and Dan Henry came to the Baskin Crossing area from their home in Georgia. Lloyd arrived before 1920, and Dan followed him a little later. By the late 1920s, the brothers began to purchase nearby land for back taxes and from grove owners. They became notable entrepreneurs in the small African American settlement. (John S. Taylor Collection, HV.)

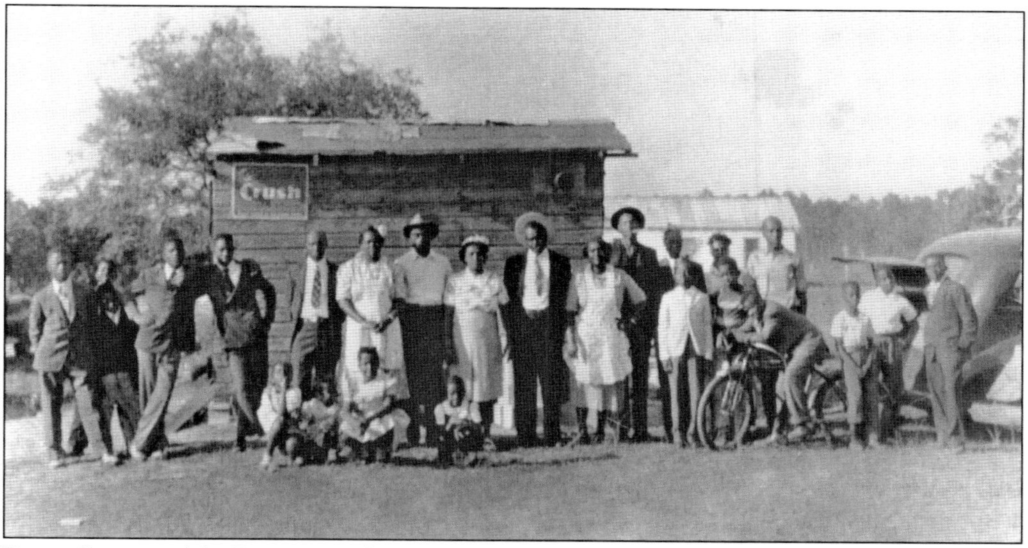

Dansville, named for Dan Henry, became the nucleus for the neighborhoods in the area nestled along the intersection of Ulmerton Road and 119th Street also known as Ridgecrest. Residents of this largely agricultural settlement lived a quiet life tucked away between the Largo and Seminole communities before Ulmerton Road bisected the area. Ridgecrest Elementary School opened to serve the area in 1958, but paved roads and county water service for most of the area had to wait until the late 1970s. New attention and concern for the community occurred after an October 1992 tornado damaged many homes in the area. Deacon J. W. Williams's grocery store, adjacent to Mount Olive Missionary Baptist Church, appears in the 1940s photograph above. The Mount Olive Church is seen below, also in the 1940s. (Both, HV.)

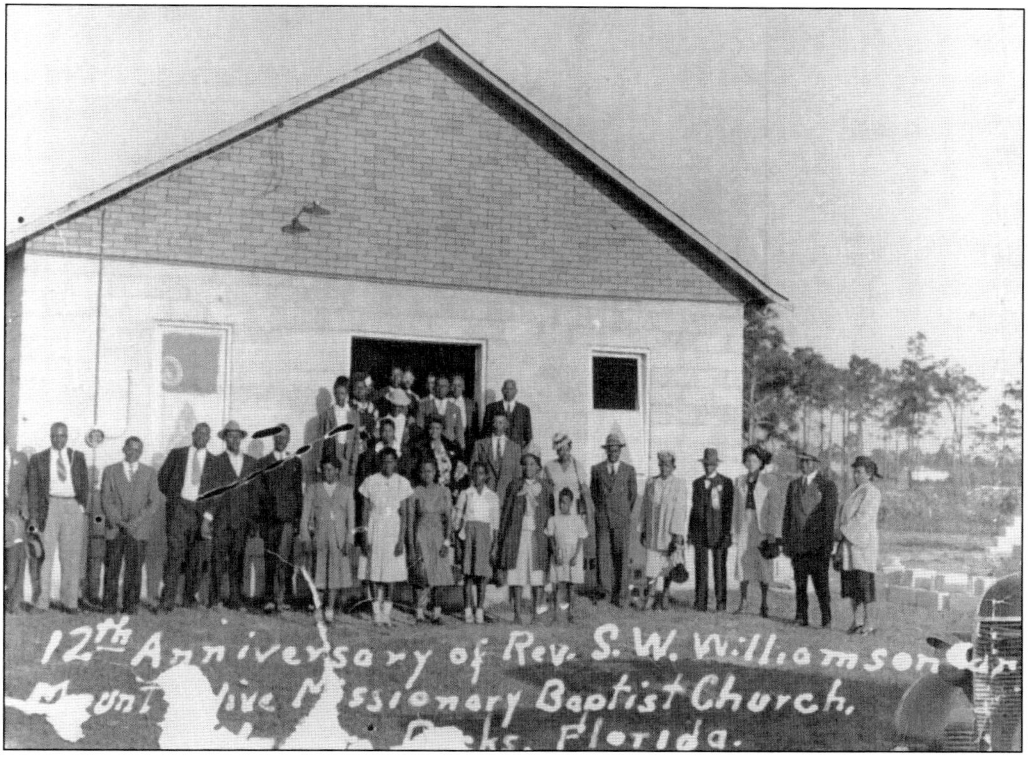

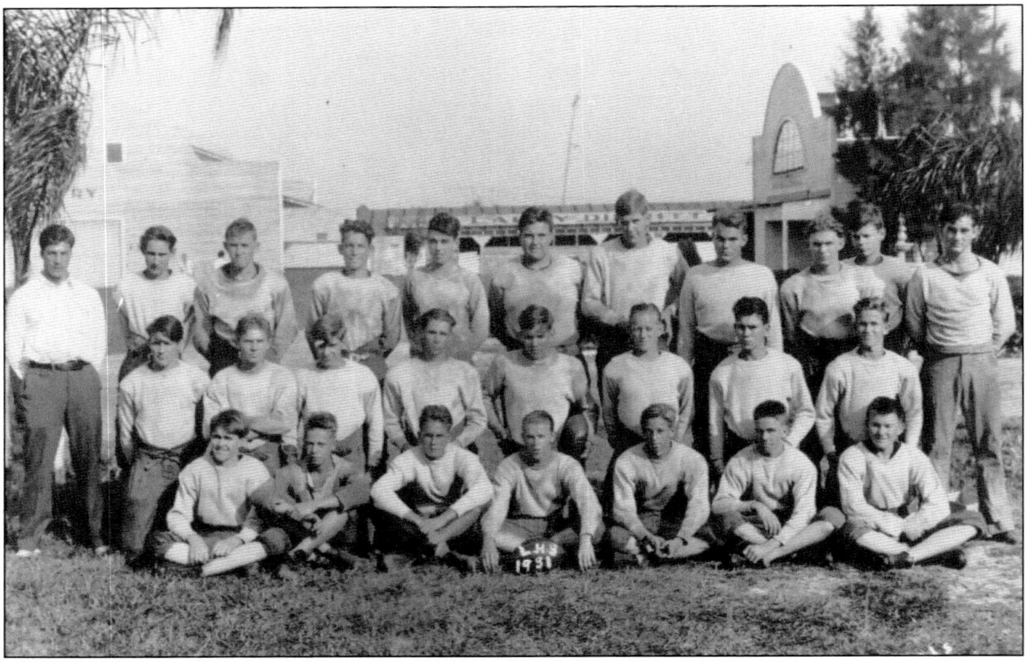

Residents of Largo and the surrounding agricultural communities rallied around their football teams, including these squads from 1931 (above) and 1934 (below). Athletic events offered an opportunity for Largo's youth to show their prowess on the field in the same way they demonstrated their talents on the farms and in the groves. Before the opening of new high schools in lower Pinellas in the late 1950s, Clearwater High and St. Petersburg High were the closest public high schools to the Largo Packers. The opening of the campus at Seminole High in 1962 brought a nearby neighbor and competitor, though Largo and Seminole shared access to the new vocational and agricultural center near the Seminole campus. (Above, HV; below, John S. Taylor Collection, HV.)

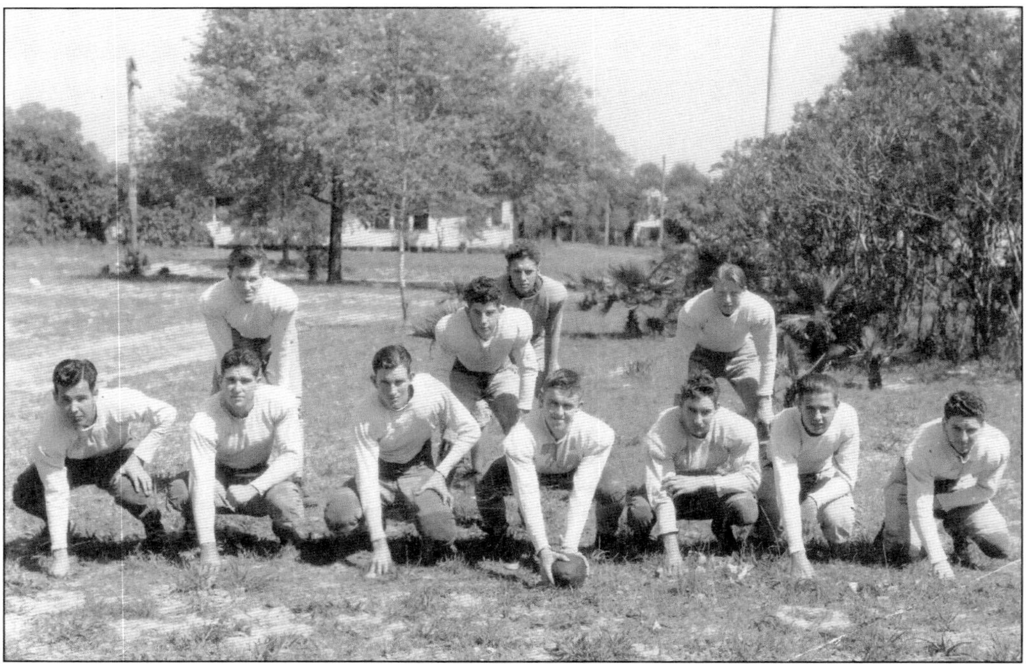

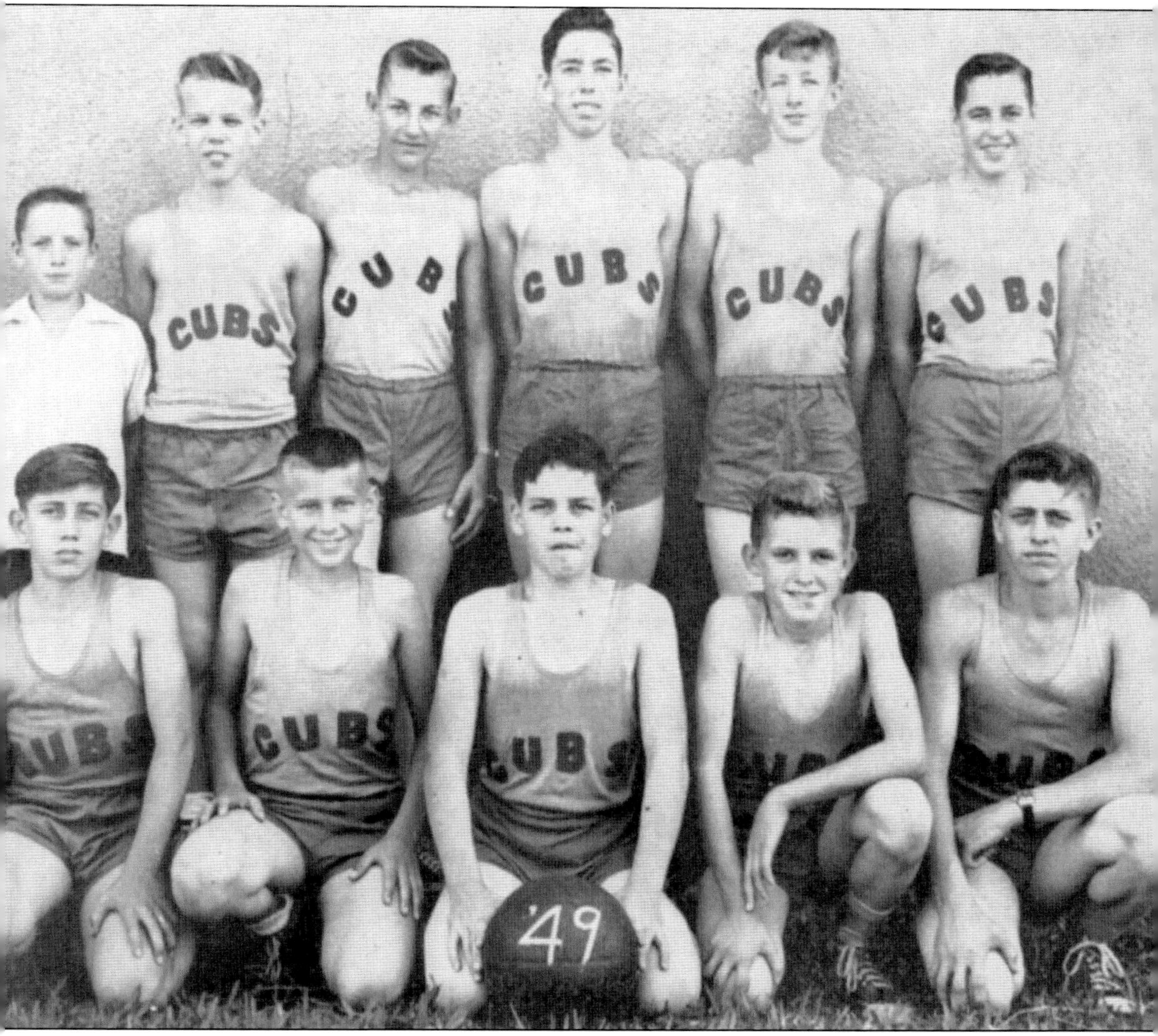

Students rooted for the home team during good seasons as well as bad. The Largo Junior High School basketball team had a tough inaugural season in 1949. The Cubs lost all of their 13 games, including two against Disston Junior High School in Gulfport with scores of 9-47 and 1-47 and a tough defeat against St. Petersburg's Mirror Lake Junior High, where they fell 3-69. Yearbook editors in the 1949 *Keystone* noted, "Although these boys were small and inexperienced, they made a fine show of excellent sportsmanship and clean play . . . The school is very proud of these boys who are taking such an active interest in athletics." (HV.)

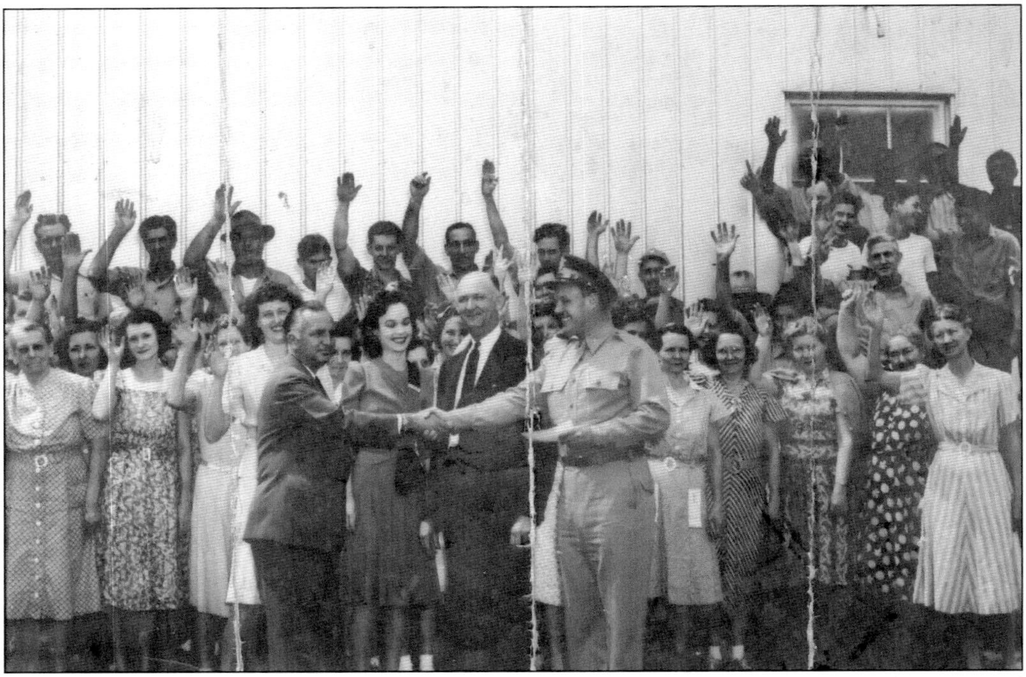

World War II forever transformed Florida. Although patrols for German submarines kept coastal residents on alert along the Gulf Beaches, much of the wartime activity in the Largo area focused on residents planting victory gardens, workers in local defense operations and industries, and those called into service making their final preparations for wartime duty. Above, workers at the John S. Taylor packinghouse make a presentation to officers from MacDill Field (now MacDill Air Force Base). Below, workers had just finished pulling roots in May 1941 from the site that would soon become Pinellas Army Air Field. After the war ended, this airbase served civilian purposes as St. Petersburg-Clearwater International Airport. (Both, HV.)

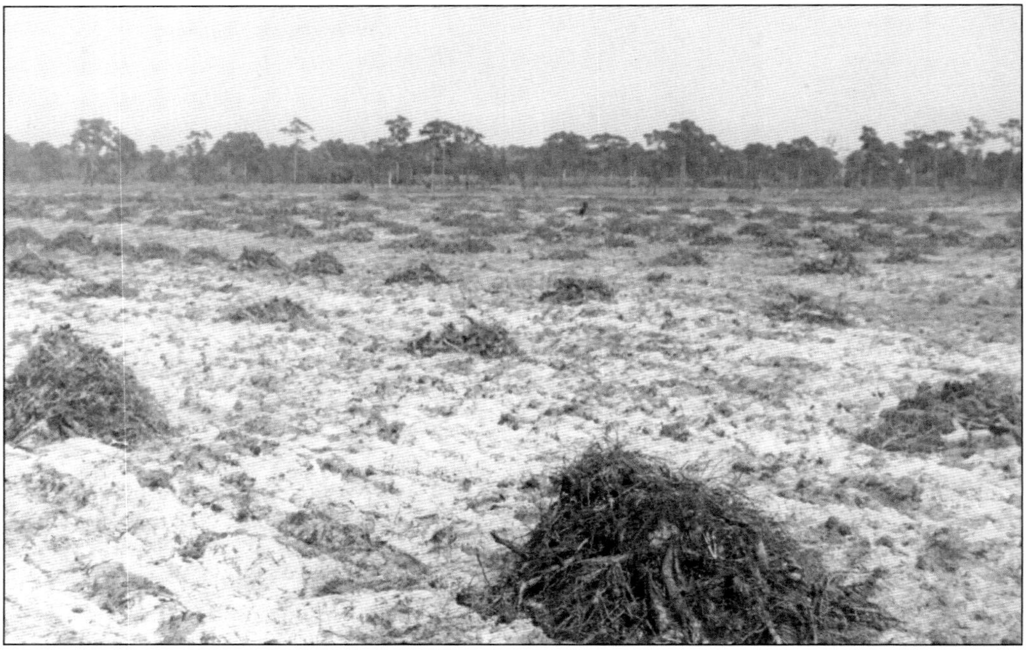

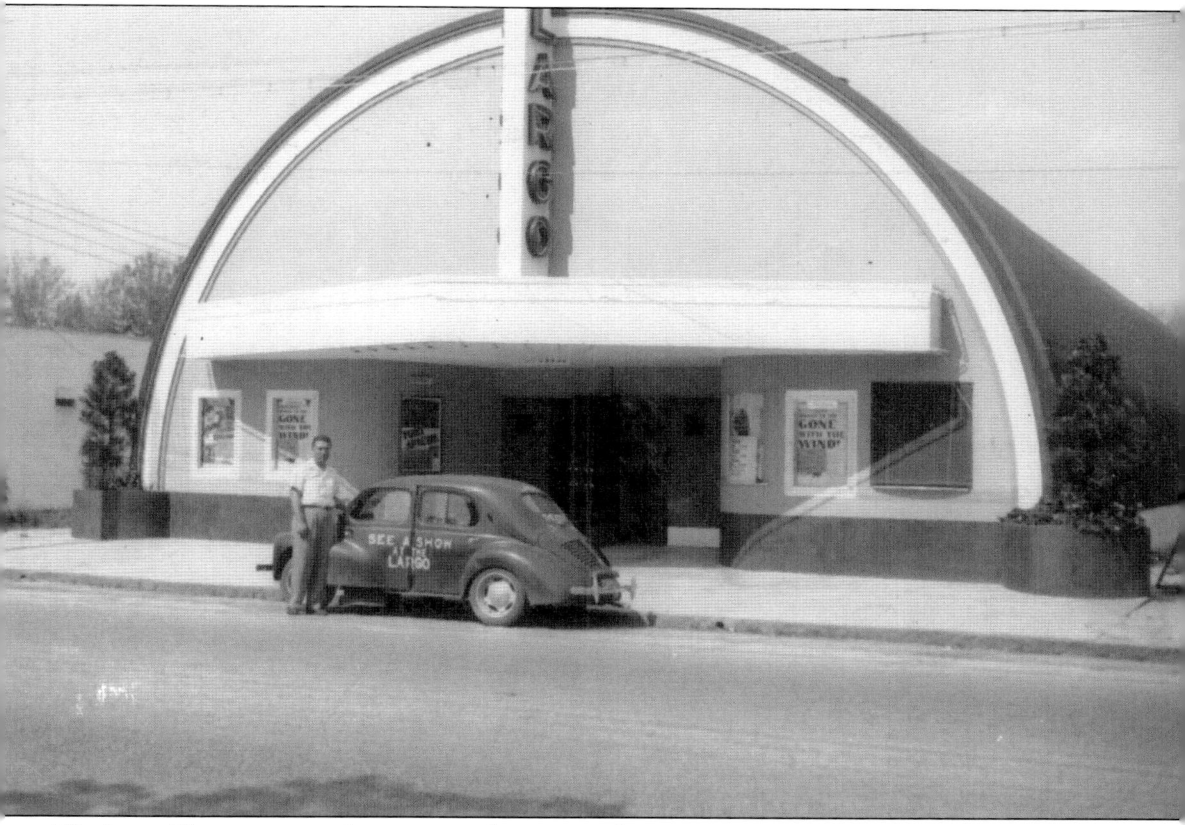

The Largo Theatre occupied a prominent location in downtown Largo at 420 West Bay Drive. The city's second downtown theater opened in 1948, about a decade after the city's old silent movie house on Railroad Avenue, the Savoy, had closed. Once dubbed the "finest small town theatre in Florida" by those in the industry, the Quonset structure accommodated 400 for matinee and evening movies and performances. As newer multiscreen complexes appeared in shopping centers and malls by the early 1970s, the Largo Theatre lost some of its appeal and began to show its age. In 1975, one movie buff complained that the interior resembled a "wartime outpost," with tattered leather seats and a musty smell that became unbearable during summer months. Despite such harsh reviews, the theater served as a popular entertainment venue and an early home for the Suncoast Sound Drum and Bugle Corps, founded in 1979. By the summer of 1980, workers disassembled the theater, lifted the large hut by helicopter, and reused it as a storage shed at the public works department. (HV.)

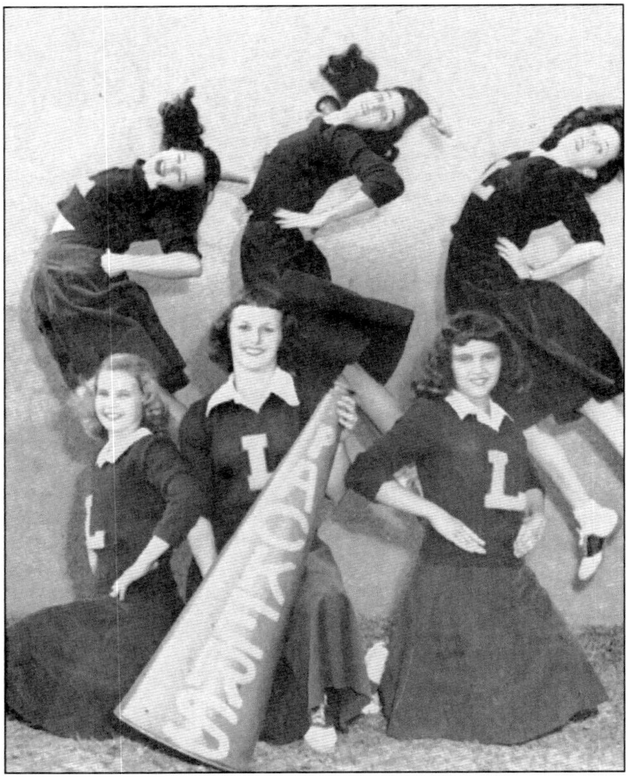

Varsity cheerleaders from the 1948–1949 school year rooted for their Packers teams. Seen here, Betty Haager, Nancy Thoman, Glenda Mix, Delina Smith, Lois Waterson (the captain), and Barbara McCready show their spirit. (HV.)

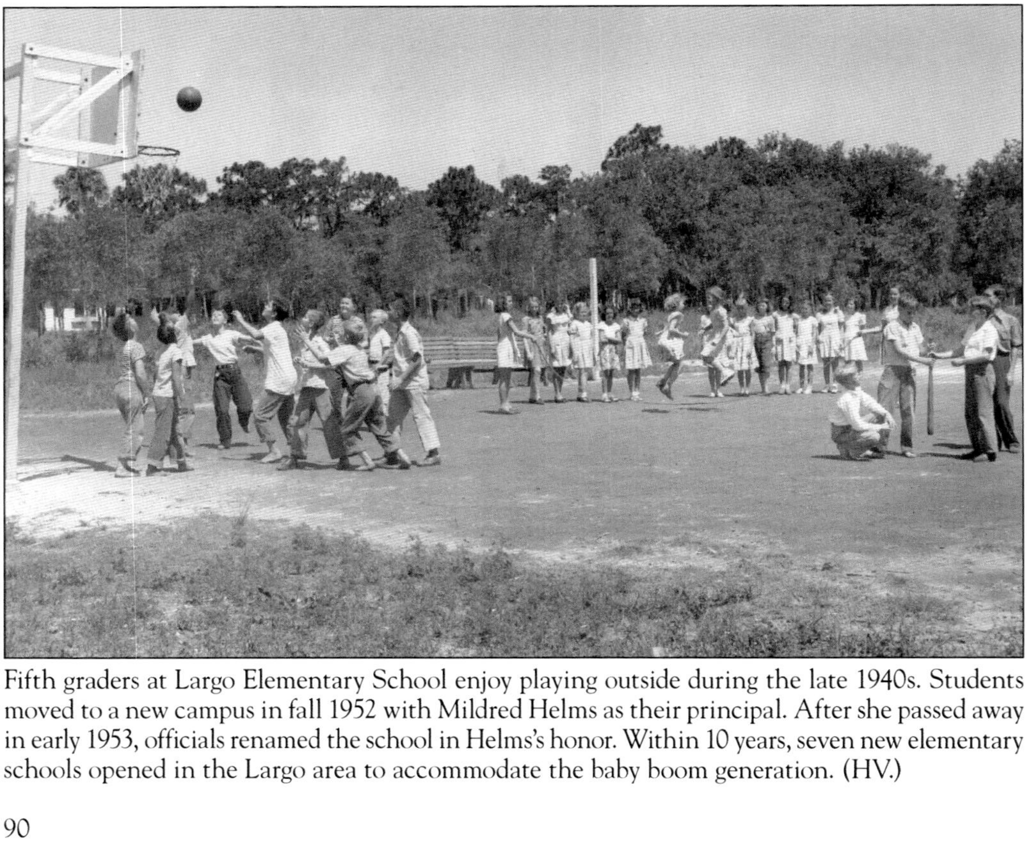

Fifth graders at Largo Elementary School enjoy playing outside during the late 1940s. Students moved to a new campus in fall 1952 with Mildred Helms as their principal. After she passed away in early 1953, officials renamed the school in Helms's honor. Within 10 years, seven new elementary schools opened in the Largo area to accommodate the baby boom generation. (HV.)

The image at right captures Jefferson Lowe (oldest son of Capt. John T. Lowe and a member of the first Pinellas County Board of Commissioners) planting a sugar, or custard, apple tree in an October 1950 ceremony. This type of apple, sometimes called an annona, became the source for the community's name when the Lowe and Meares families settled there in the 1850s. Jefferson served as Anona's only postmaster during his tenure from 1883 until 1922. Although many of the original annonas died after freezes in the 1890s, the legacies of the early families took root. Below, a group of pioneers gather at Anona Church 10 years earlier in October 1940. Those in attendance included Jefferson Lowe, "Dr. Bob" McMullen, "Uncle Birt" McMullen, and other members of the Booth, Dieffenwierth, Hammock, Hardage, Lowe, McMullen, Meares, Plumb, and Sellers families. (Both, HV.)

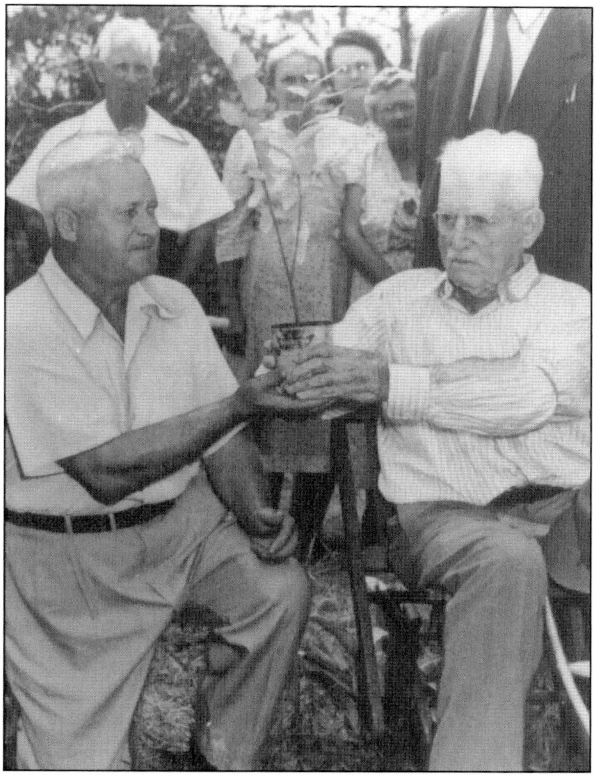

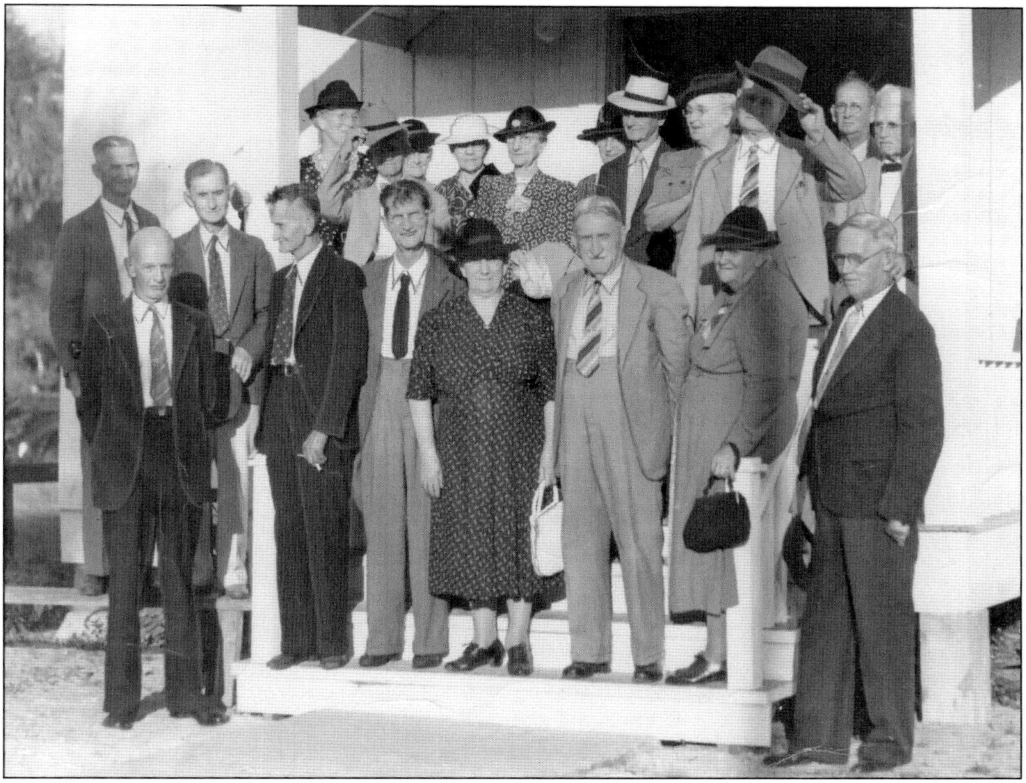

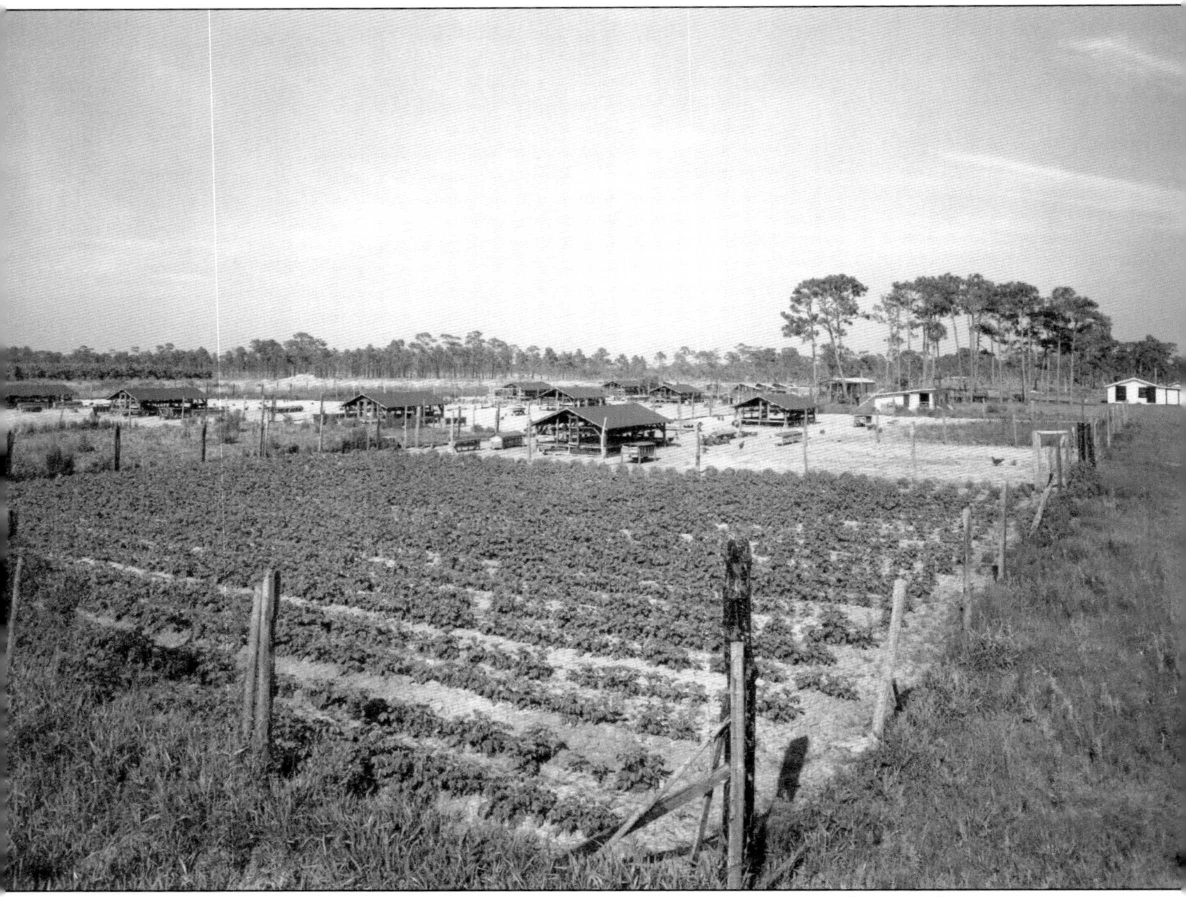

More than 170 military installations dotted Florida's landscape during the World War II. However, as this April 1946 image clearly reveals, the period immediately following World War II was a time when residents of the Largo area continued to count eggs in chicken coops and bushels harvested from the field in greater numbers than cars on the road or building permits issued. Residential developments soon replaced much of the farmland. (THPL.)

Four

Clean Air Industries and Homes Built to Please 1955–1979

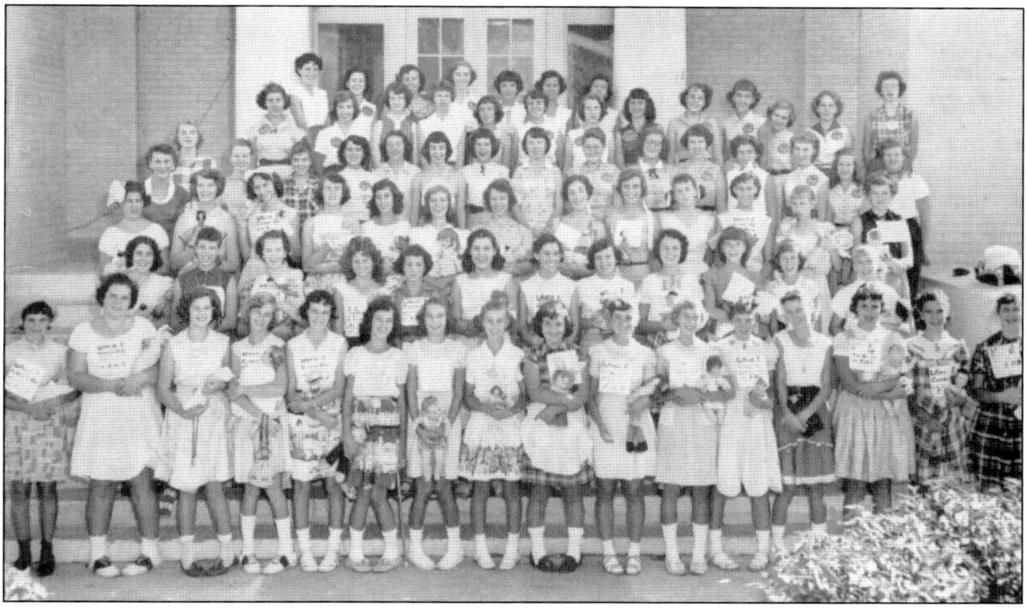

The Largo area experienced explosive growth by the mid-1950s. Enrollment surged on school campuses as baby boomers entered school. This image from the 1954 Largo High School yearbook shows members of the Future Homemakers of America preparing for motherhood with baby dolls in their hands and "When I Grow Up" signs on their shirts. They came of age as Largo also went through some growing pains. (HV.)

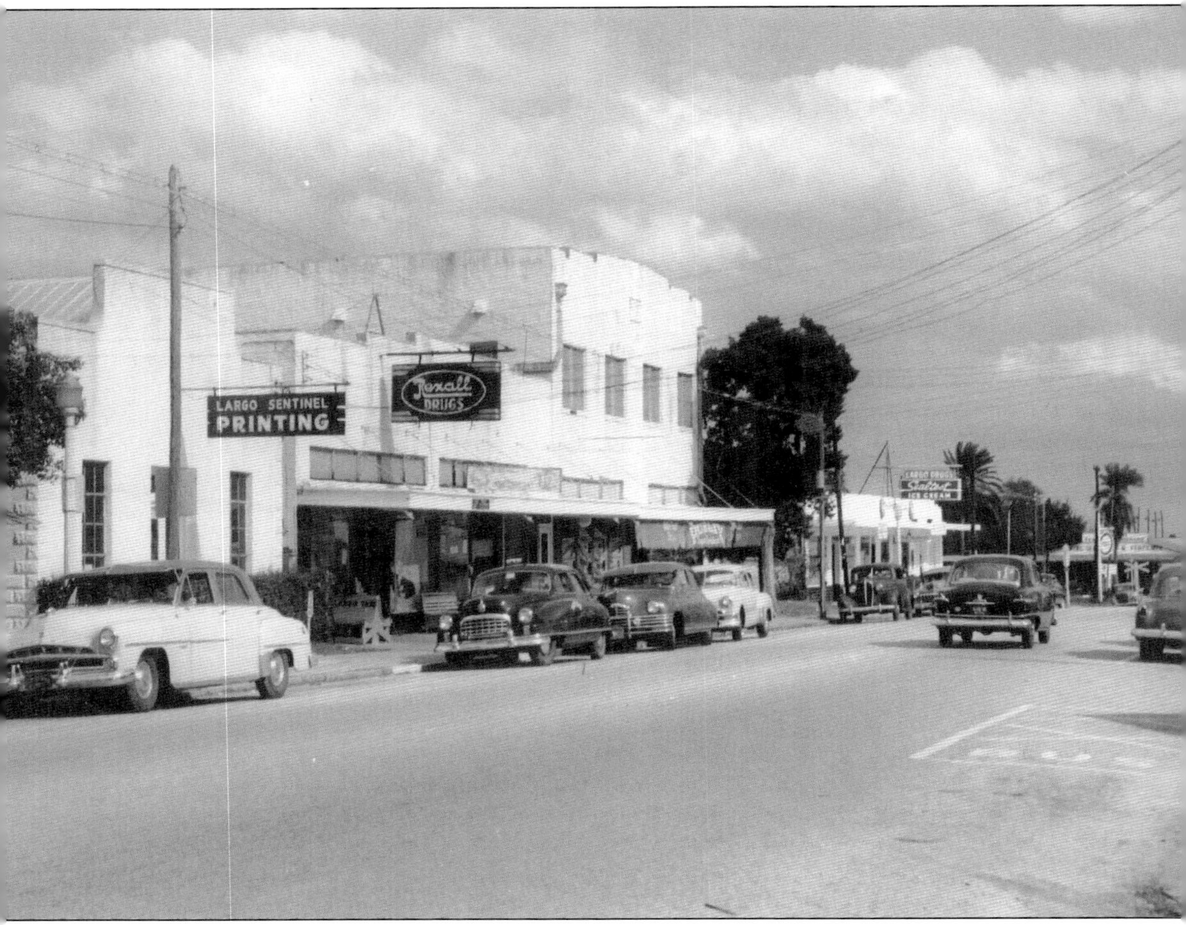

This snapshot of Largo's downtown looking east along Bay Drive illustrates some of the businesses on the north side of the road in the early 1950s. The weekly *Largo Sentinel* occupied a place in the heart of the community, alongside a Rexall drugstore and the Publix supermarket. The Largo Feed Store appears beyond the Largo Drugs building and railroad crossing on the right side of this image. (HV.)

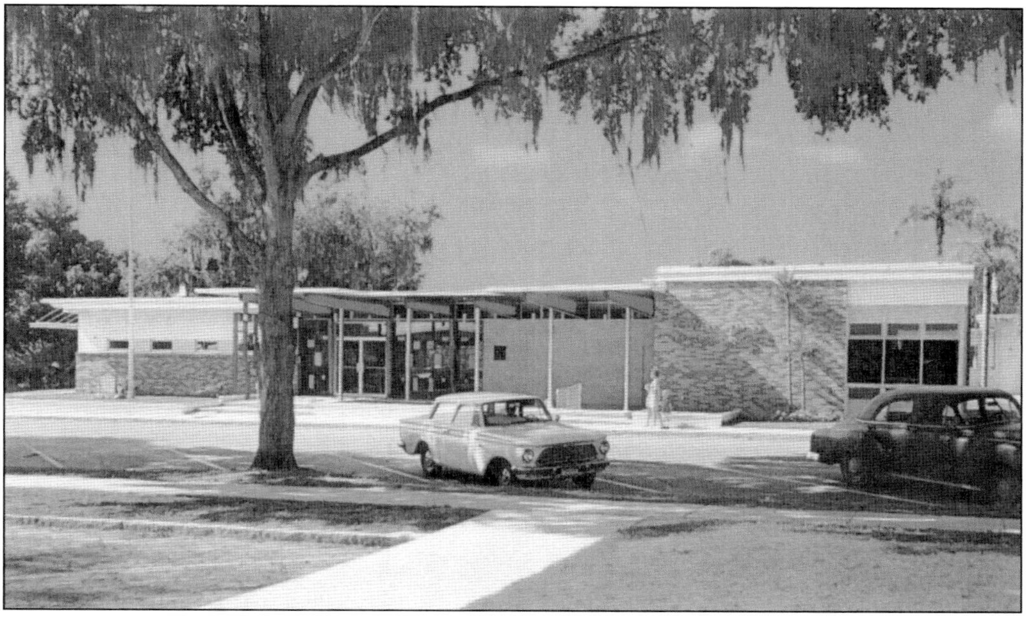

Older municipal facilities no longer met the needs of the growing city. Voters within the Largo city limits and surrounding unincorporated areas overwhelmingly approved a November 1955 annexation referendum that expanded the size of the city to approximately 3 square miles. The 10-foot-by-10-foot police station building was no longer sufficient, and neither was the town hall in an old school building in Ulmer Park. In July 1962, a new city hall, seen above, replaced the old building in Ulmer Park. By 2004, this site became part of the West Bay Village townhomes located between First Avenue Southwest and Cleveland Avenue. The fire station below opened in 1963 to replace inadequate facilities used since the late 1920s. Public safety facilities have increased significantly since the 1960s as the community continues to grow. (Both, HV.)

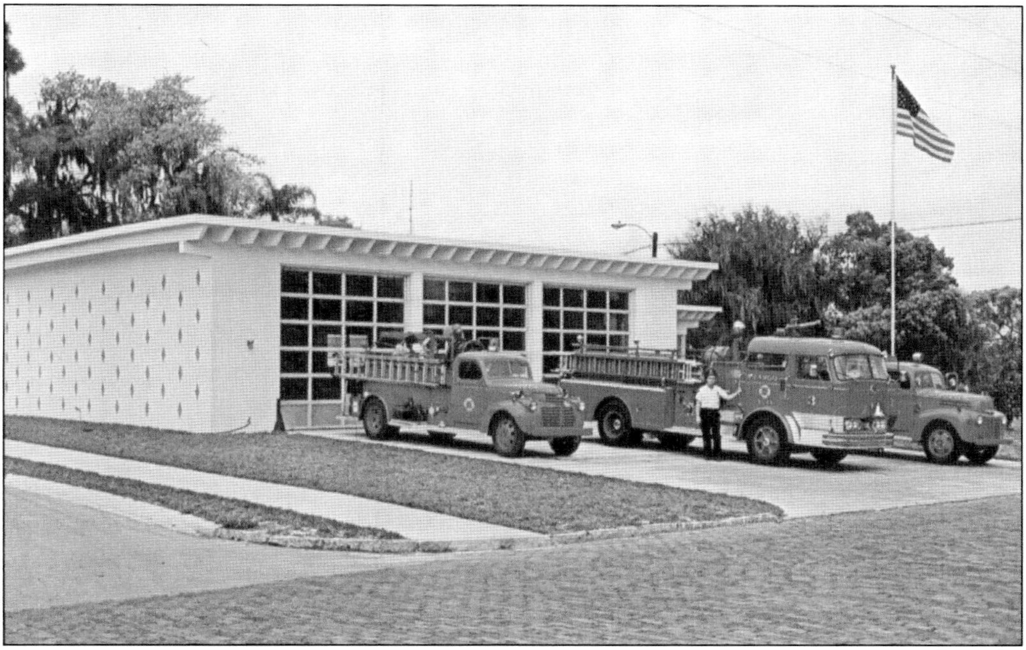

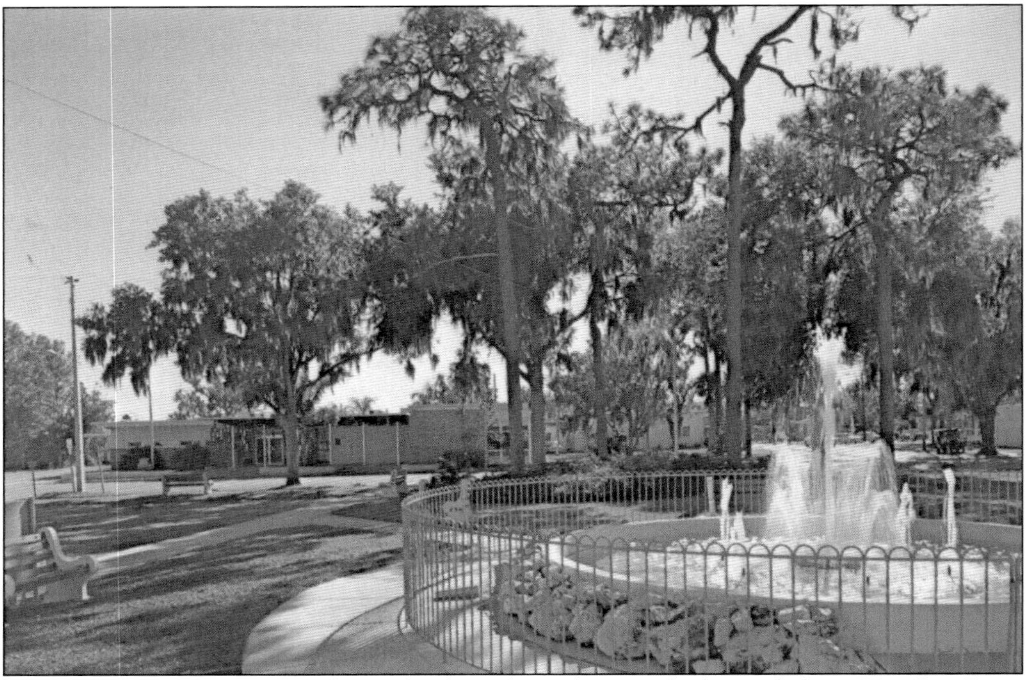

Another view of the municipal complex from the early 1960s looks south from West Bay Drive beyond First Avenue Southwest. Years later, the city sold much of the public land in this area in an attempt to reinvigorate the downtown. By 2004, developers had replaced the city hall with townhomes and transformed land along Bay Drive next to the remaining portion of Ulmer Park into commercial establishments. (HV.)

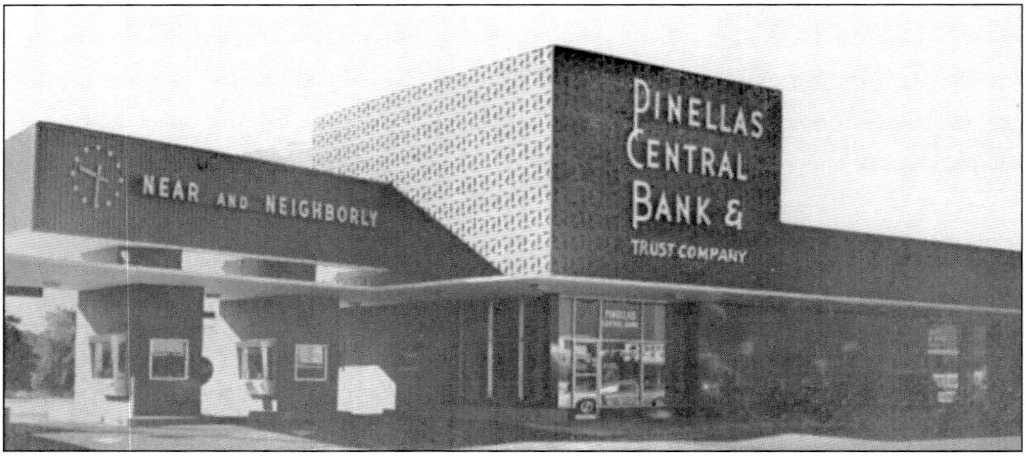

Businesses also expanded to meet the needs of the growing community. Pinellas Central Bank and Trust began operations in the revamped 1907 Bank of Largo building (see page 45) in February 1952. The bank then moved to the new Pinellas Shopping Center at the intersection of Clearwater-Largo Road and West Bay Drive in October 1954. This 1963 picture shows the structure as it appeared between 1959 and 1974. (HV.)

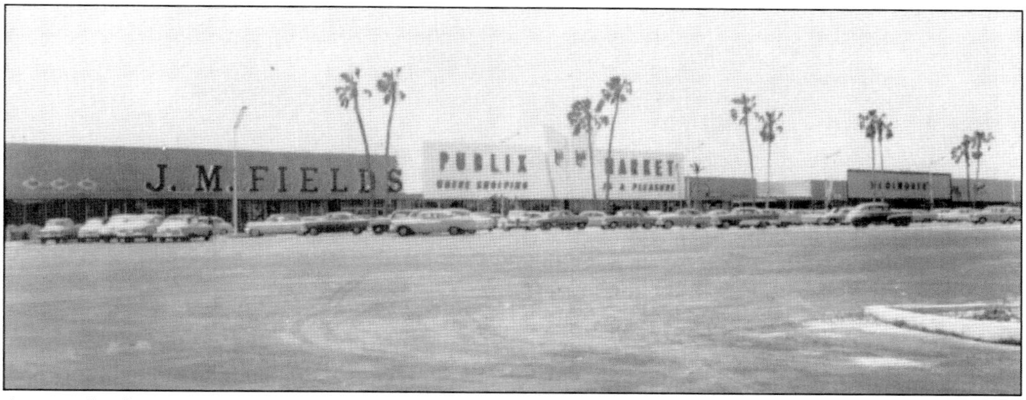

At nearly the same time that Pinellas Shopping Center took shape in western Largo, Midway Shopping Center, above, opened in northern Largo in the late 1950s. Located along the intersection of Missouri Avenue and Rosery Road, Midway offered convenience to residents of Largo, Belleair, and southern Clearwater. Although lunch counter sit-ins and demonstrations to desegregate facilities took place throughout Florida in 1960, the W. T. Grant and Woolworth stores at Midway agreed to open their dining areas to African Americans without delay in December 1960, earlier than similar venues in St. Petersburg. Even as new suburban developments spread in all directions from Largo, the 1960 aerial image of the north side of Bay Drive looking east from Clearwater-Largo Road shown below demonstrates that much of central Largo maintained its residential character. (Both, HV.)

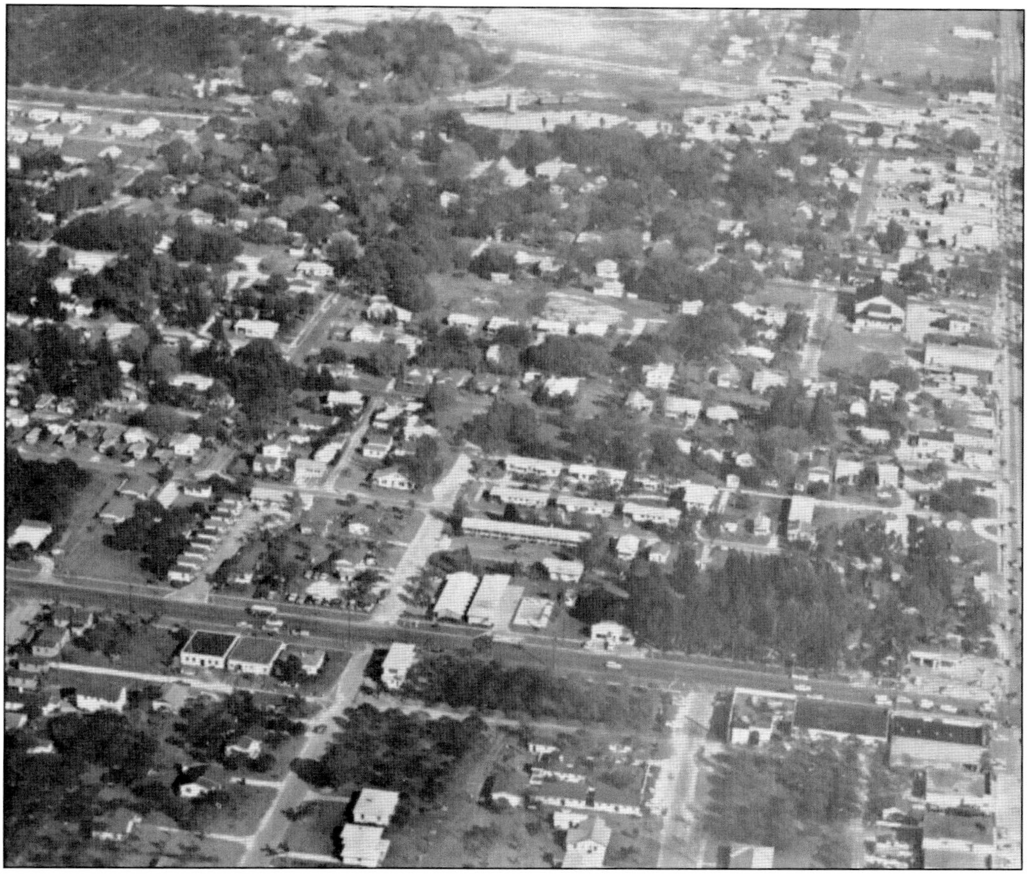

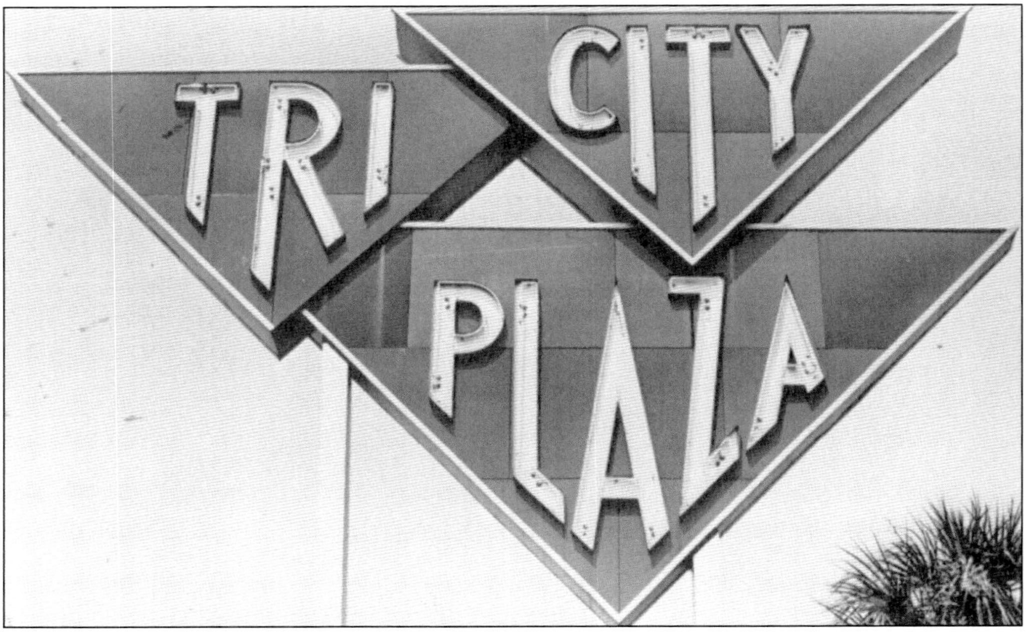

The intersection of U.S. Route 19 with Bay Drive/Roosevelt Boulevard presently marks a southeastern area of the Largo city limits. In the 1940s, this area was unincorporated and largely uninhabited. By 1949, plans to reroute U.S. Route 19 to the east as part of the Gulf Coast Highway and rename the older road Alternate U.S. Route 19 came to fruition. The Tri-City Plaza shopping center soon became a landmarkat this intersection. (HV.)

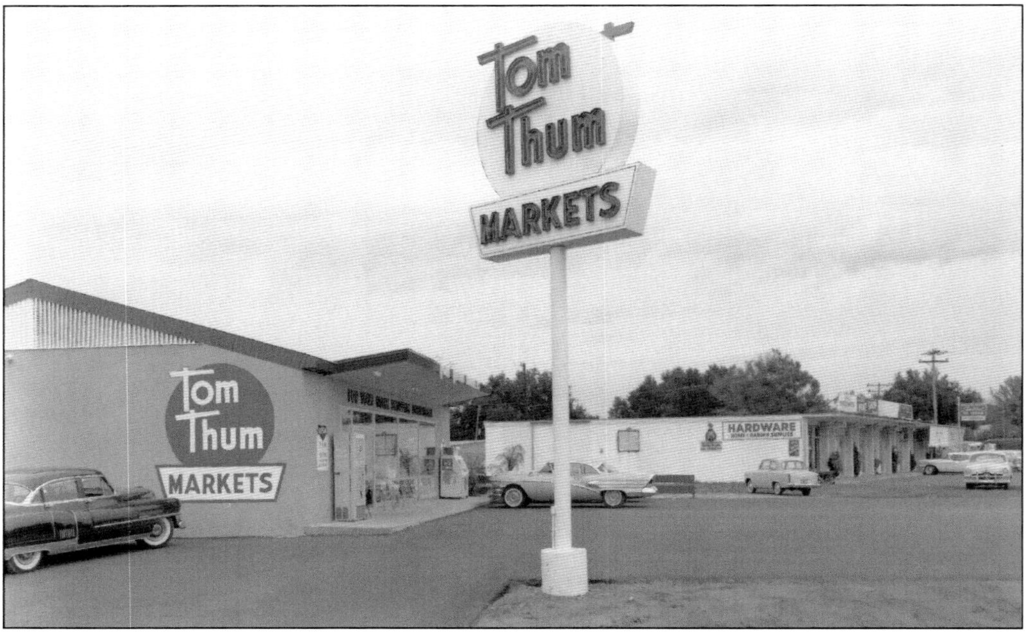

The new bridge that opened between Largo and Indian Rocks Beach in June 1958 promoted development south and west of Largo. Groves and scrubland between Anona and Largo disappeared at an alarming pace between the late 1950s and the 1980s. This October 1958 photograph shows one of the first mainland convenience stores to serve this area along Indian Rocks Road, Tom Thum Markets. Other stores soon followed. (THPL.)

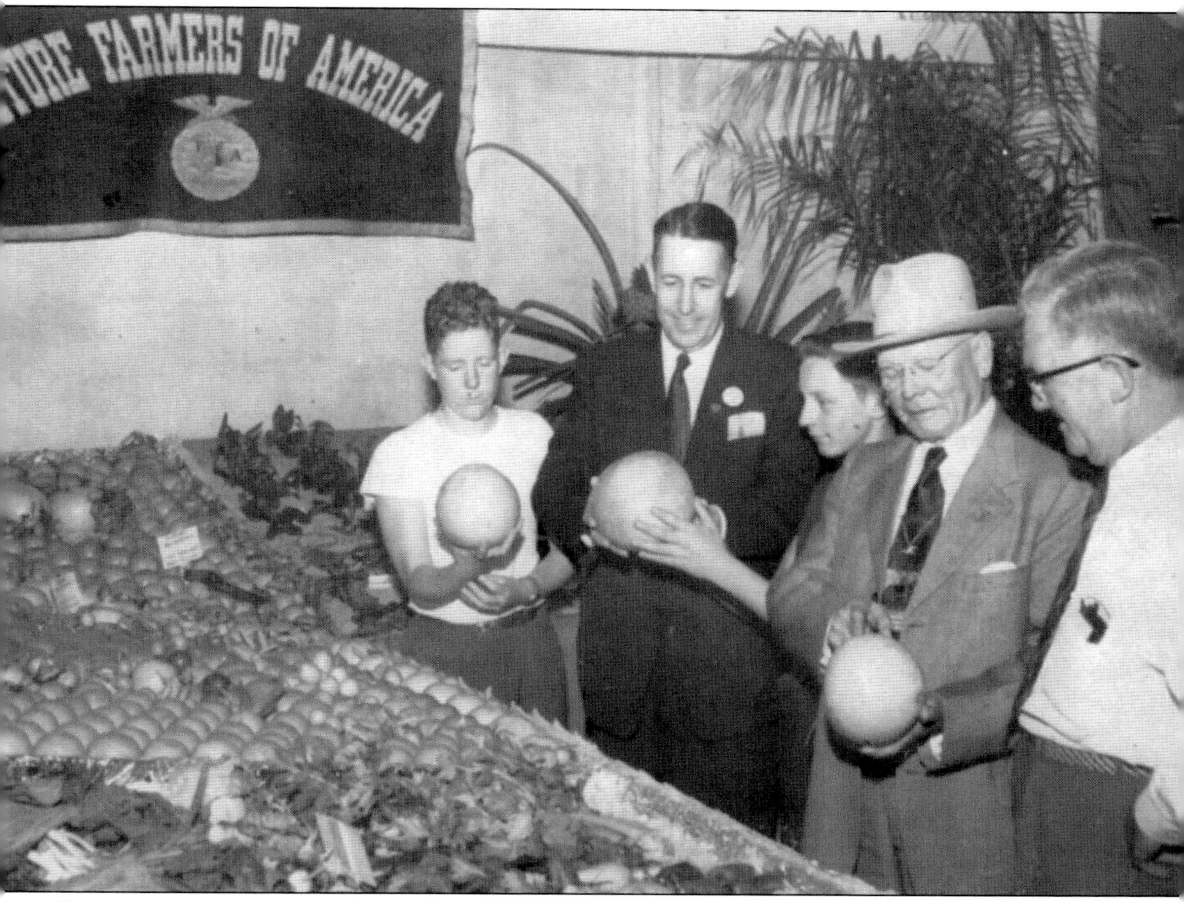

Despite postwar patterns of growth and suburbanization, Largo retained an agricultural flair, especially during the annual gatherings at the Pinellas County Fair. This image from 1954 shows future farmers Lloyd Larimore and Elmer Williams standing on either side of acting governor Charley E. Johns (second from left), longtime Commissioner of Agriculture Nathan Mayo (in hat), and Pinellas County commissioner Sidney Parry (right). (HV.)

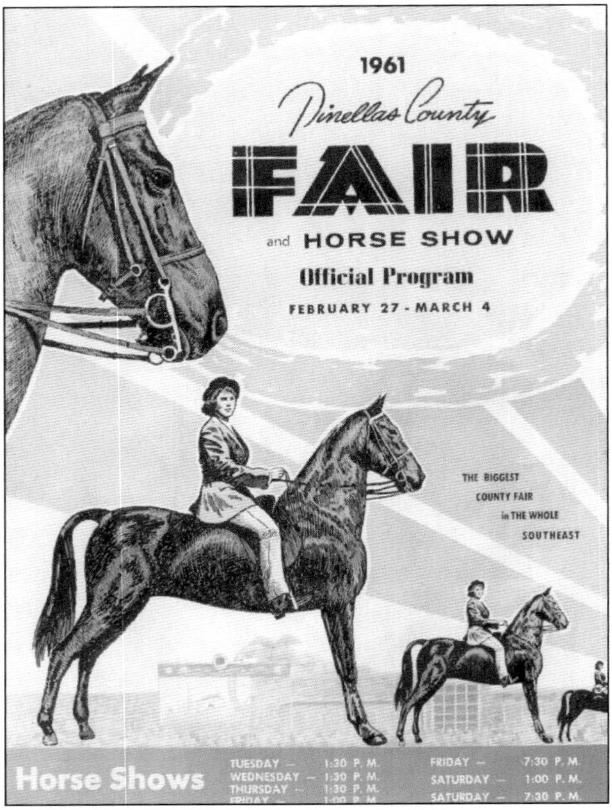

The stature of the Pinellas County Fair grew during the late 1950s and early 1960s. Ironically, at the same time developers began to bulldoze citrus trees and farmland from one end of the county to the other, from Tarpon Springs to St. Petersburg, the fair earned a reputation as one of the best of its kind in the southeastern United States. (HV.)

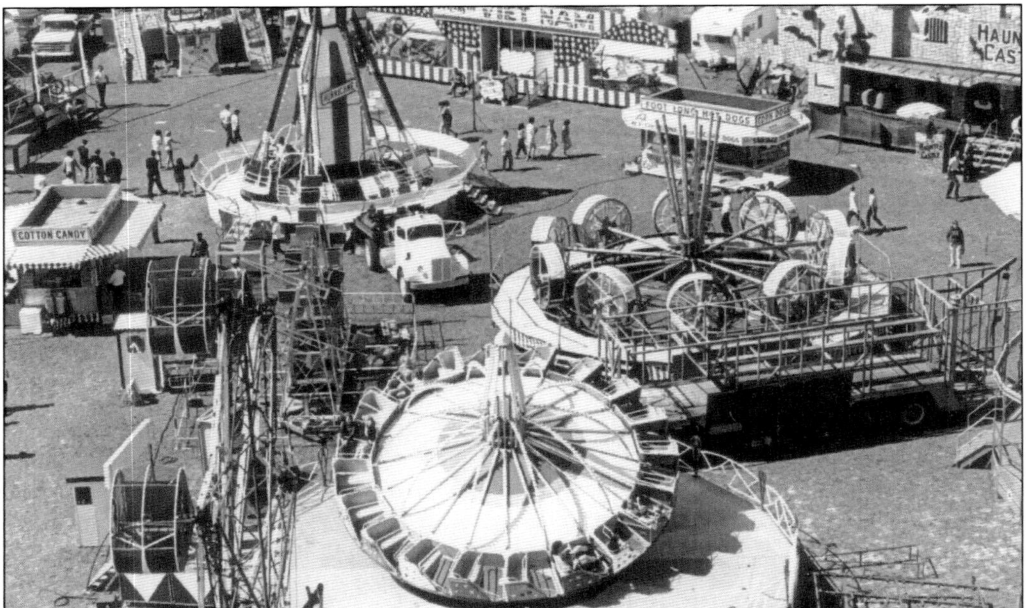

Crowds along the midway at the Pinellas County Fair enjoyed a variety of rides, attractions, square dancing performances, agricultural exhibits, and bluegrass concerts. A popular evening event was the adult tractor operators' competition, something one would never find in Pinellas County today. By the mid-1960s, the fair even had a ride known as the Killers of Vietnam. (HV.)

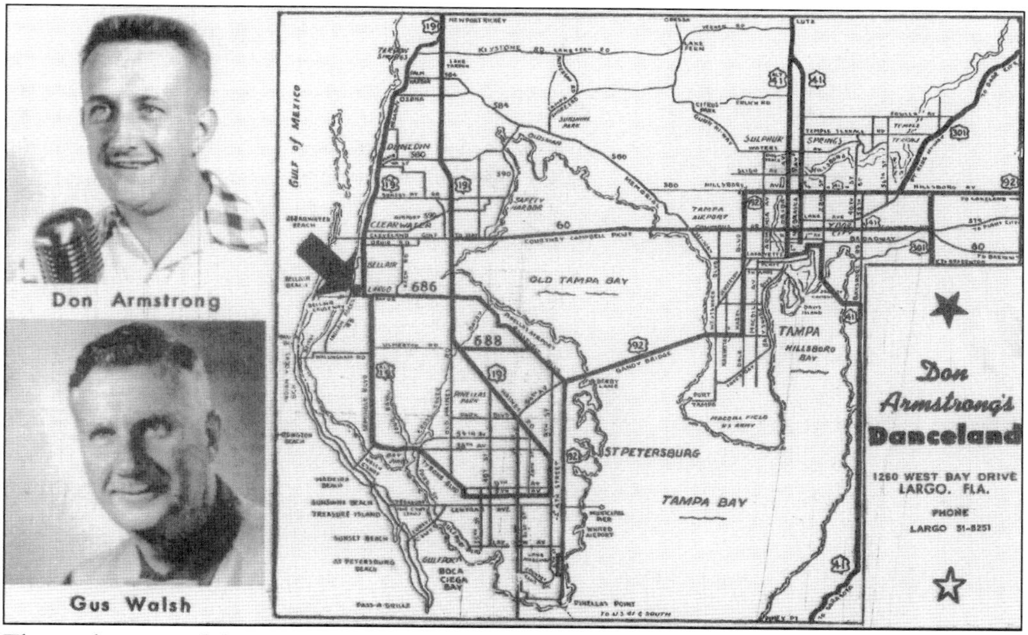

Those who enjoyed dancing to country tunes did not have to wait for the annual fair to sing and move along with the music. Don Armstrong's Danceland offered square and international folk dancing lessons. Opened in November 1953 near the current site of the Pinellas Trail, tuition per class in 1954 was 50¢. This postcard dates from 1957. (HV.)

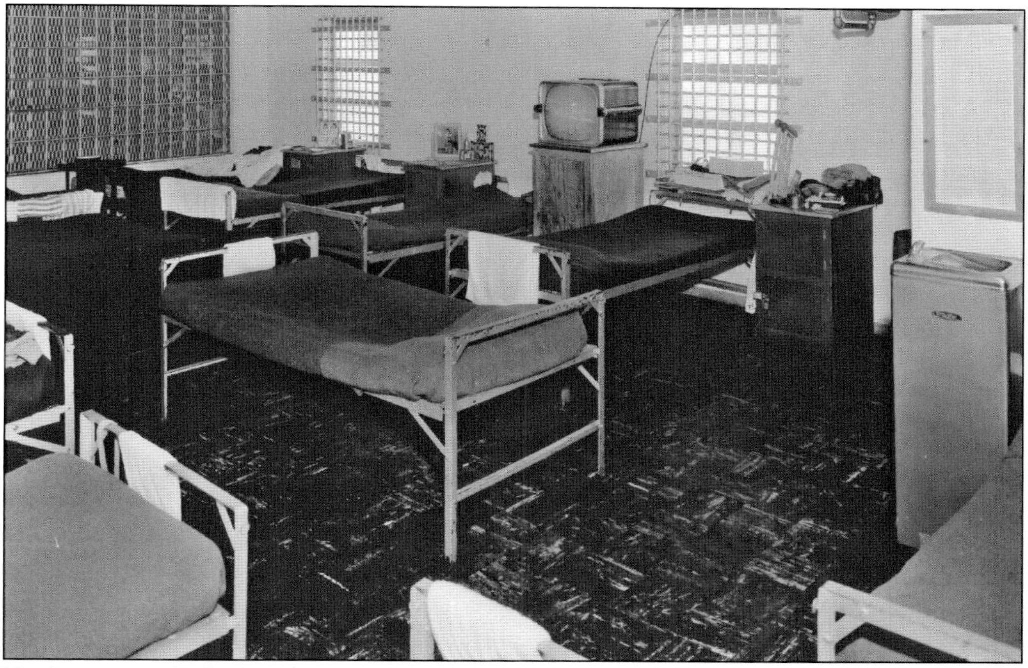

No dancing took place at this prison camp located along Ulmerton Road between Cross Bayou and Forty-ninth Street. This April 1956 image shows the sparse accommodations encountered by those sentenced to work on road crew detail. Long before the Pinellas County Jail moved from downtown Clearwater to Forty-ninth Street, work farms such as this existed in the remote areas near Largo, including sites near the sheriff's department. (THPL.)

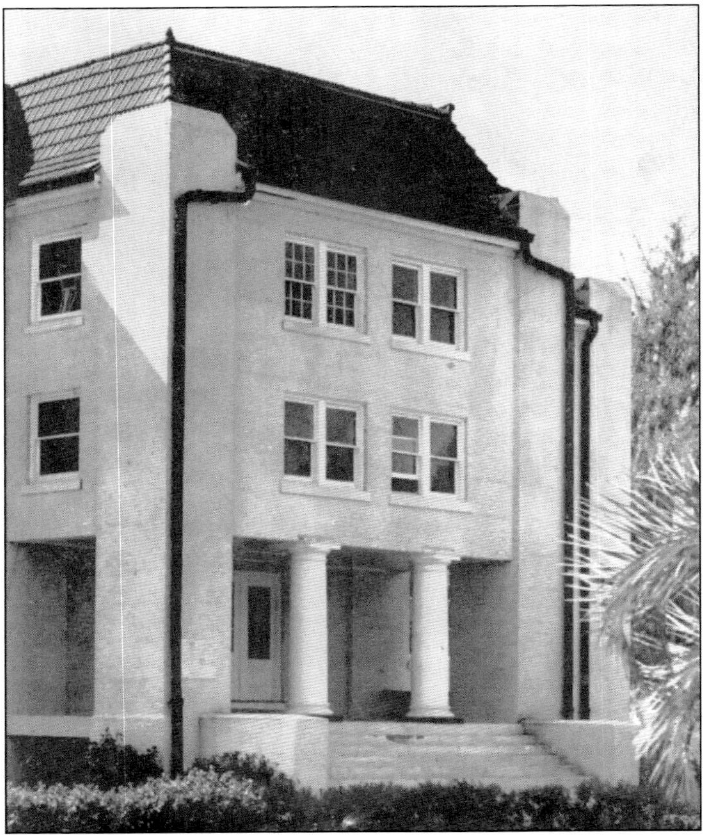

As it reached the half-century mark, the campus that served as Largo Junior/Senior High School began to show its age. Located along Fourth Street Southwest, the campus remained in the center of the Largo area. However, encroaching residential developments made it impossible to expand facilities at that site. The image at left shows the structure before it was remodeled to convert part of the porch into rooms. (HV.)

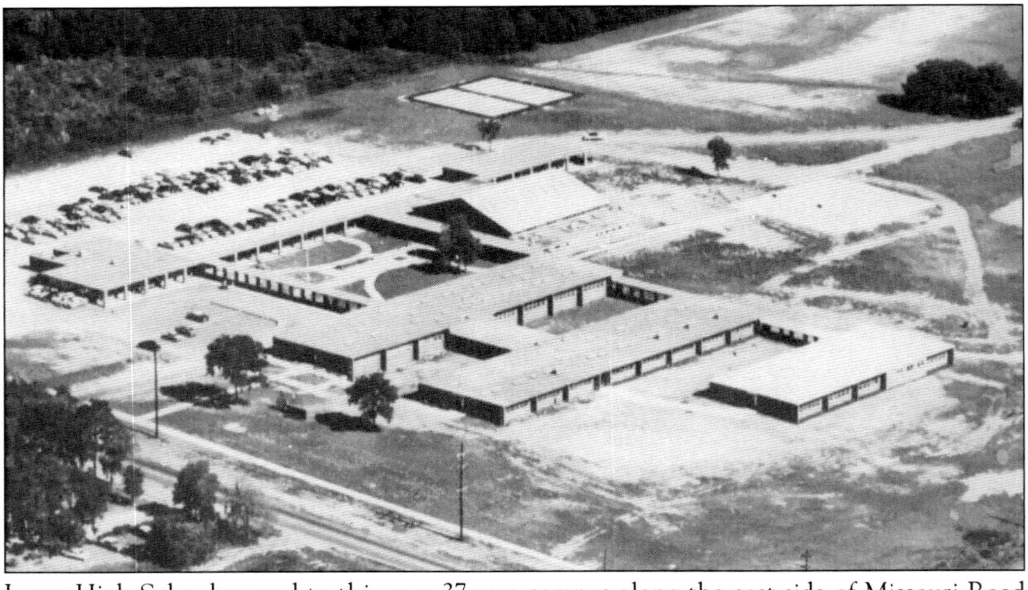

Largo High School moved to this new 37-acre campus along the east side of Missouri Road in 1957. Constructed at a cost of $625,000, the original buildings housed 37 teachers and 707 students in 1957. Five years later, 75 teachers and 1,350 students called Largo High their home. Students in Largo Junior High (now Largo Middle) moved to a new facility along Eighth Avenue SE in 1968. (HV.)

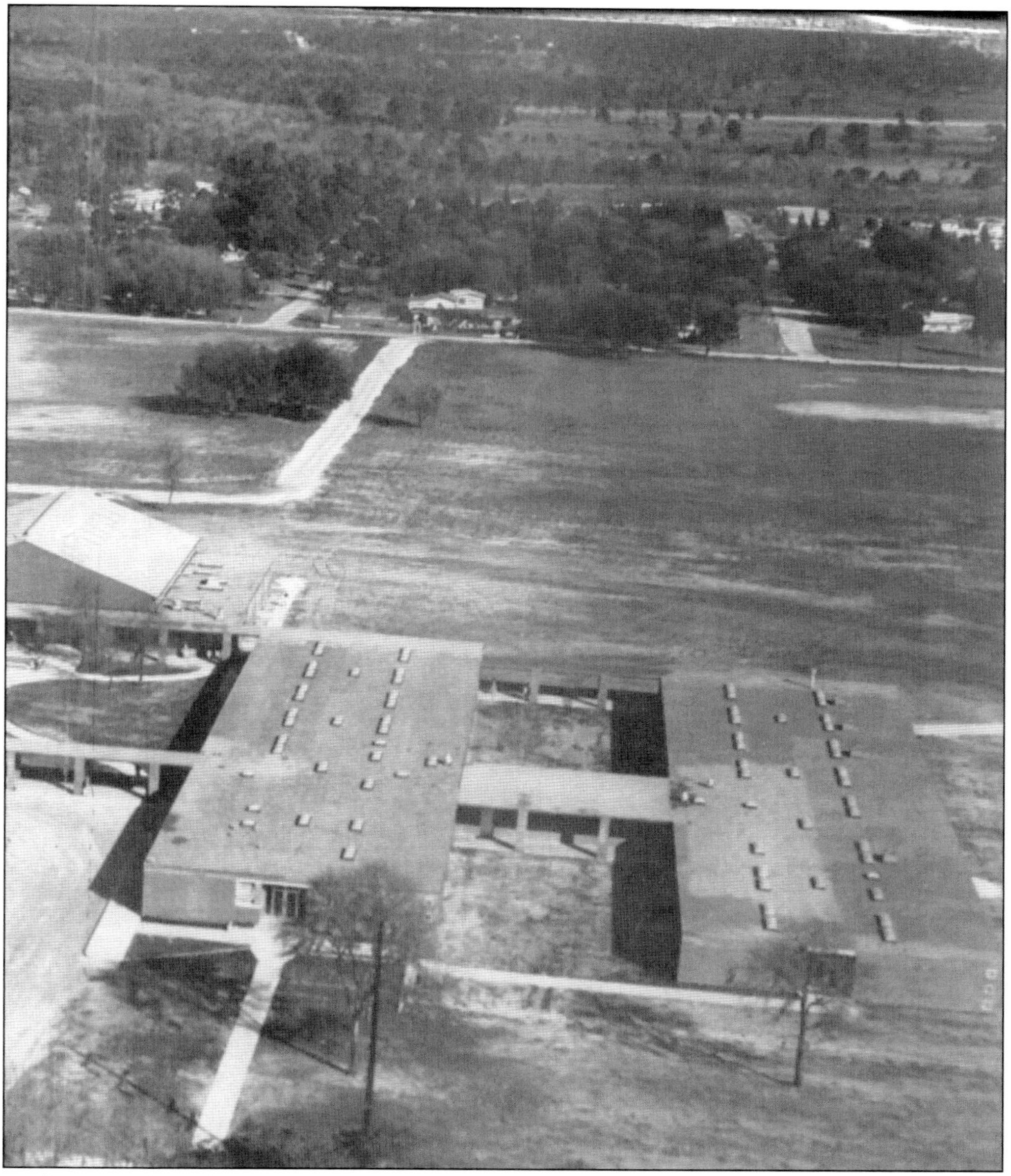

Looking east from the new Largo Senior High School campus in 1958, one certainly notices the absence of houses and other buildings between Missouri Avenue (a two-lane road at the time) and Highland Avenue in the distance. Seven years later, the Largo Chamber of Commerce used the wide-open spaces in this area of central Pinellas as a marketing tool after a 1965 federal air quality study of over 160 sites indicated that Largo averaged the second fewest number of pollution particles in the survey. As cars multiplied on the roadways and buildings appeared in the horizon, the chamber proclaimed Largo the "Clean Air Capital." (HV.)

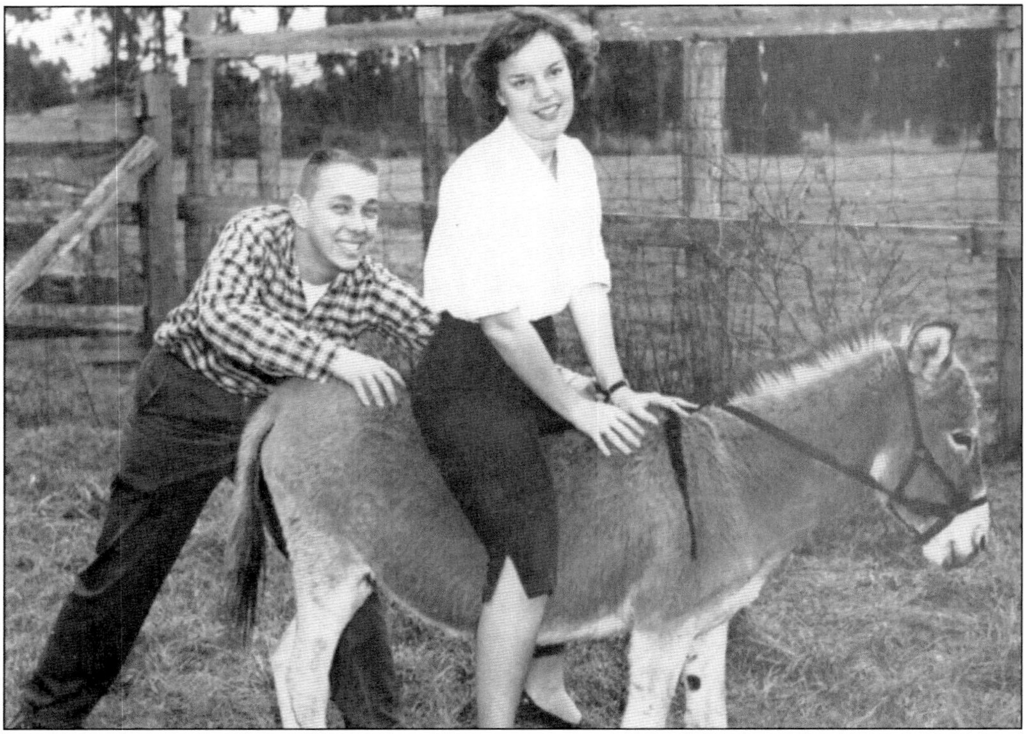

As these yearbook images from the 1958 *Keystone* reveal, agricultural themes continued to serve as a popular focal point on the senior superlative pages for those soon to graduate. Above, Georgia Zubrod and Emmette Jackson shared accolades as the most original graduates. Below, Sandy O'Neil and Jay Kellerman plowed their way through the competition to garner honors as the most humorous. (Both, HV.)

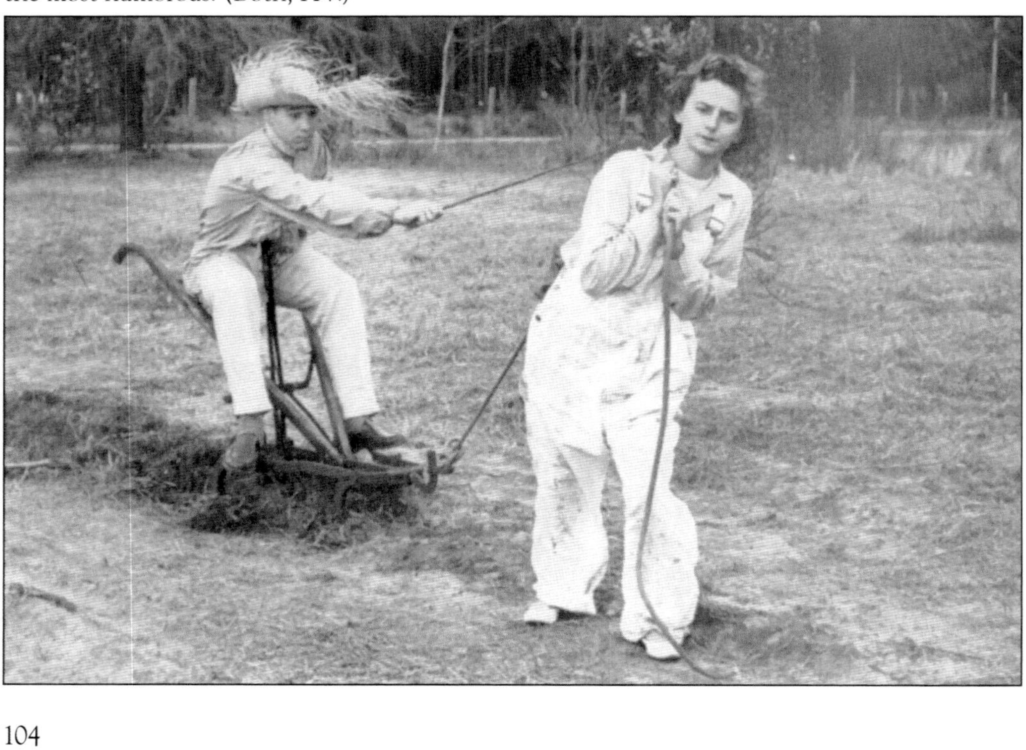

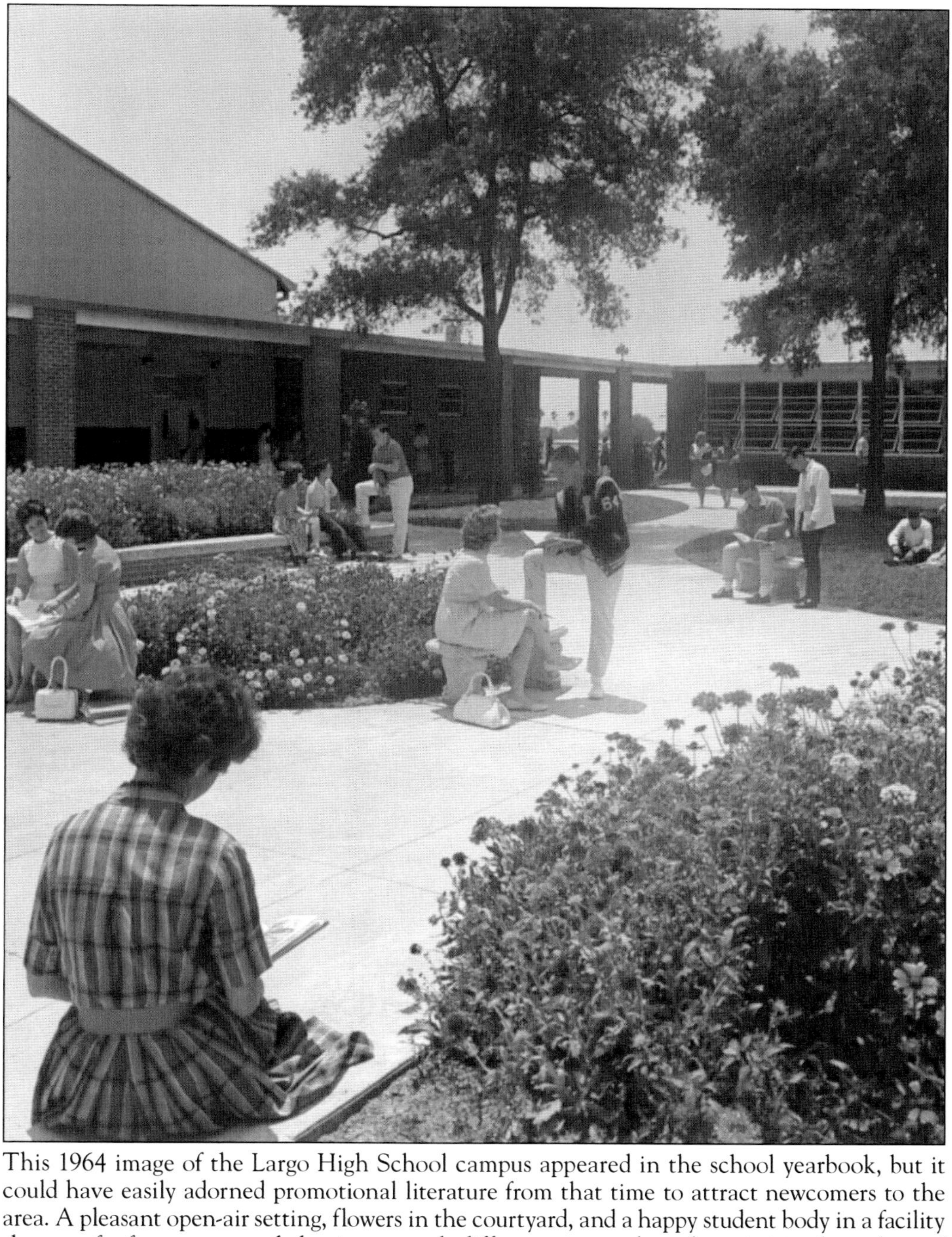

This 1964 image of the Largo High School campus appeared in the school yearbook, but it could have easily adorned promotional literature from that time to attract newcomers to the area. A pleasant open-air setting, flowers in the courtyard, and a happy student body in a facility that was far from overcrowded paints a much different picture than the primitive log cabins of yesteryear or the crowded classrooms of today. Under the surface, another event in 1964 would redefine educational opportunity and access in Pinellas County: in May 1964, Leon W. Bradley Sr. of Clearwater filed a class action suit in the United States District Court that asked for federal intervention to accelerate school integration. Little progress on this front had taken place in Pinellas since the 1954 and 1955 Supreme Court decisions in *Brown v. Board of Education*. By 1971, the county fell under a federal court order that mandated school busing and other methods of desegregating facilities. (HV.)

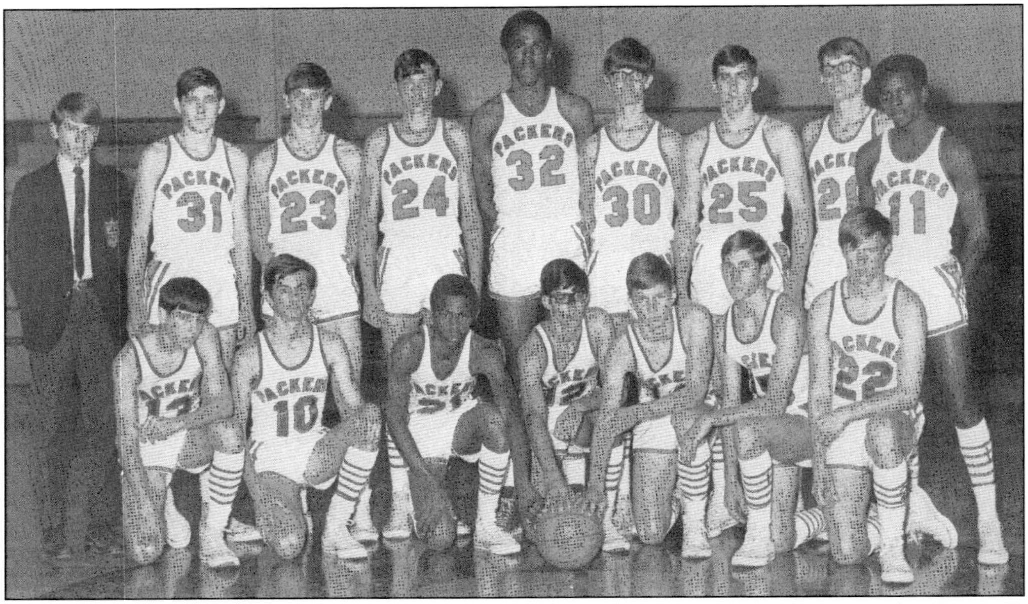

Integration of many Largo area schools took place before the 1971 federal court order. By 1967, African American students enrolled at the high school. For the most part, the transition to integrated schools in the greater Largo area did not meet with the tension or resistance found in some south Pinellas schools, such as Boca Ciega High or Dixie Hollins High. This is a photograph of the 1970 varsity basketball squad. (HV.)

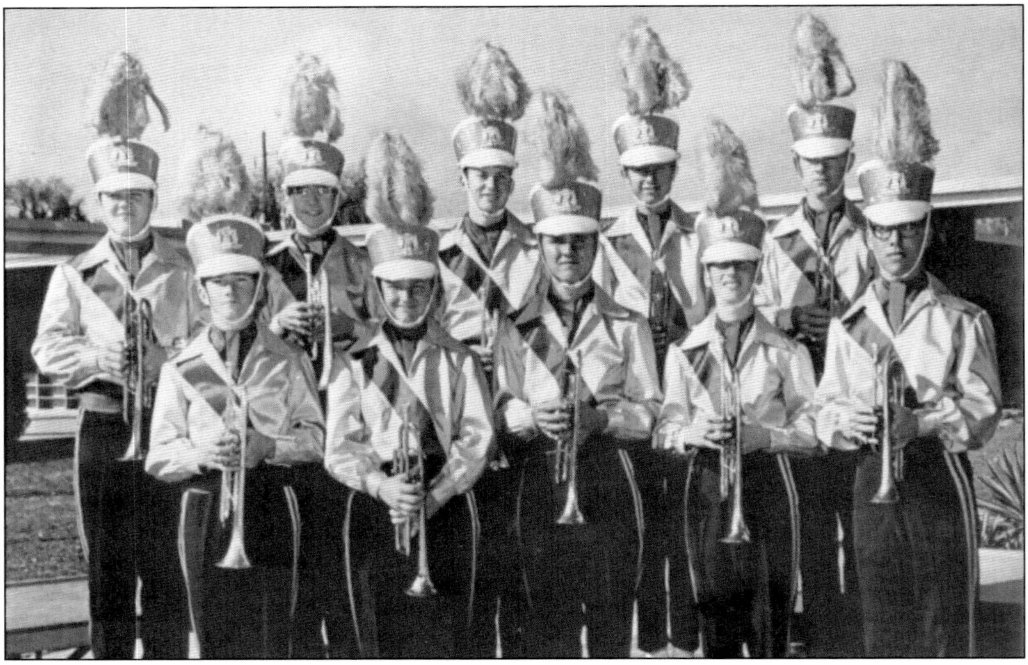

The Band of Gold took musical performances to a new (and international) level. Shortly after the 1968 statewide teacher strike decimated instructional ranks, Robert Cotter assumed leadership of Largo High's band. Until his retirement in 1980, Cotter encouraged band members to reach for new heights. After winning national competitions, they took top honors as the 1978 World Music Contest Champions in Holland. This image shows the band in 1969. (HV.)

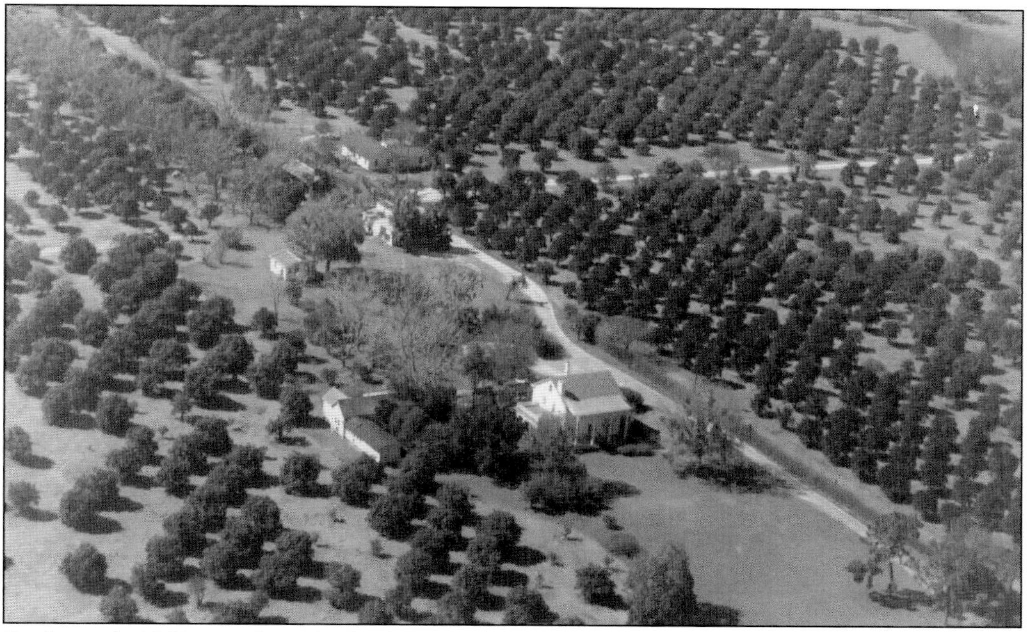

By the early 1960s, residential suburbs started to appear alongside the remaining John S. Taylor property at Keene Road. This image shows the site in the 1960s, with Belleair Road in the upper right corner. Once used for cattle grazing and citrus cultivation, the property was acquired from the Taylor family by Pinellas County. It opened in early 2010 as Eagle Lake Park. (John S. Taylor Collection, HV.)

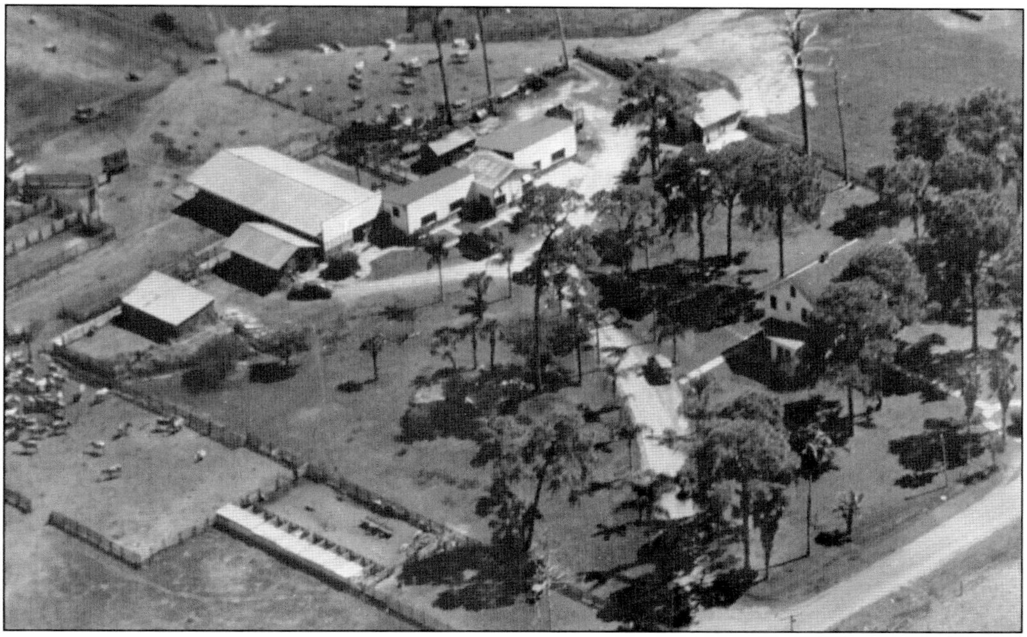

Charles E. Donegan opened a dairy southeast of the city limits in 1924. He and his wife, Cecel, selected the location near the former lakebed of Lake Largo because it offered an excellent site for their cattle to graze. This view shows the Donegan Dairy in 1953. At one time, the 250 cows at the dairy provided milk to customers throughout the county. After the dairy closed, mobile homes rested where the cows once roamed. (HV.)

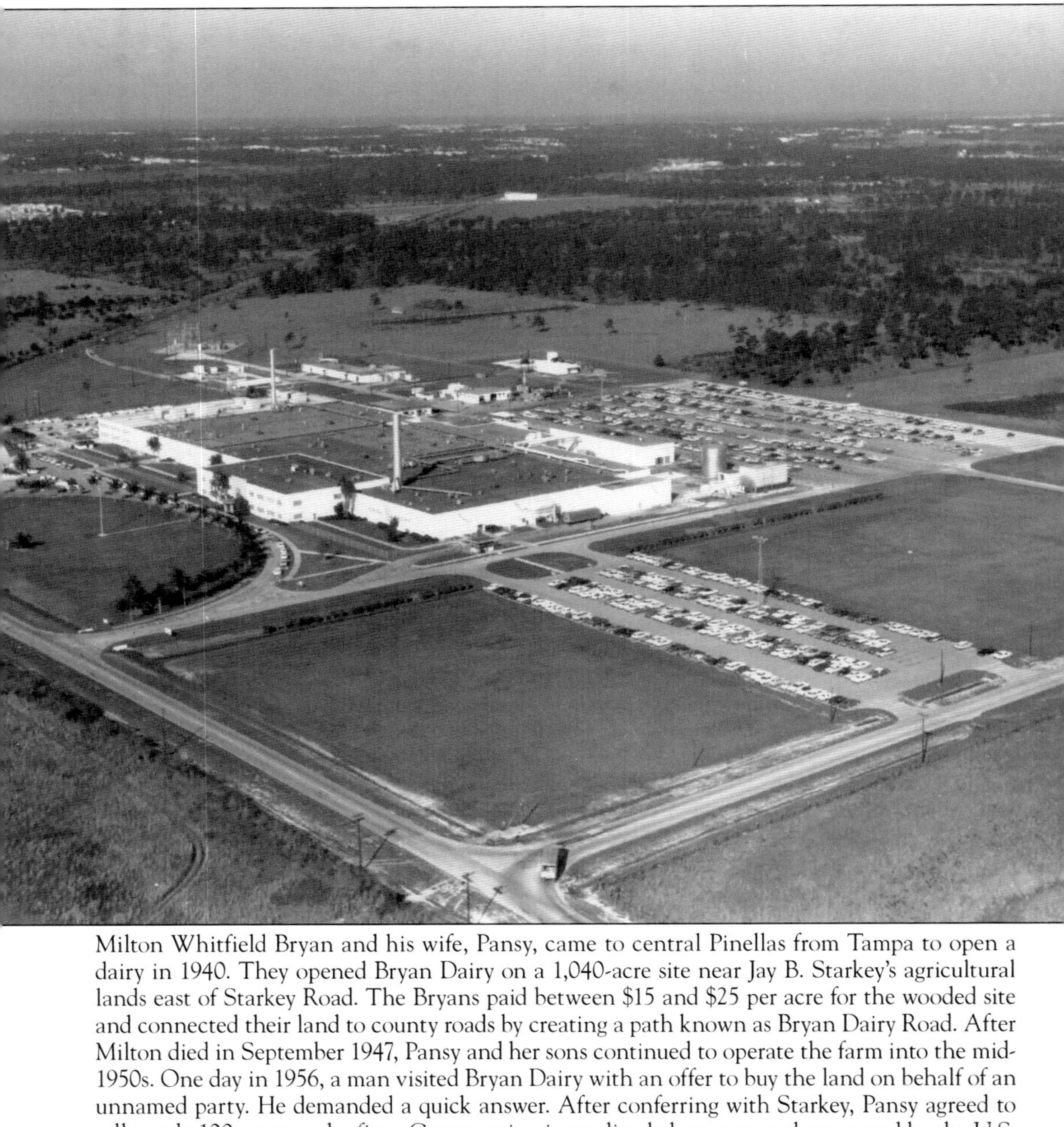

Milton Whitfield Bryan and his wife, Pansy, came to central Pinellas from Tampa to open a dairy in 1940. They opened Bryan Dairy on a 1,040-acre site near Jay B. Starkey's agricultural lands east of Starkey Road. The Bryans paid between $15 and $25 per acre for the wooded site and connected their land to county roads by creating a path known as Bryan Dairy Road. After Milton died in September 1947, Pansy and her sons continued to operate the farm into the mid-1950s. One day in 1956, a man visited Bryan Dairy with an offer to buy the land on behalf of an unnamed party. He demanded a quick answer. After conferring with Starkey, Pansy agreed to sell nearly 100 acres to the firm. Construction immediately began on a plant owned by the U.S. Atomic Energy Commission and operated by General Electric. This aerial view from the 1960s looks northwest at the plant and the intersection of Bryan Dairy and Belcher Roads. An extension of Belcher Road would later connect this area with Seventy-first Street. (HV.)

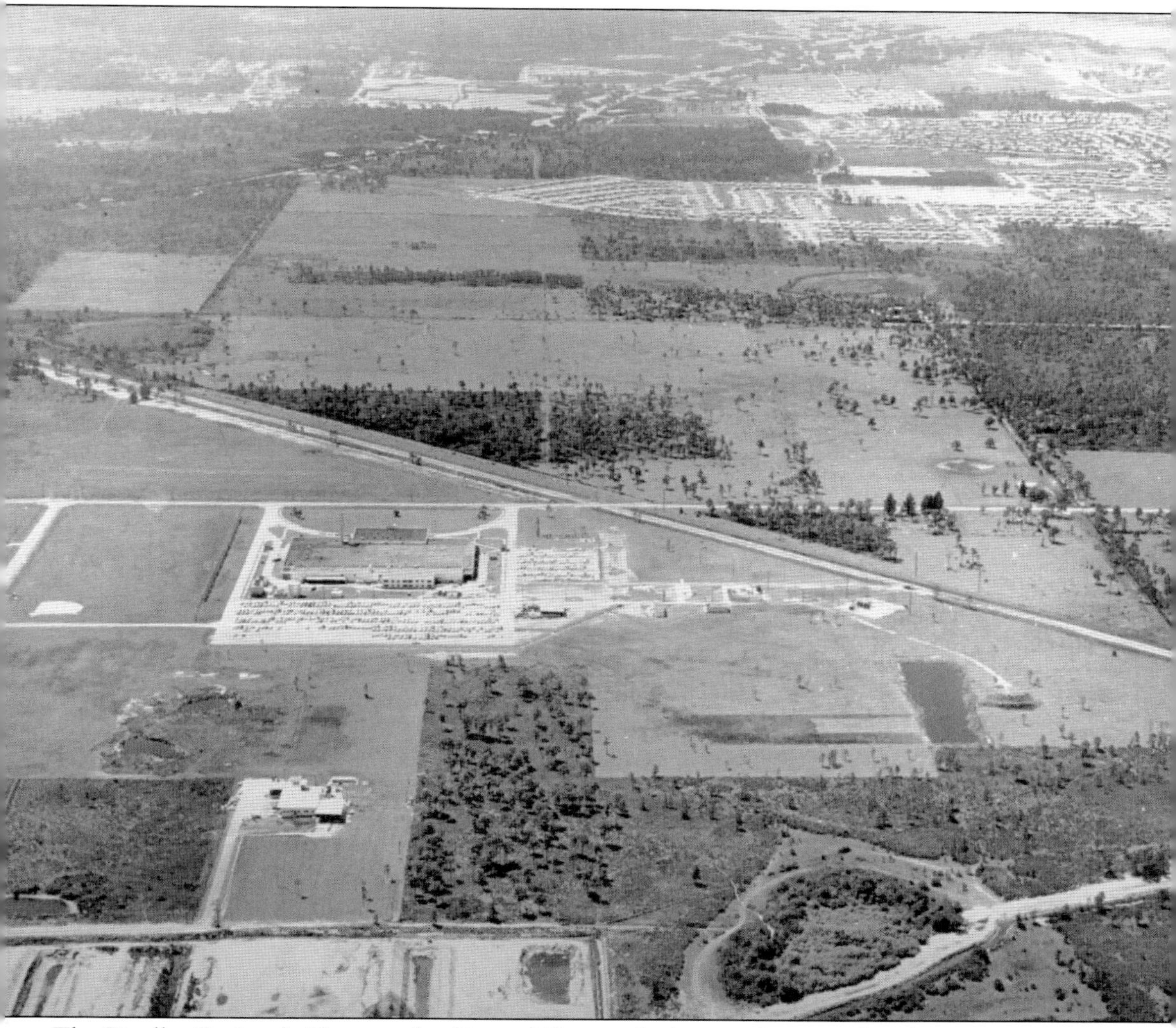

The Pinellas Peninsula Plant, as the General Electric facility was known, played an important role during the Cold War years as the first large scale manufacturing plant in Pinellas County. Its opening in January 1957 also ushered a new era of explosive development in the mid-county region between Largo, Pinellas Park, and Clearwater. Within a few years, subdivisions sprouted on acreage between Lake Seminole and Pinellas Park sold by Pansy Bryan and Jay Starkey. Although outside of Largo's city limits, much of this area, such as the upscale Bardmoor subdivision, continues to maintain a Largo mailing address even as Pinellas Park and Seminole have annexed large segments. By the 1970s, homes sat atop most of Starkey's former holdings along the eastern side of Lake Seminole. Also, the opening of Honeywell and other manufacturing plants in this area brought new service and industrial jobs to an area once dependent on agriculture. This 1960s view of the plant scans the horizon southward toward Cross Bayou and Long Bayou. (HV.)

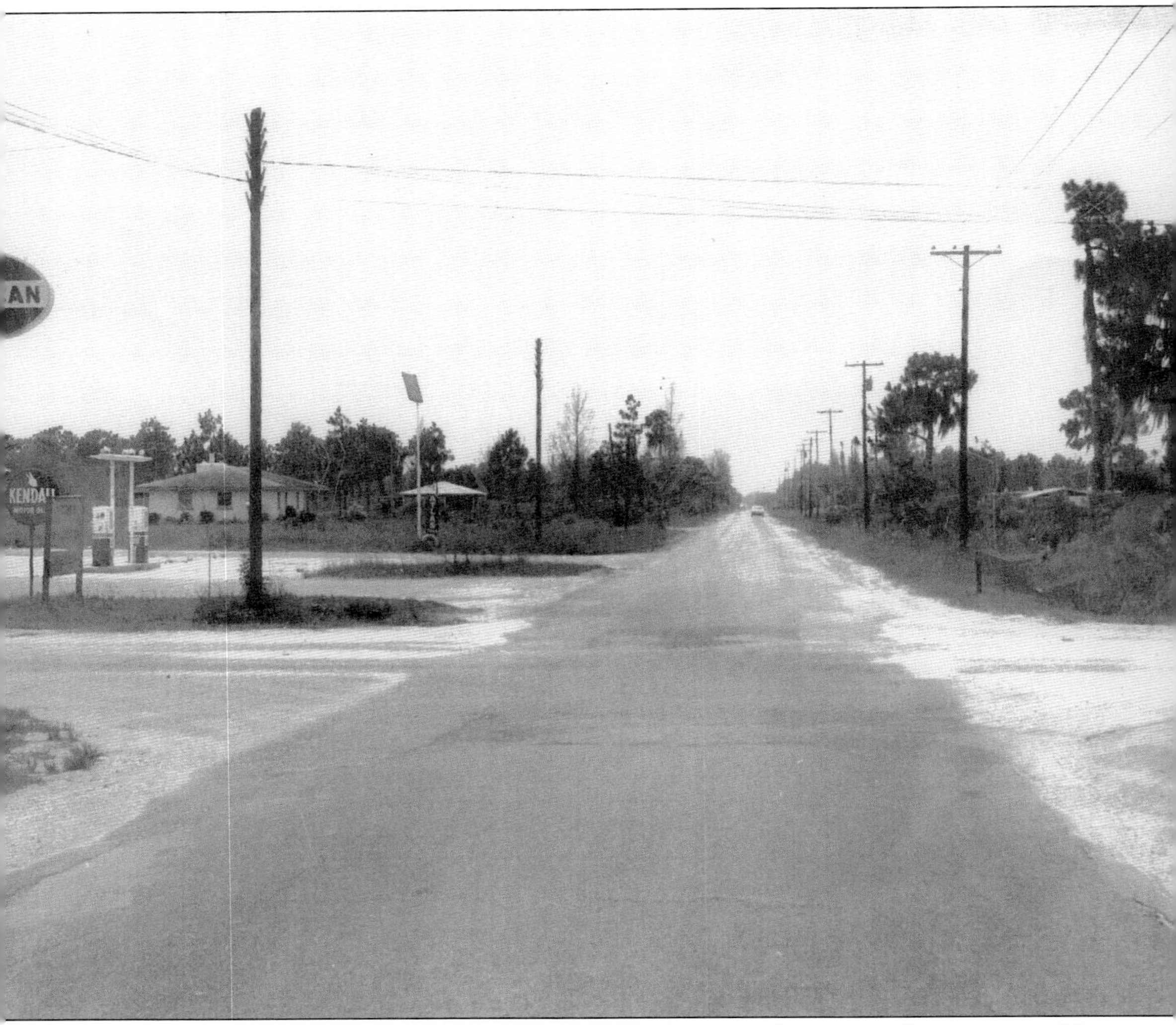

This August 1963 image of a remote intersection shows a scene that is virtually unrecognizable to present-day Largo residents. Today this corner is one of the busiest in southern Largo. This photograph follows a two-lane Ulmerton Road at Belcher Road, facing west toward Starkey Road. (HV.)

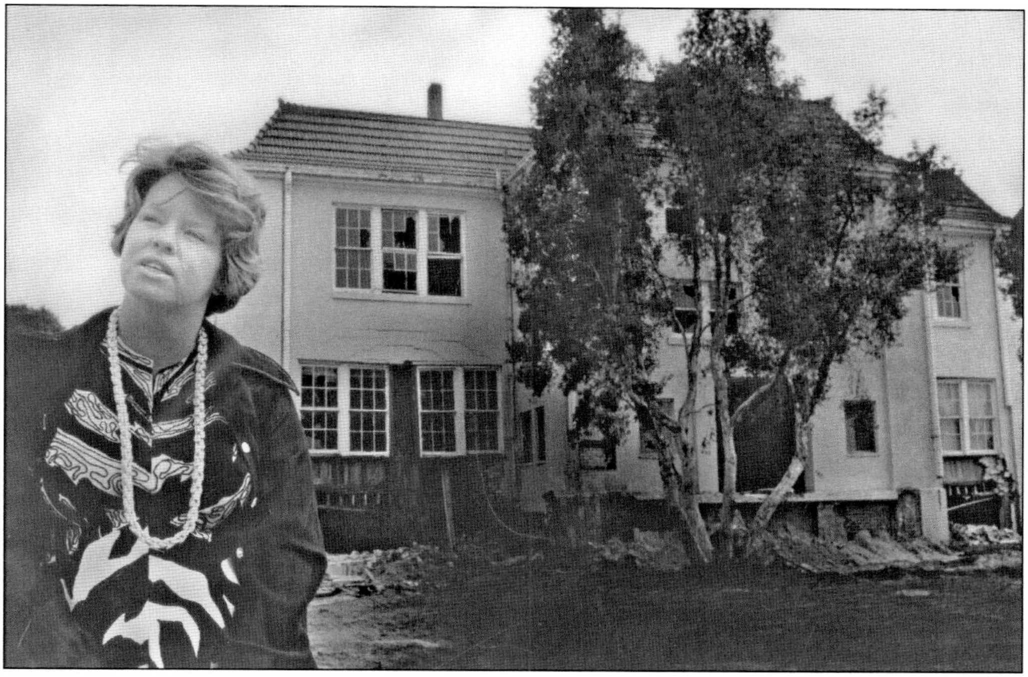

Faye Johnson Prince, shown above, made a painful discovery when she returned to Largo for a vacation in July 1975. While passing by the 1914 red brick school she had attended many years earlier, she noticed crews demolishing her old school. They began tearing down the corner where her kindergarten class once met. The site later became the headquarters for Pinellas County Schools. That same year, First Federal of Largo proudly placed the advertisement below in the Largo yearbook. After the savings and loan closed, the building sat vacant for years. Finally, in July 1997, the building-turned-eyesore at West Bay and Clearwater-Largo Road came down. One city official proclaimed, "It was a symbol of what is wrong with downtown Largo . . . Now we can look forward to a more vibrant city." (Both, HV.)

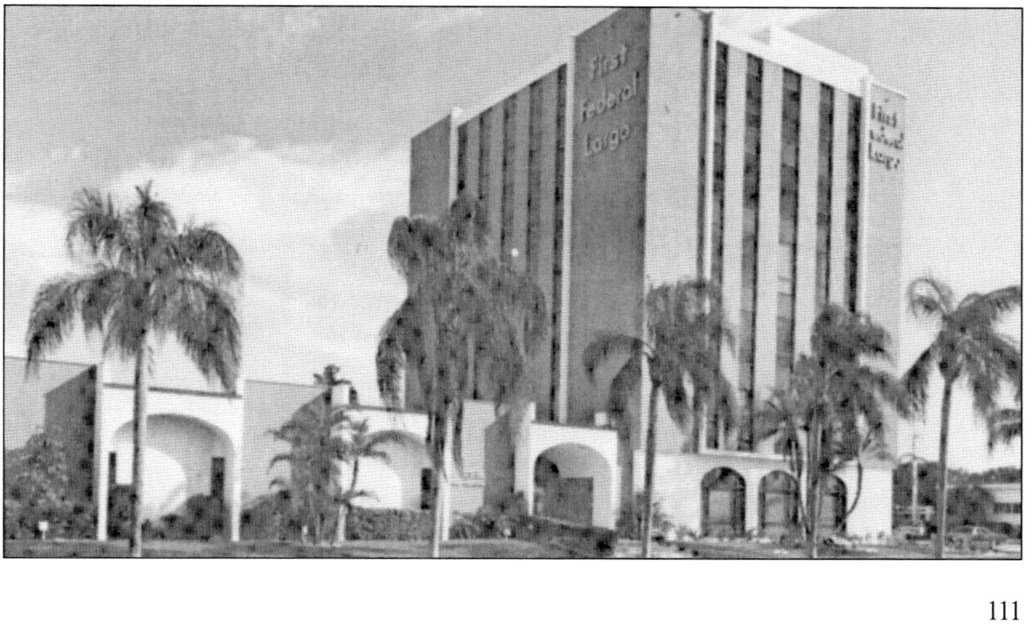

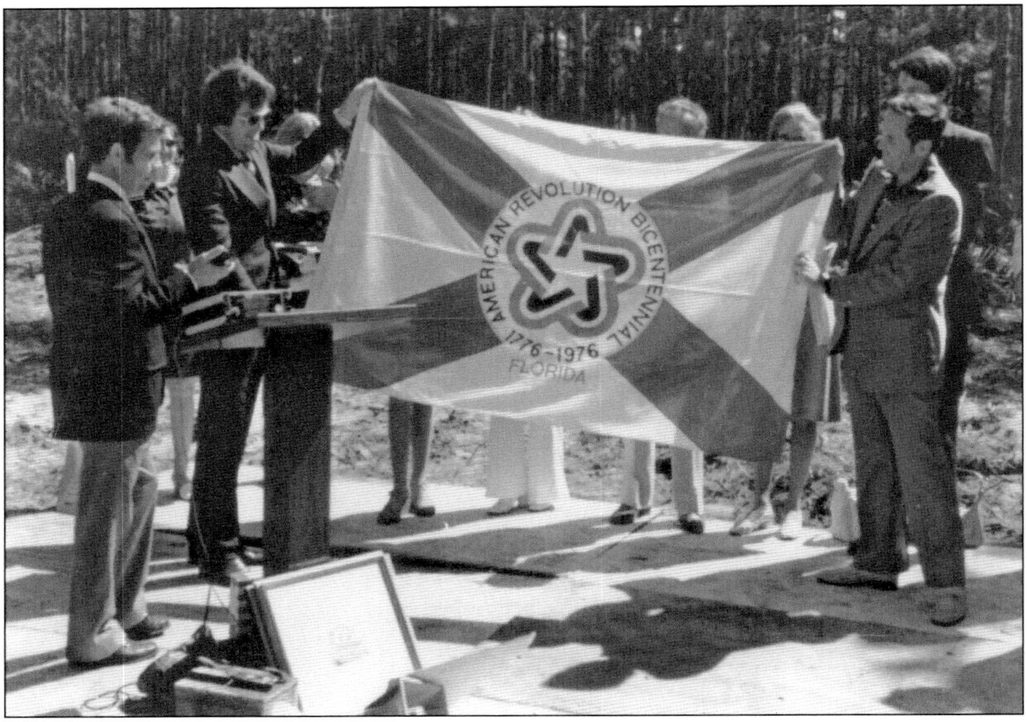

Heritage Village opened on a tract of land near Largo in the mid-1970s as the historical museum for Pinellas County. Ground-breaking ceremonies in March 1976 ushered in the bicentennial. Many Largo treasures, including the Lowe barn; the Lowe, McMullen, and Walsingham houses; and the pillars from old Largo High School have found a safe haven at the village. The image below shows the 1912 Lowe barn as it appeared before moving to Heritage Village in 1976. (Both, HV.)

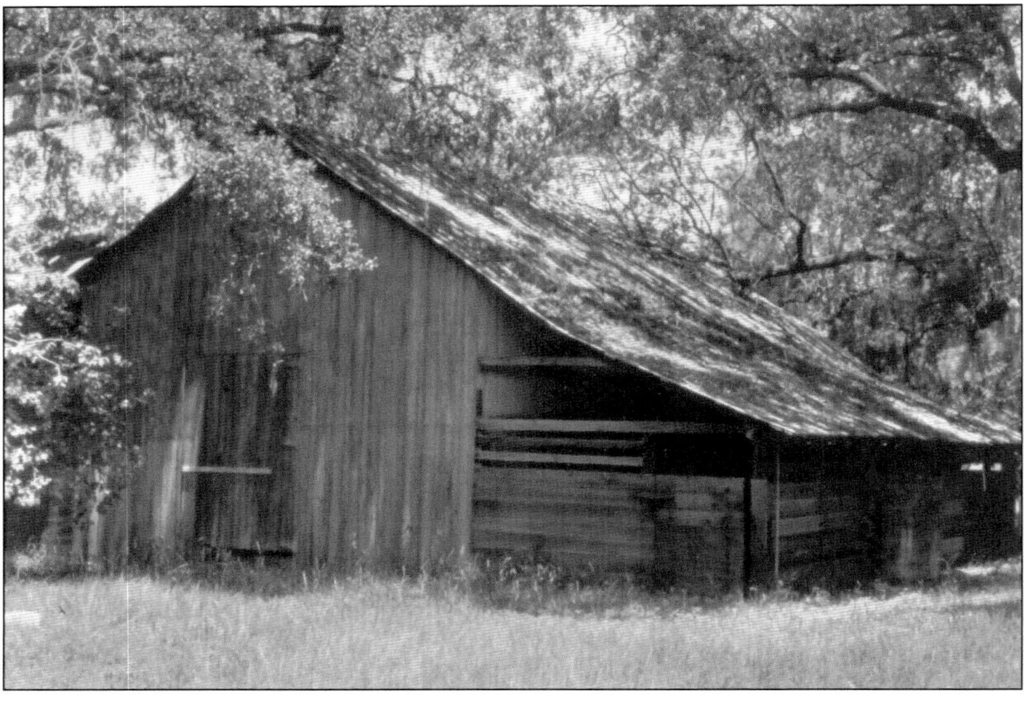

Five

A Progressive City on a Populated Peninsula 1980–2010

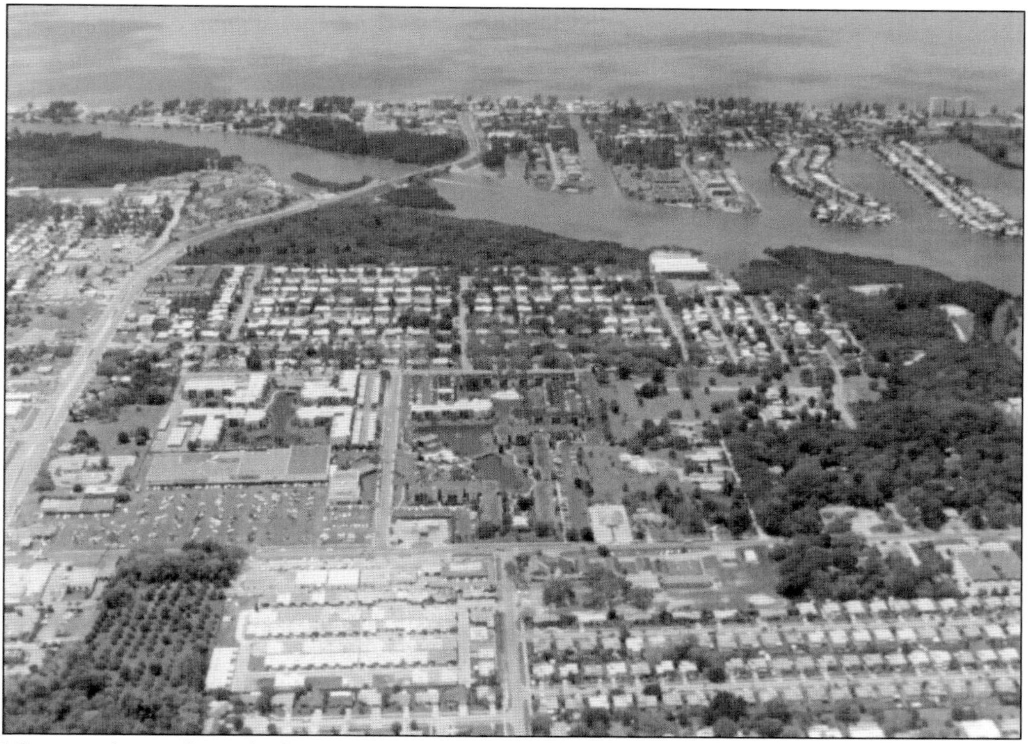

This aerial view from the late 1980s, looking westward from Largo and the Anona area toward Indian Rocks Beach and the Gulf of Mexico, differs greatly from the sights and surroundings witnessed by early members of the Lowe, Kilgore, Meares, and McMullen families. The lower left corner shows the intersection of Walsingham Road with Indian Rocks/Oakhurst Road. (HV.)

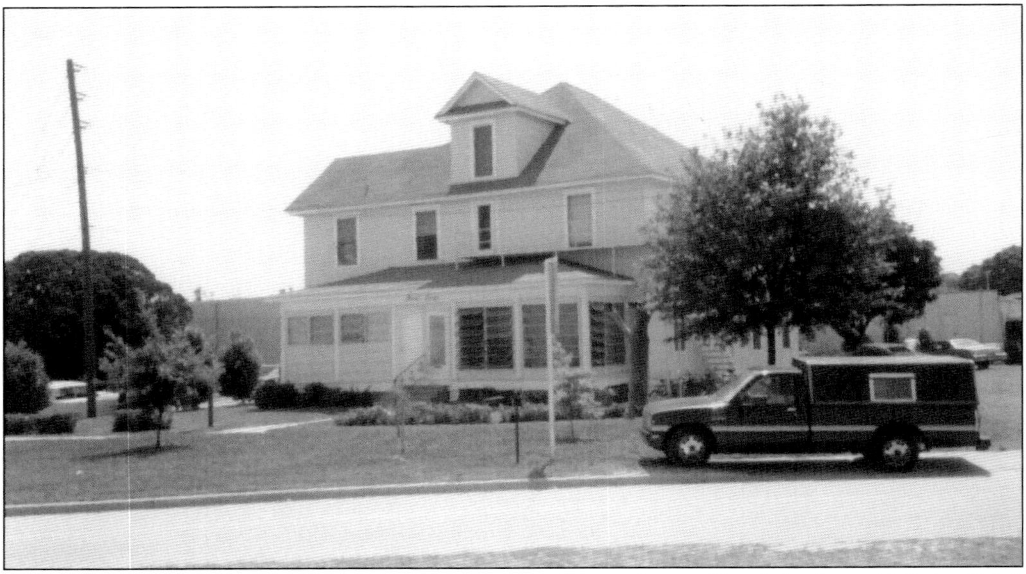

Subsequent owners had enclosed the porch of the former Largo Hotel, built in 1908 by F. M. Campbell. Shown above in a May 1983 photograph looking west from Seminole Boulevard, the structure that once perched near the Taylor Building and across Railroad Avenue from the early train depot appeared haggard. Over the next two decades, the old hotel's condition further deteriorated as it became a rooming house for transients. In August 2006, the city paid $775,000 to acquire the property for redevelopment purposes. After investigating the old hotel's condition and comparing the costs of moving and preserving the building ($2 million) versus demolishing it ($29,400), the city condemned the building in September 2007 and it disappeared soon thereafter. Another early structure, the old barn of W. A. Belcher's property, below, also awaited the wrecking ball. (Both, Lyn Friedt Collection, HV.)

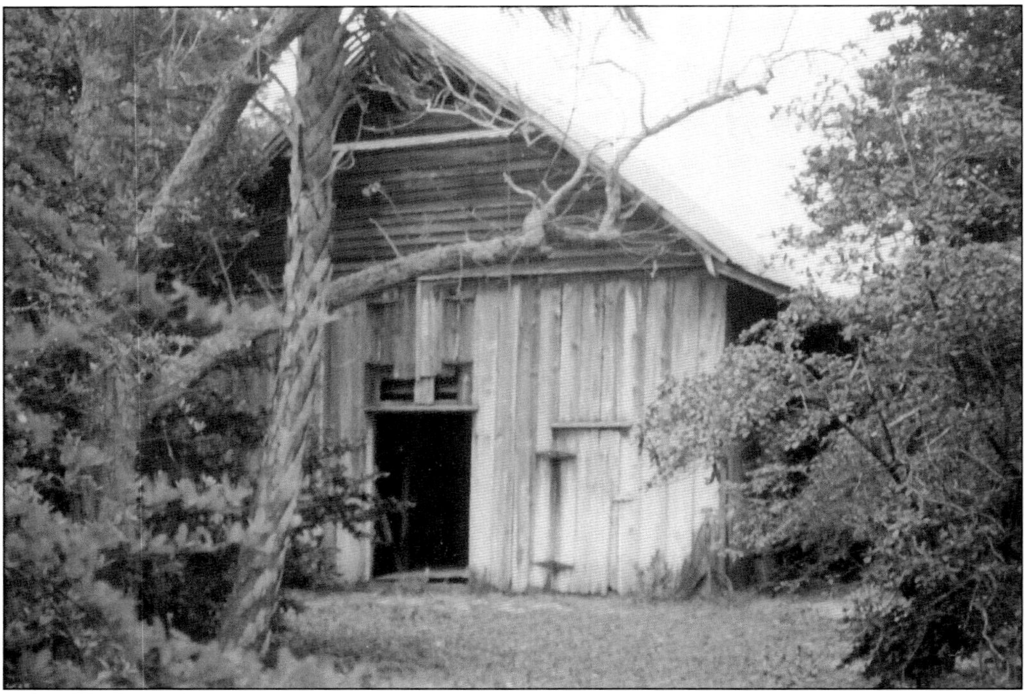

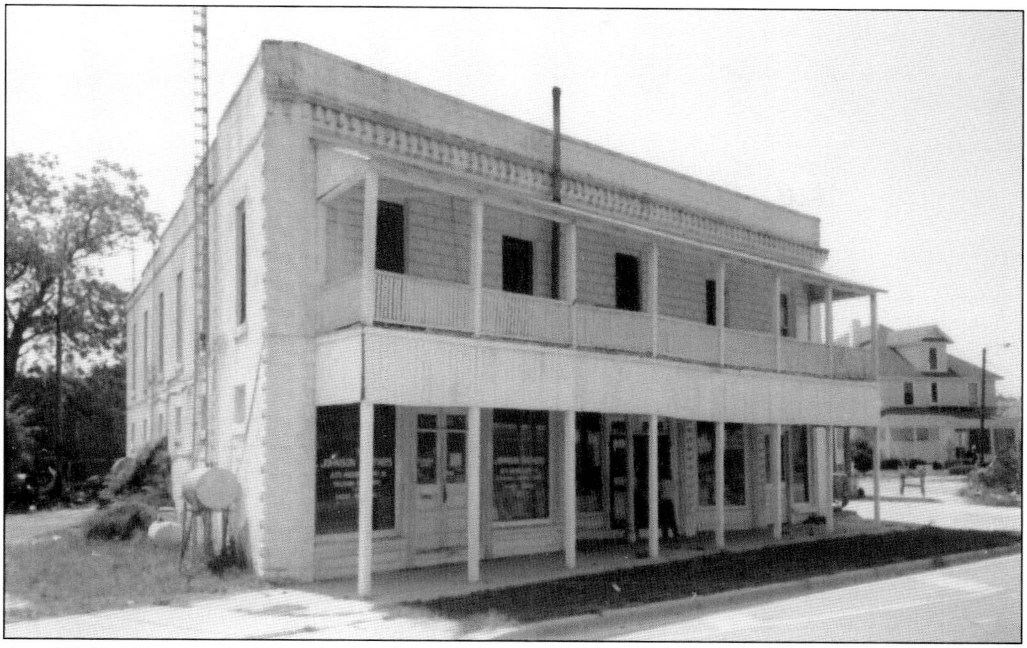

As of 2010, the only structure within Largo's city limits listed on the National Register of Historic Places is the Johnson Building along the former Railroad Avenue (First Street Southwest) between First Avenue Southwest and Cleveland Avenue. Constructed in 1910–1911 by Louis Steele Johnson, this edifice is one of the few remaining buildings from Largo's early years that still occupies its original site. The early 1980s photograph above shows the rusticated block structure with a view of the old Largo Hotel (mentioned on the previous page) to the right (or northwest) of it. At that time, some of the windows still displayed the Johnson family businesses that once thrived there. The image below, taken in October 2010, indicates that the building has suffered further neglect as it reaches the century mark. (Above, Lyn Friedt Collection, HV; below, author.)

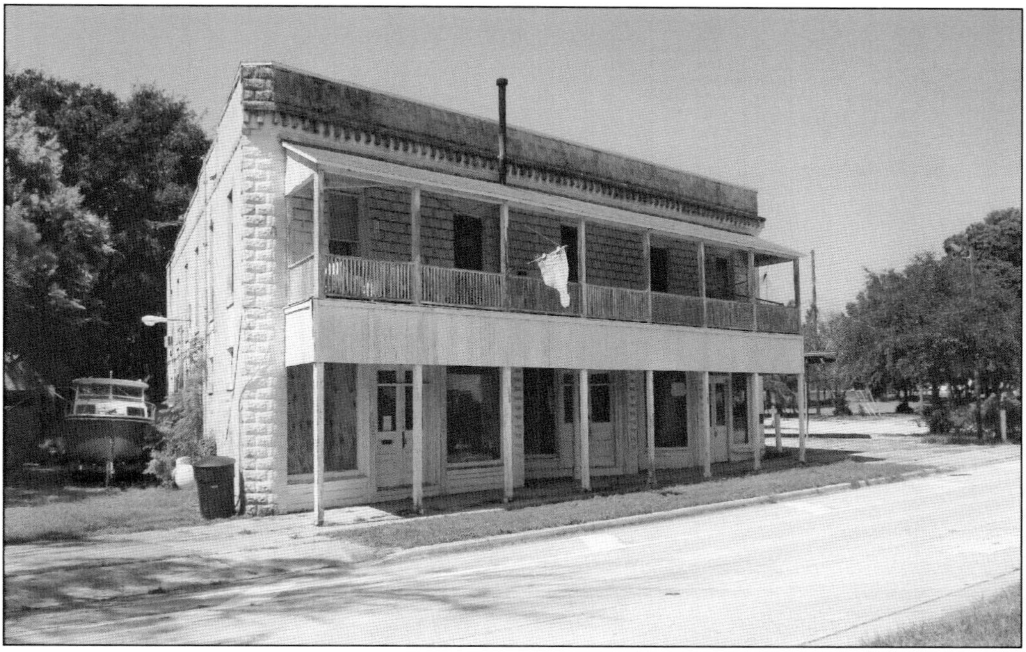

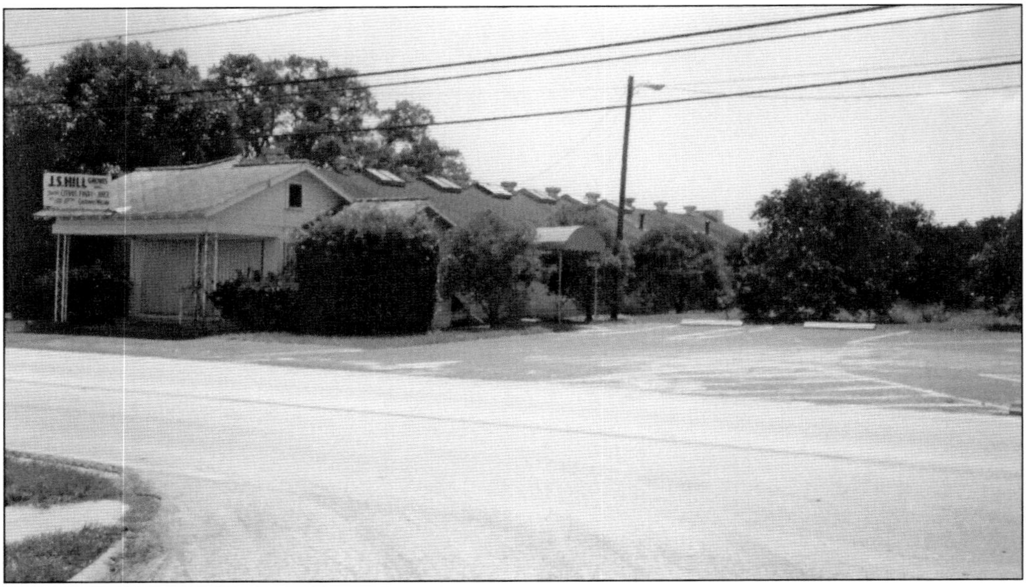

The land booms of the last 40 years have blurred boundaries and altered the sense of community. Largo and neighboring municipalities engage in annexation battles that try to bring unincorporated areas of Pinellas County into their tax base. Few remnants of the once-vibrant citrus industry remain, and those that do have had to find new purposes to survive. An Oakhurst grove established in 1915 became the basis for the J. S. Hill packinghouse. From the 1920s through the 1980s, the plant thrived, and customers regularly visited for the packed fruit, marmalades, and juices. The family closed the plant in the mid-1980s and sold much of the 60-acre grove to developers. For awhile beginning in the mid-1990s, a family member even sold kayaks at this location. From kumquats to kayaks, the landscape of Largo has certainly changed. (Both, Lyn Friedt Collection, HV.)

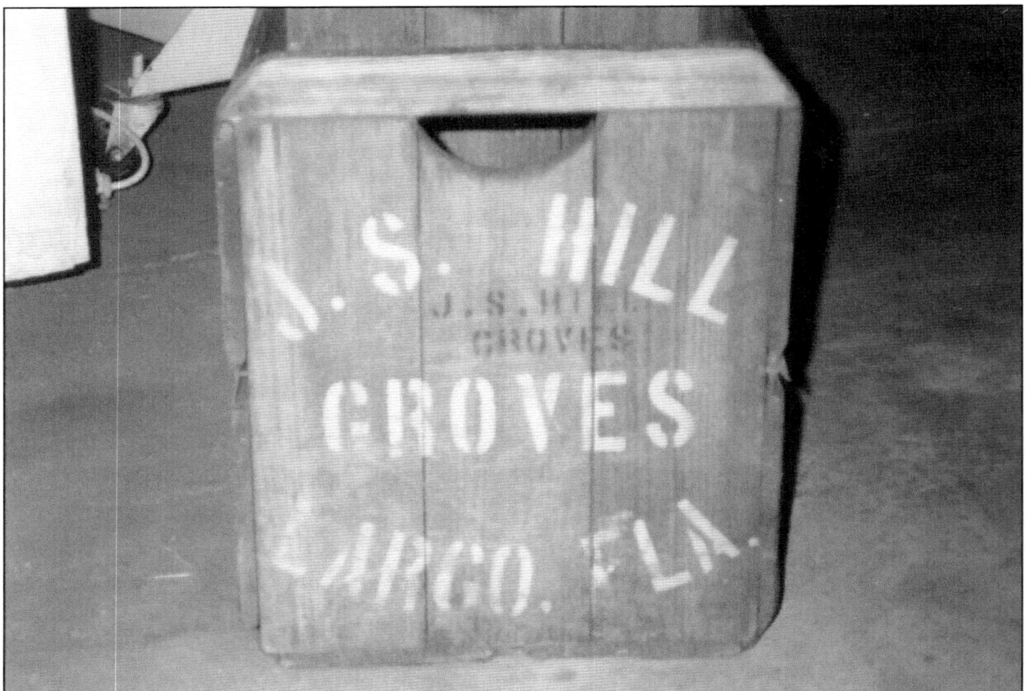

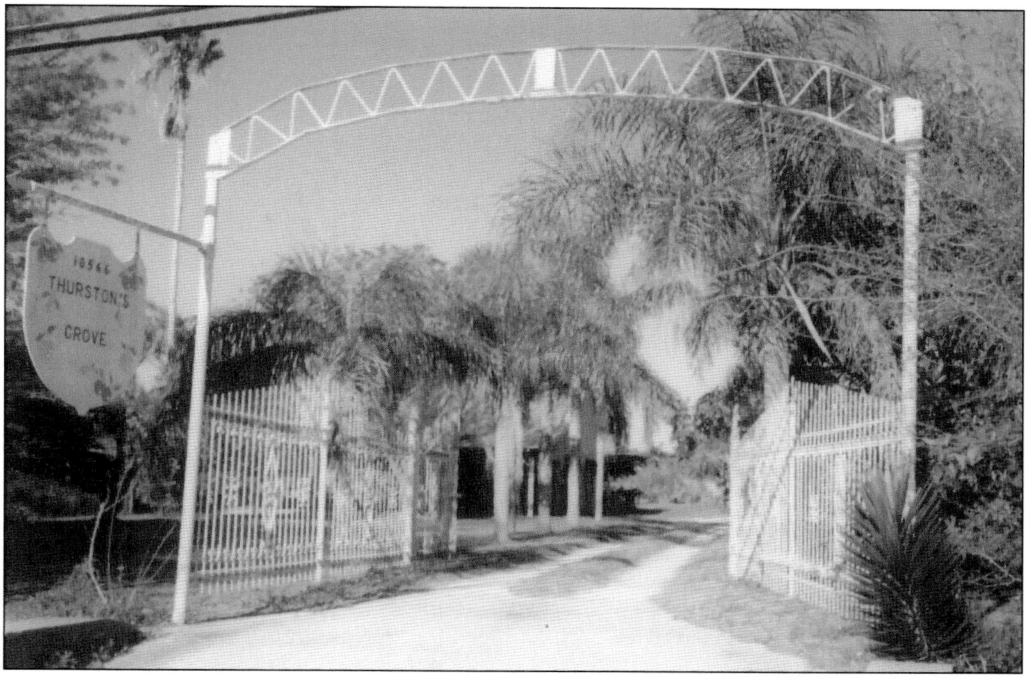

Since the 1962 freeze, developers had asked Margueritte Thurston to sell the grove her husband had acquired in 1917. By the 1990s, as subdivisions sprouted around her land, she operated the largest surviving citrus grove in Pinellas County. As Thurston told a reporter in 1989, "My land's going to stay right here, just like it is, like it always has been." She added, "I think about all the nice land, all covered with concrete. It shouldn't have happened." Although Thurston wanted her acreage to remain under cultivation, after she passed away in 1998 at the age of 92, her family sold the 37-acre tract to cover estate taxes. Sadly, the only round oranges found between 102nd Avenue North, Ridge Road, and the Pinellas Trail today appear on the street signs. (Above, Lyn Friedt Collection, HV; below, author.)

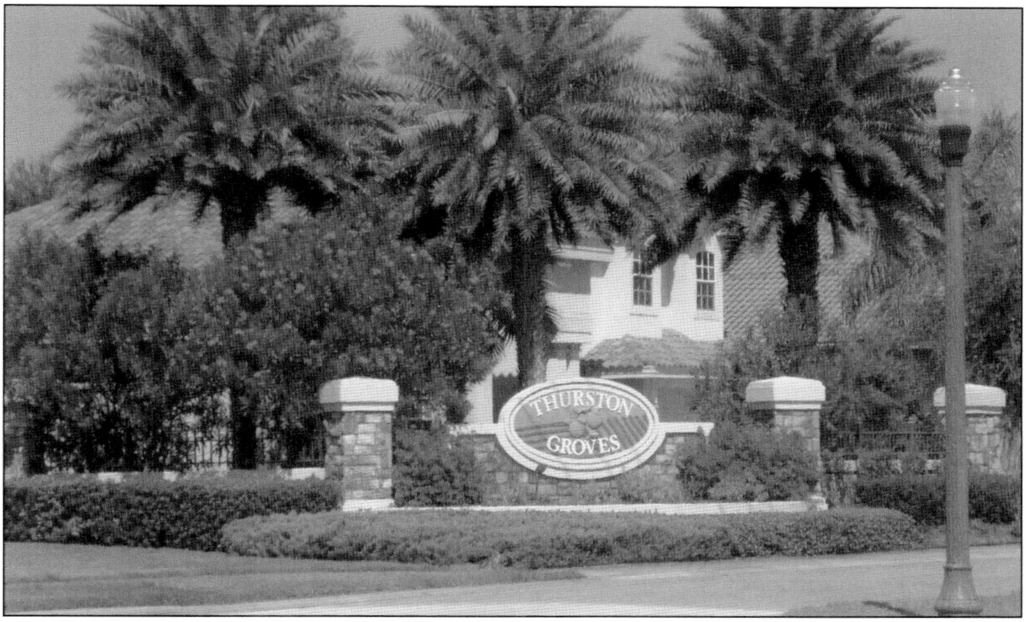

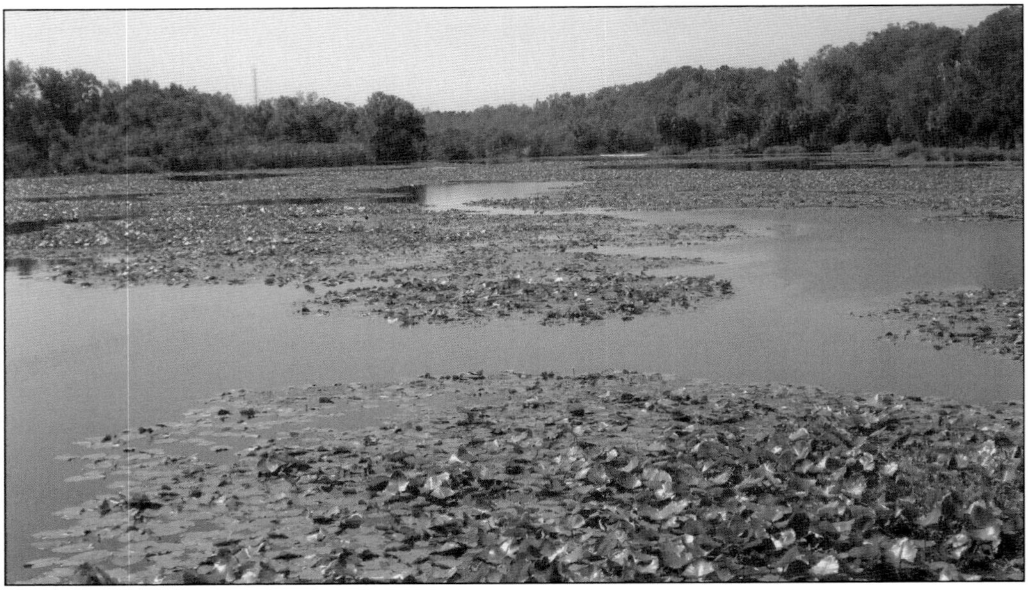

City and county officials met with members of the Largo Chamber of Commerce in April 1957 to discuss creating a park on the Taylor Avenue Reservoir. At that time, the county held title to a long corridor of land running from the dam alongside Taylor Avenue (Eighth Avenue Southwest) to land south and west of Baskin Crossing that included present-day Ridgecrest Park, Heritage Village, and Walsingham Park. The park opened in 1958, and as the result of a contest that took place in April 1959, it was eventually named in honor of John S. Taylor Sr., a former city commissioner, state legislator, and Citrus Fruit Exchange president. Other names under consideration included Largoland and Playland Park. Although officials originally wanted to add a sandy beach and bathing pavilions, the omnipresent alligators in the 53-acre freshwater lake forced them to abandon their plans. (Both, author.)

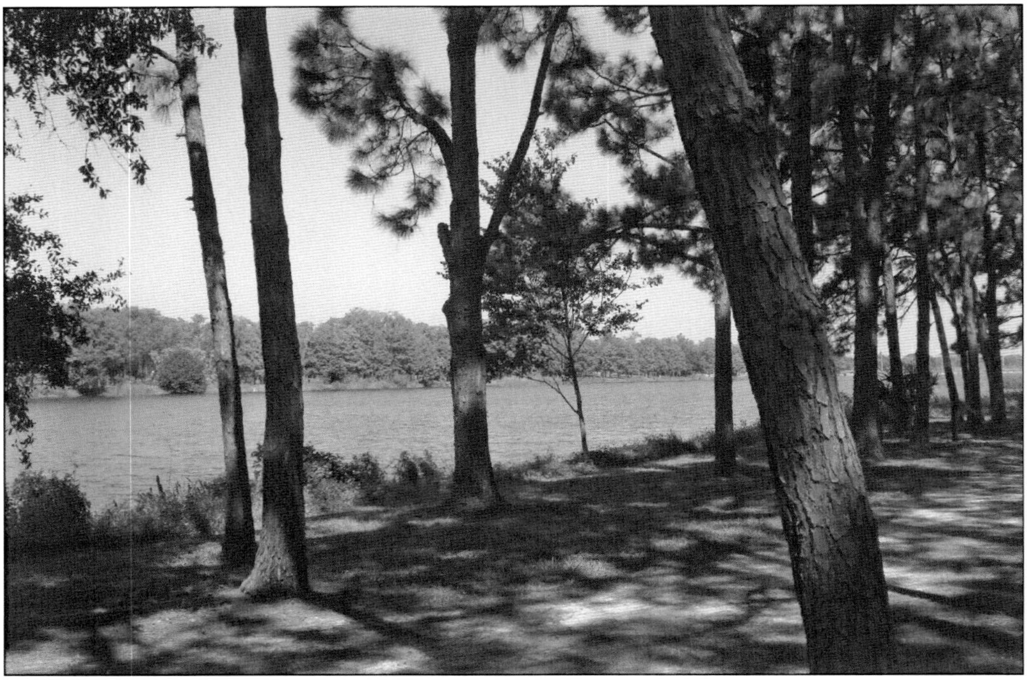

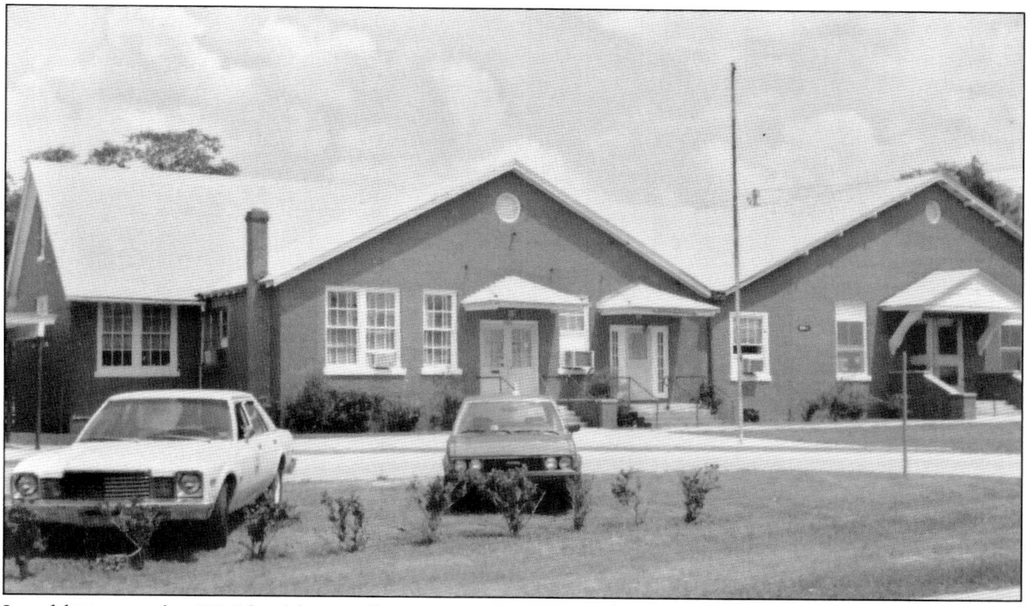

In addition to the 1915 building still in use on the Seminole Elementary School campus, the 1917 section of Anona Elementary School, shown above in this 1984 photograph, is one of the few educational facilities in Pinellas County with more than 90 years of continuous service. Many classrooms built after these have disappeared. In the mid-1980s, for example, the Pinellas County School Board decided to demolish the remaining 1924 building from the old Largo High/Junior High campus along Fourth Street SW between Second and Fourth Avenues. In its place, the board voted to construct a new school district headquarters and move the school board's offices from Clearwater, the county seat, to Largo. During a time of increased enrollment and reduced resources, some condemned the new building, below, as a "Taj Mahal." (Above, Lyn Friedt Collection, HV; below, author.)

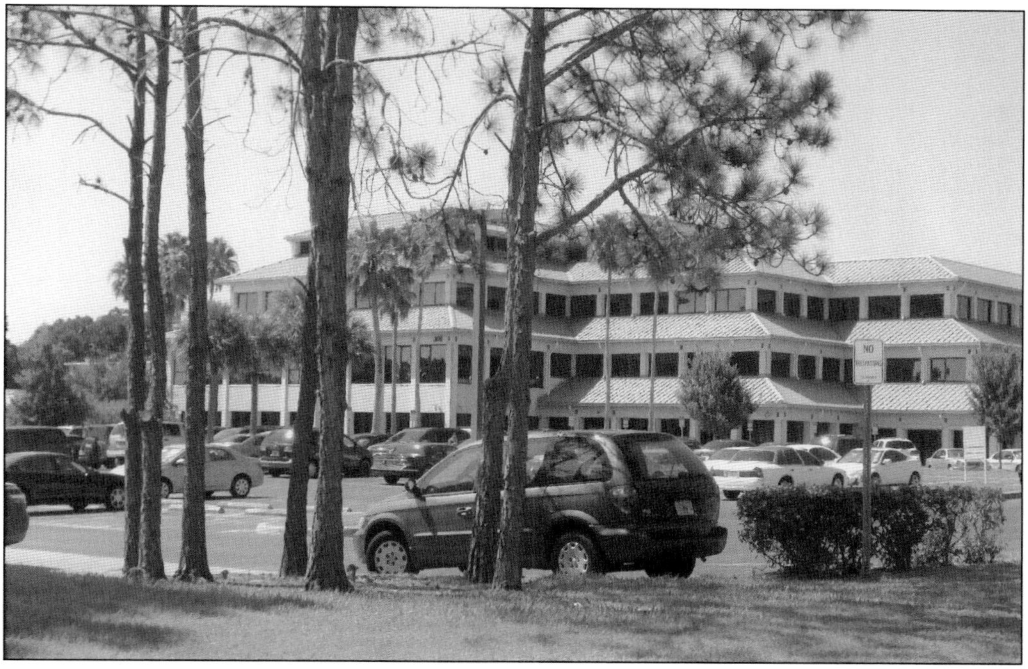

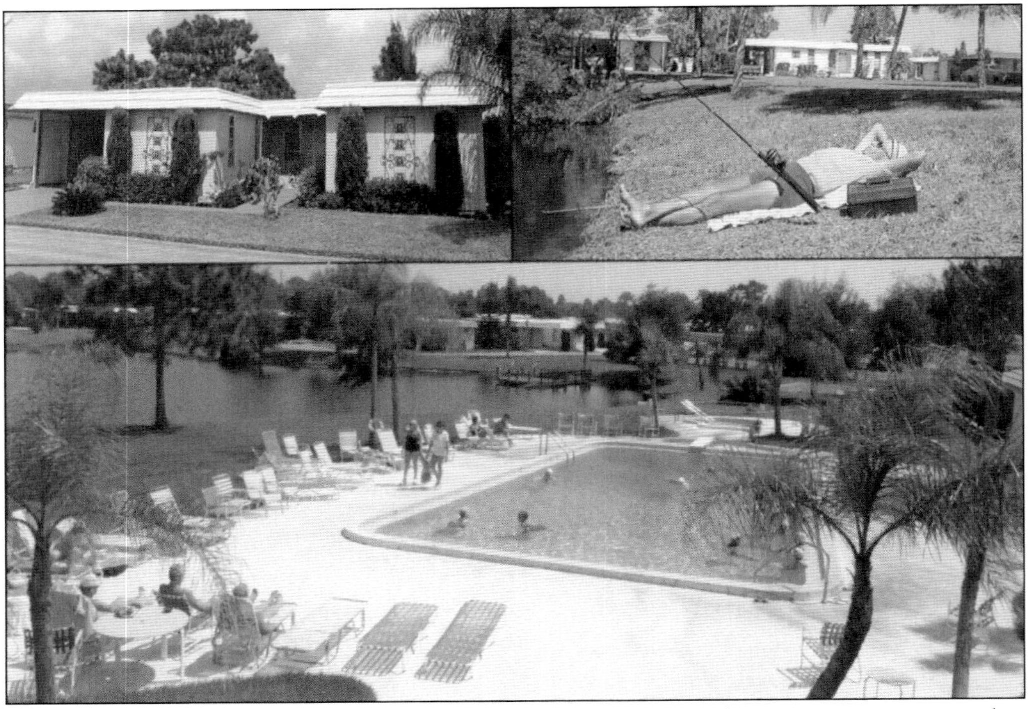

Adult communities such as Ranchero Village attracted newcomers and retirees to communities that possessed all of the amenities of "Florida-fun living." This development, located on Ulmerton Road between Belcher Road and Sixty-sixth Street, sported three recreation clubhouses, three swimming pools, lakes regularly stocked with fish, and championship shuffleboard courts. (HV.)

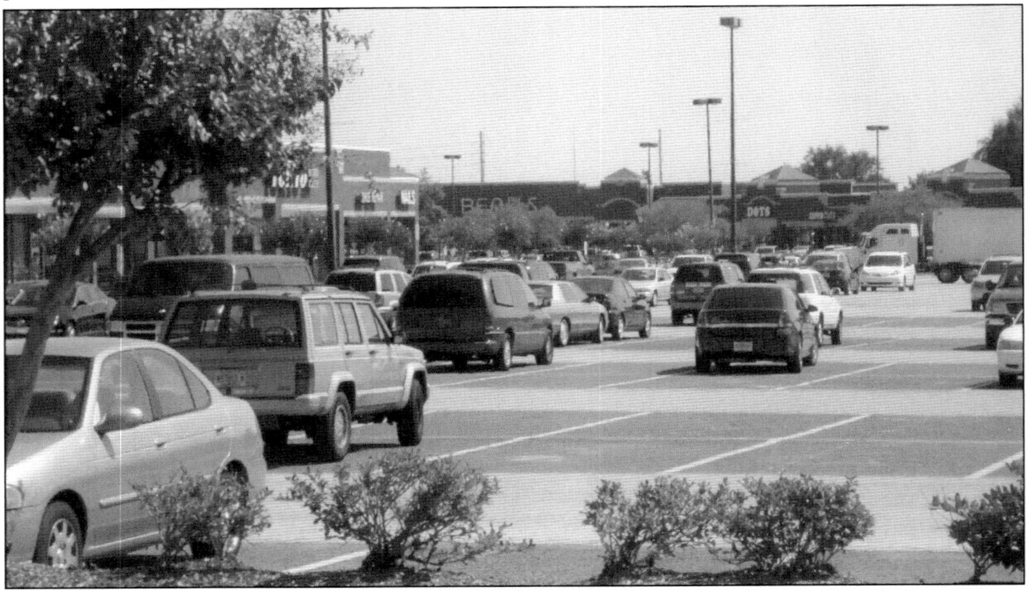

To meet the demands of a growing population, companies scrambled to acquire the remaining land available. At Ulmerton Road and Seminole Boulevard, bulldozers leveled 63 acres of pine scrubland to build Largo Mall, a place a reporter once called "a vast oasis in a desert of mobile home parks and traffic." Its opening in March 1988 accelerated the trend of businesses abandoning downtown for high-profile suburban locations. (Author.)

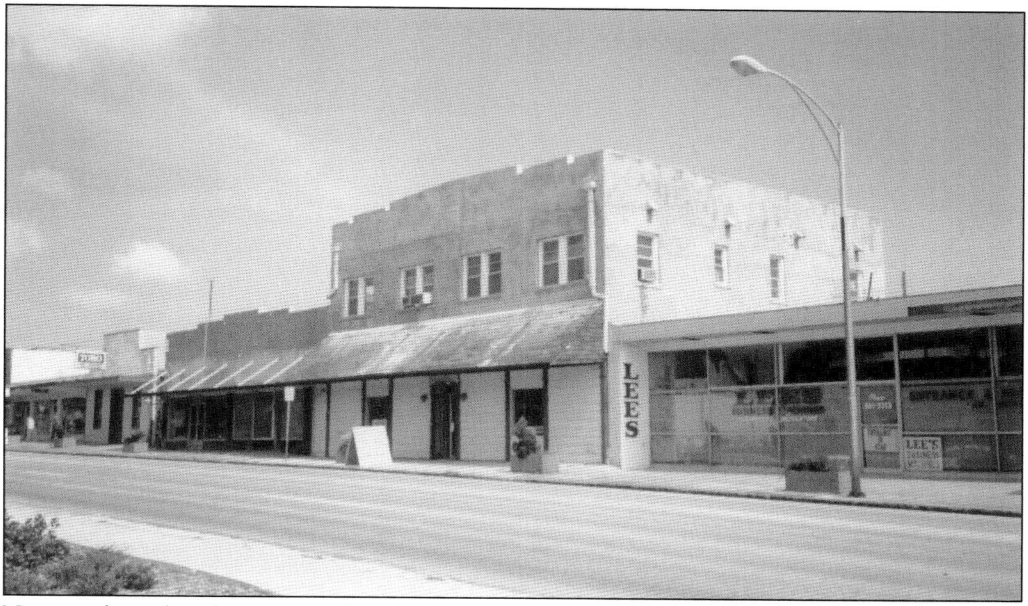

New residential and commercial establishments far from the city's core had led people to shop away from downtown Largo long before Largo Mall opened. Shopping malls perched between Largo and communities such as Belleair Bluffs, Clearwater, Pinellas Park, and Seminole pulled customers away from older mom-and-pop establishments. By the early 1980s, vacant storefronts and tired edifices along the 200 block of West Bay Drive, above, became the norm rather than the exception. Owners had repurposed many elegant homes and private residences in the city, such as the dwelling at 409 West Bay Drive seen below, to the point that much of their past grandeur had disappeared. With the glory days of the citrus industry behind them, leaders boldly changed Largo's motto to "City of Progress." Would their words be followed by actions? (Both, Lyn Friedt Collection, HV.)

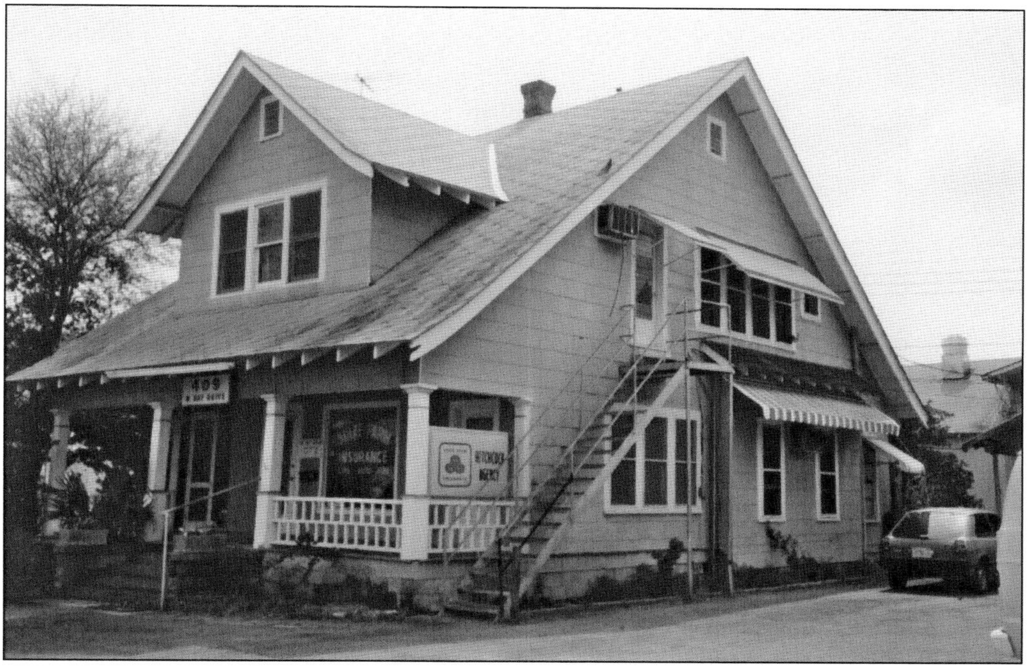

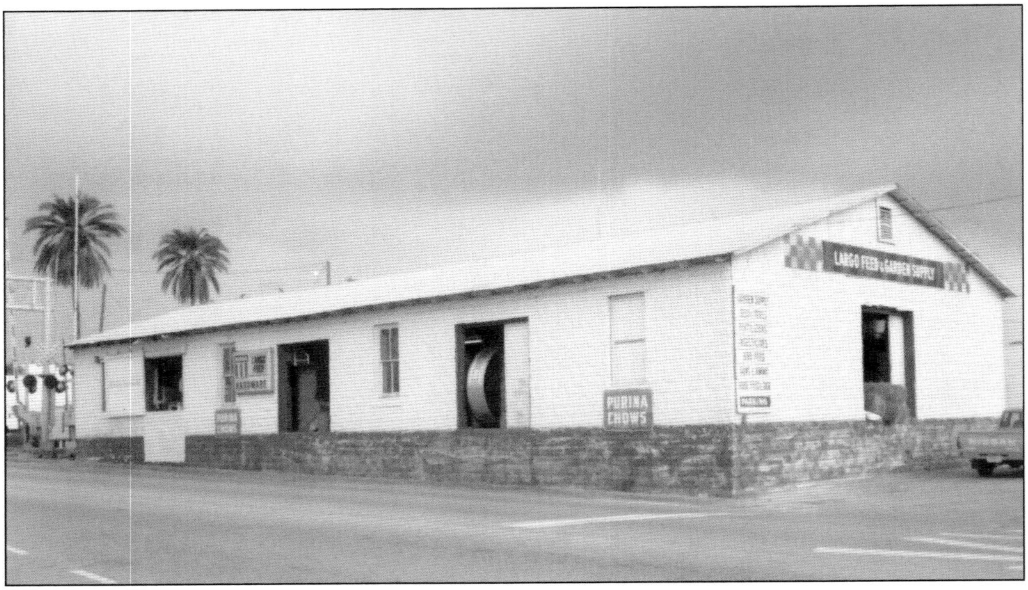

The Largo Feed and Garden Supply store faced imminent demolition after the state department of transportation announced long overdue plans to widen Bay Drive through Largo. As the July 1984 image above illustrates, the narrow roadway already hugged the south wall of the store. Longtime historian Sadie Johnson reminded the mayor and commission that the building represented Largo's oldest continually operating business center. Her initial pleas fell upon deaf ears. (Lyn Friedt Collection, HV.)

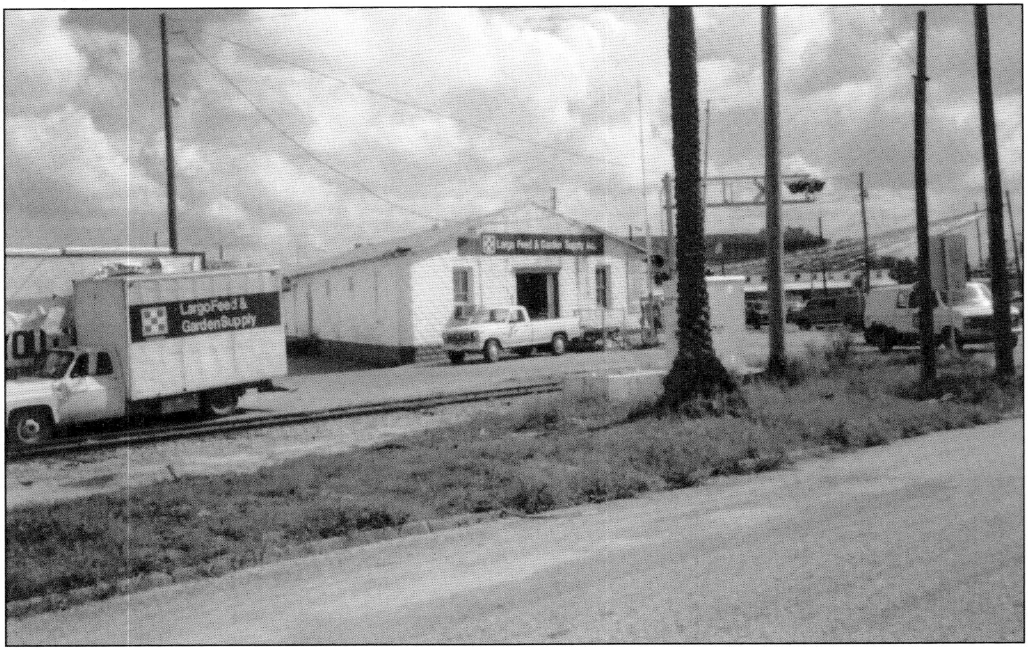

Members of the Largo Area Historical Society proposed to move the feed store diagonally across the busy intersection. This 1986 eastward view of the Largo Feed and Garden Supply store from First Street Northwest shows the old Taylor packinghouse on the right rear, an area slated for redevelopment and a possible spot for the feed store. After extensive negotiations, the society entered into an agreement with the city to save the building. (Lyn Friedt Collection, HV.)

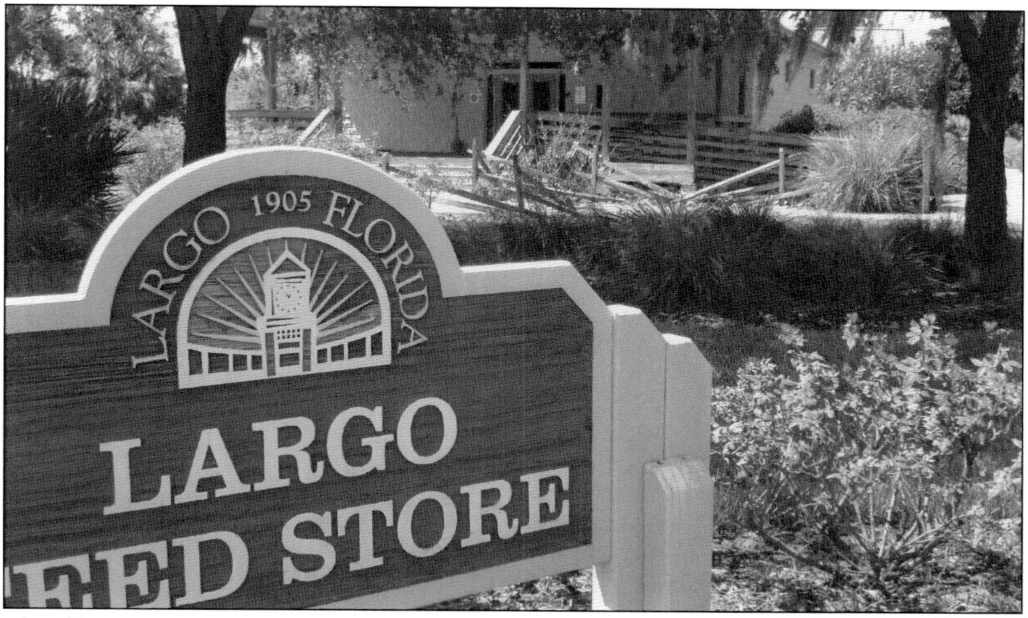

The older Largo Feed and Garden Supply building relocated to the southern area of Largo Central Park, near the old fairgrounds site, in November 1992. The Largo Area Historical Society raised funds to help with the move and subsequent structural renovations. As the sturdy building begins its second century of existence, it serves as the home for the historical society's meetings, including the popular potluck "Cracker Suppers" that commemorate the community's roots. (Author.)

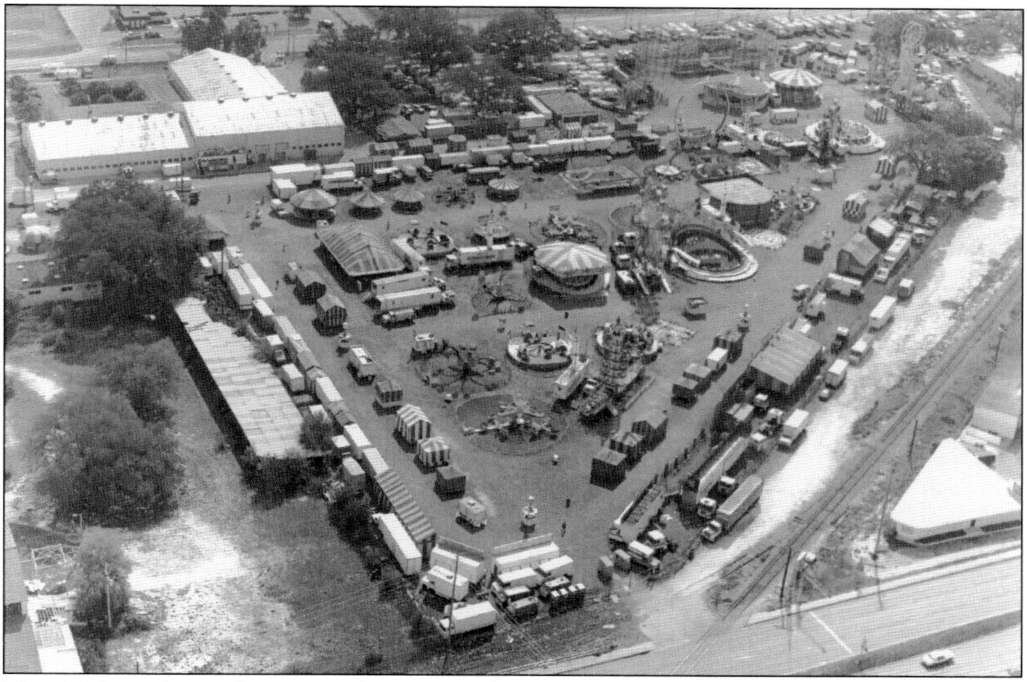
This 1980 aerial view facing east from Seminole Boulevard shows one of the last Pinellas County fairs that took place on the old fairgrounds. The event later moved to the Wagon Wheel Flea Market near Pinellas Park. City leaders acquired the fairgrounds from the county for $1.25 million with plans to transform it into a new park complex with a cultural center and other amenities. (HV.)

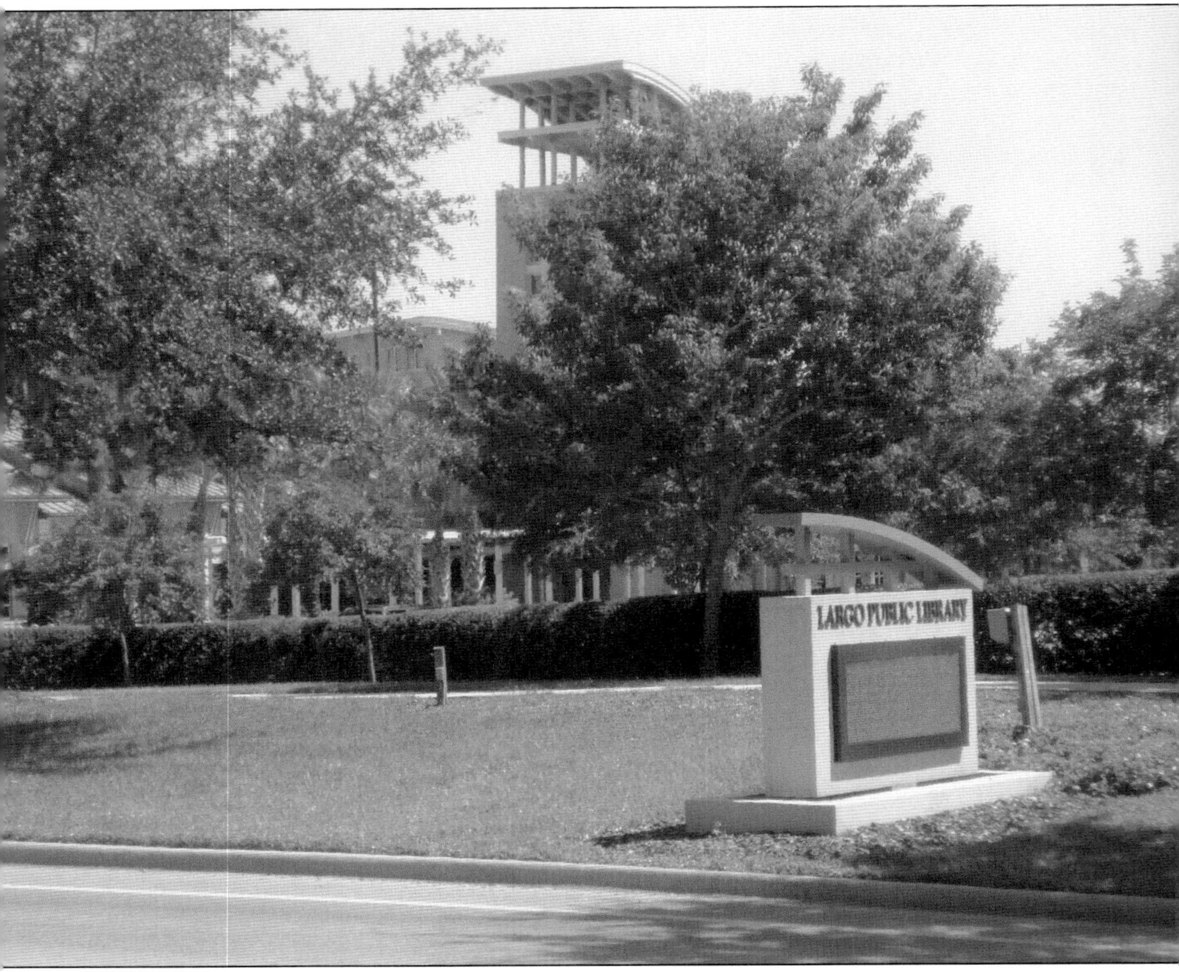

The Largo Public Library, one of Pinellas County's busiest, opened at its present site in 2005 after occupying three other locations in the city. The original library, started by the Largo Woman's Club in 1914, filled a room in the town hall. The collections moved into a stand-alone building at Cleveland Avenue and Fourth Street Southwest in 1962. By 1977, a larger library sat along East Bay Drive. The impressive facility includes the best genealogical research collection in Pinellas County and excellent local history sources. It occupies a prominent place across the street from the Cultural Center (home of the Eight O'Clock Theatre community performances) and the renovated feed store at Largo Central Park. The land on this site formerly used for crops and the county fair also served the home of the Bay Area Renaissance Festival for two decades, beginning in 1981. People once gathered here to see the annual assembly of mimes, jugglers, singers, jousters, and other performers in medieval costumes. (Author.)

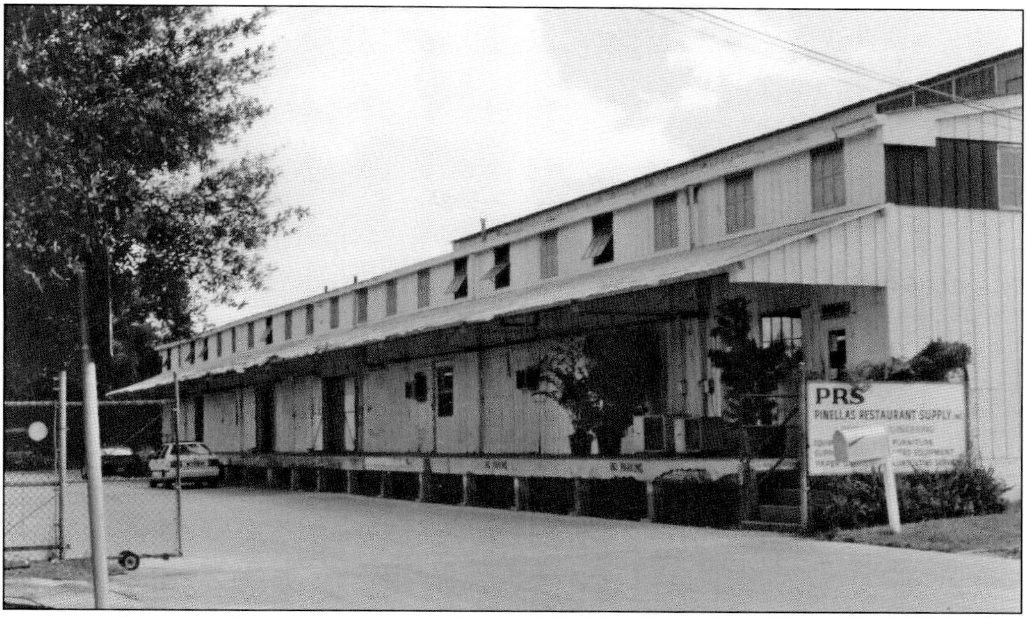

As groves disappeared, the Taylor packinghouse at the southeast corner of Seminole Boulevard and East Bay Drive found new life as a warehouse leased by the Taylor family. One occupant, the Pinellas Restaurant Supply Company, satisfied the hefty diet of the growing hospitality industry. Second-hand deep fryers sat on the concrete floors once filled with citrus crates. The city entered into negotiations with the Taylor family to purchase the former plant, some outbuildings, and 4 acres for $1.5 million. Underground fuel storage tanks and other environmental concerns slowed the process. The deal closed in October 1993. Soon thereafter, a newspaper writer promoting a fundraiser for the new park referred to the structure as a "big gray eyesore … not a part of history worth preserving." Wrecking crews demolished the building in 1994. (Both, Lyn Friedt Collection, HV.)

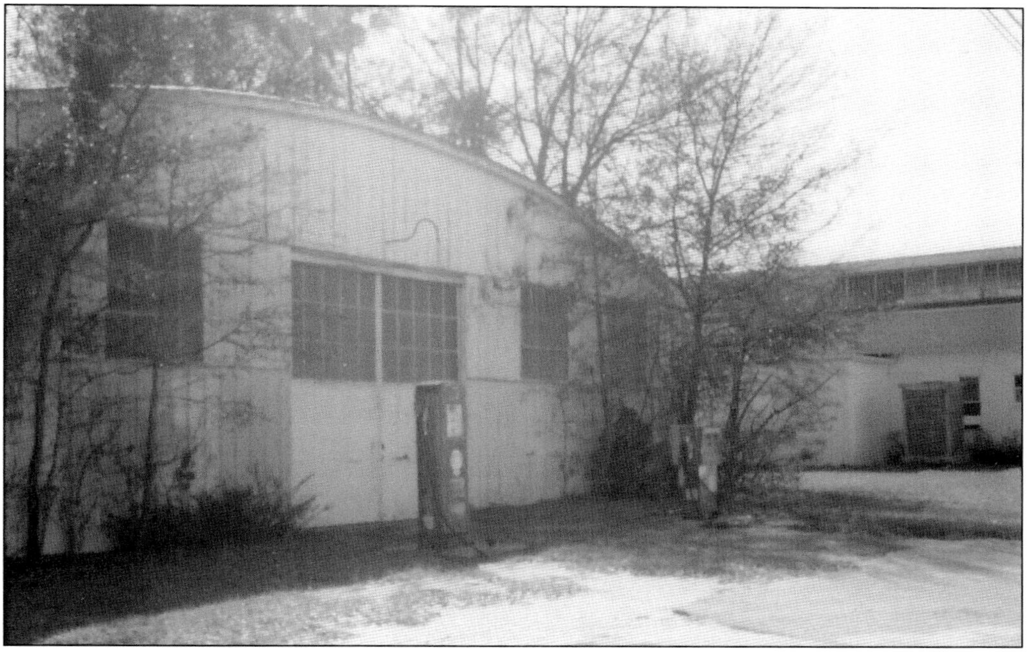

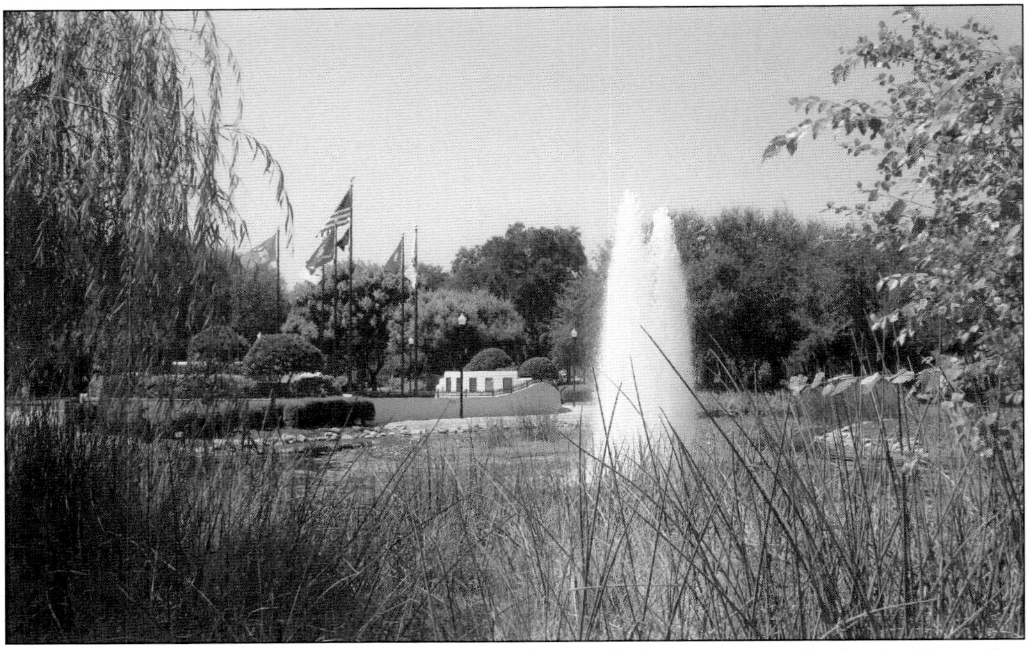

Largo Central Park encompasses 70 acres on the former Taylor property and other holdings that once formed the heart of the business and economic community. This image shows the park in October 2010 near the Military Court of Honor. Just to the east, on the former site of Lake Largo, the 31-acre Largo Central Park Nature Preserve offers a place to see otters, birds, rabbits, and alligators. (Author.)

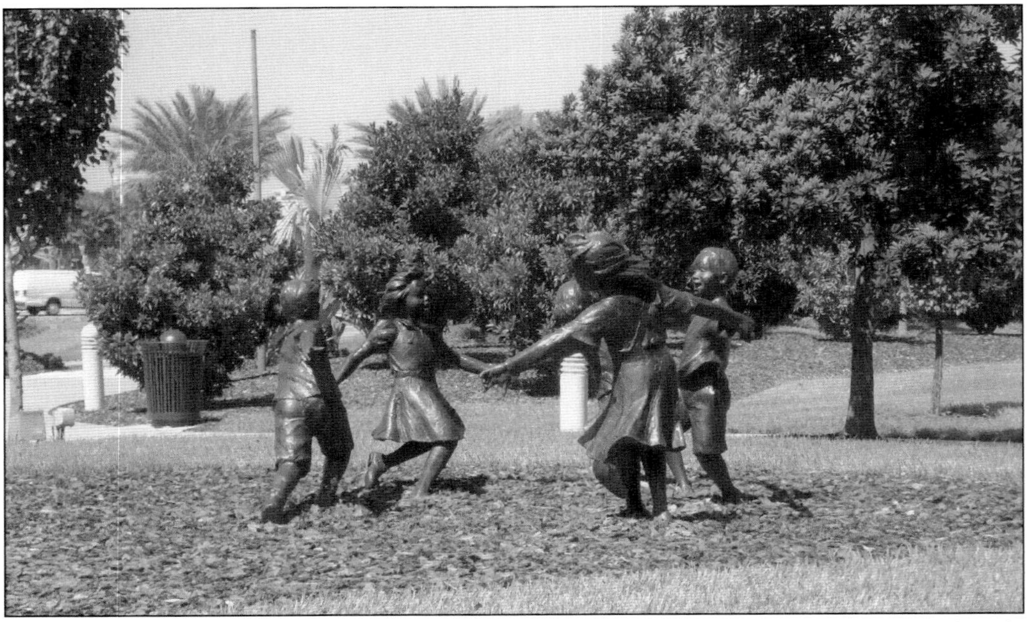

Taylor's packinghouse once sat at the spot now occupied by this statue at Largo Central Park. Throughout the park, the tracks for a large-scale model railroad operated by the nonprofit Largo Central Railroad meander for more than a mile. Today people of all ages can enjoy a place of natural beauty by visiting a location where railroad operators and citrus farmers first settled Largo more than a century ago. (Author.)

BIBLIOGRAPHY

Ayers, R. Wayne. *Tampa Bay's Gulf Beaches*. Charleston, SC: Arcadia Publishing, 2002.

Campbell, F. Leon. *A History of Seminole Pioneers*. Undated, typewritten manuscript in possession of the Seminole Historical Society.

Costrini, Patricia Perez, ed. *A Tradition of Excellence: Pinellas County Schools, 1912–1987*. Clearwater, FL: School Board of Pinellas County, 1987.

Goldman, Sue Searcy. "Baskin-Dansville: An African-American Community in Transition." *Punta Pinal: Newsletter of the Pinellas County Historical Society* 17 (Spring/Summer 1994): 8-9.

Indian Rocks: A Pictorial History. Indian Rocks, FL: Indian Rocks Area Historical Society, 1980.

Largo Area Historical Society. *From Pines and Palmettos: A Portrait of Largo, Florida*. Virginia Beach, VA: Donning Publishers, 2005.

———. *Largo, Florida, then 'Til*. Largo, FL: Bicentennial History Book Committee, 1979.

Miller, Marian, comp. *Index for Largo . . . then 'Til*. 1994.

Pinellas County. *The Golden Anniversary of Pinellas Schools, Celebrating 50 Years of Educational Progress*. Clearwater, FL: Pinellas County Board of Public Instruction, 1962.

Schnur, James Anthony. *Heritage Villagers: A Social History of the Pinellas Peninsula as Revealed through the Structures at Heritage Village*. Largo, FL: Heritage Village-Pinellas County Historical Museum, 2004.

Starkey, Jay B. *Jay Starkey's Things I Remember, 1899–1979*. Brooksville, FL: Reprint by Southwest Florida Water Management District, 1980.

In addition to the publications above, those wanting additional information about the history of the Largo area should visit the Largo Public Library and the Archives and Library at Heritage Village.

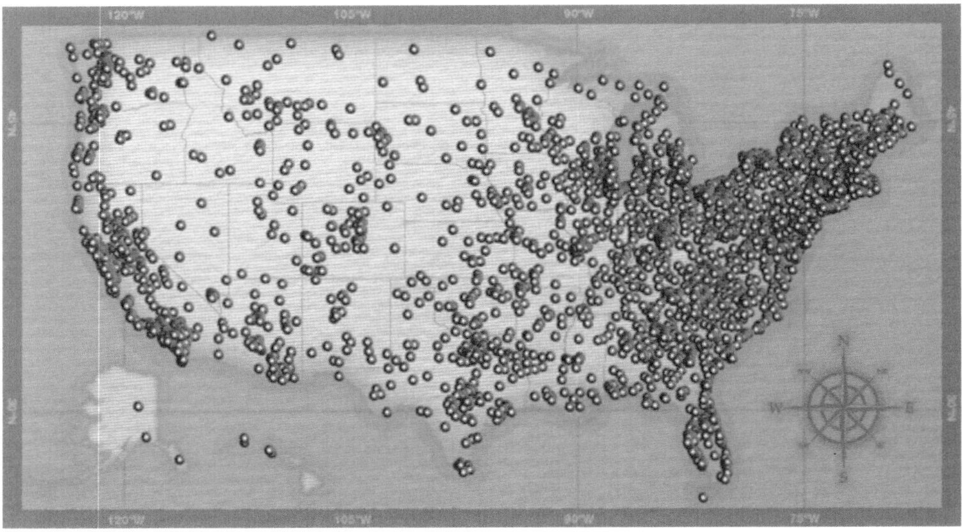

Consistent with our mission to preserve history on a local level, this book was printed in South Carolina on American-made paper and manufactured entirely in the United States. Products carrying the accredited Forest Stewardship Council (FSC) label are printed on 100 percent FSC-certified paper.

MADE IN THE USA